The
Hyperactivity
Hoax

The
Hyperactivity Hoax,

Sydney Walker III, M.D.

ST. MARTIN'S PRESS NEW YORK

Library of Congress Cataloging-in-Publication Data

Walker, Sydney.
      The hyperactivity hoax / by Sydney Walker III.
          p. cm.
      Includes index.
      ISBN 0-312-19287-8
      1. Hyperactive children—Medical care.   2. Attention-deficit-
disordered children—Medical care.   3. Methylphenidate
hydrochloride—Side effects.   4. Diagnostic errors.   5. Medication
abuse—Complications.   I. Title.
RJ506.H9W353   1998
618.92'8589—dc21   98-8013
                                                                                      CIP

First Edition: December 1998

10   9   8   7   6   5   4   3   2   1

To the memory of my beloved father, always
a child advocate, a prince among men, who
taught me the perseverance and optimism
that I hope are reflected in this book

Acknowledgments

I am grateful to my editor, Heather Jackson, for recognizing the importance of this book's message, and to my agent, Margot Maley, for getting my draft into the right hands. I am also fortunate to have the assistance of Alison Blake, whose journalistic skills and grasp of the subject, along with her ability to translate my medicalese into readable form, have been indispensable. Also, I thank Amy Butros and the UC San Diego reference library staff for their cheerful response to my many requests for information. Finally, I am grateful to my staff, Danielle Williams and Andra Fisher, for keeping me on schedule and assisting with my communications.

As always, I am very fortunate in having the ongoing support and encouragement of my beloved wife, Ann-Songmin.

IMPORTANT NOTE FOR READERS

The information in this book is not intended to be a substitute for medical care.

If your child is taking Ritalin or any other prescription drug, do not discontinue it without medical supervision. Children who stop taking Ritalin can suffer serious "rebound" effects, in which severe symptoms can occur. Sudden discontinuation of any drug used to treat hyperactivity can cause serious harm. Consult a doctor to taper your child off drugs if you choose to do so.

Contents

Contents

PART 4
Getting *Real* Help for Your Child

Introduction

IS HYPERACTIVITY A DISEASE? DOES RITALIN SUCCESSFULLY treat it?

No and no.

That may sound radical. After all, nearly every classroom in America now has several "hyperactive" students, and approximately two million children are taking Ritalin. Surely doctors wouldn't be giving an amphetamine-like drug, whose biochemical properties are quite similar to cocaine, to millions of children without good reason—would they?

I argue that the answer is yes. In this book, I explain why—and how you can obtain a *real* diagnosis, *real* treatment, and frequently a cure for your "hyperactive" child.

First, however, let me emphasize that I'm not another quack or guru with a quick-fix treatment for hyperactivity. I'm a practicing neurologist and psychiatrist, trained in neurosurgery, physiology, and pharmacology. I trained at Boston University Medical School and National Hospital in Queen's Square, London. And in more than three decades of practice, currently as the director of the Southern California Neuropsychiatric Institute, I've evaluated and treated hundreds of children labeled "hyperactive."

Most of these children were on Ritalin when they came to me. Most of them, after brief interviews with other doctors, had been given labels such as attention deficit hyperactivity disorder (ADHD) or attention deficit disorder (ADD). In almost every single case, I was able to find a cause for the child's symptoms. In most cases, I was able to prescribe treatments that reduced the symptoms without drugs. And in many cases, the children's disorders were curable.

If your child is one of America's two million "hyper"

children, I'm sure you'll recognize him or her in the stories of my patients. And I believe you'll gain hope—not the false hope of Ritalin but the *real* hope that there may be an effective treatment or even a cure for your child.

PART 1

Dangerous Labels for Troubled Children

CHAPTER 1

Symptoms in Search of a Diagnosis

Why did they give him Ritalin for diabetes?
Mother of a hyperactive child later diagnosed with subclinical diabetes
after years of drug treatment

It's one of the biggest frauds ever perpetrated on the educational
system, on parents, on their children. Every medical person
involved should be held accountable for it ethically.
Dr. Michael Valentine, school psychologist, on the labeling of
millions of children as hyperactive[1]

HAS YOUR CHILD BEEN LABELED HYPERACTIVE? IF SO, you're not alone. According to doctors, there's an epidemic of hyperactivity in America today. Three to 5 percent of all U.S. schoolchildren, and more than 10 percent of elementary school-age boys, currently take Ritalin or other drugs for hyper behavior, attention deficits, and impulsiveness.

These children are labeled hyperactive by family practitioners, neurologists, and psychiatrists. Some of them are initially "diagnosed" by teachers, school counselors, or nurses. There's only one problem with this scenario: *Hyperactivity is not a disease. It's a hoax perpetrated by doctors who have no idea what's really wrong with these children.*

ARE YOU SKEPTICAL? IF SO, I'M NOT SURPRISED. THE MED-
ical community has elevated attention deficit disorder (ADD)
and attention deficit hyperactivity disorder (ADHD) to the
status of diagnoses, and most people believe that these are
real diseases. They aren't—and doctors who label children
ADD or ADHD don't have a clue as to what's really ailing
them.

Why? Because hyperactivity and attention deficits are
merely *symptoms*.

What's the difference between a symptom and a diagnosis? Here's an example. Let's say you come down with a
chronic cough. Should your doctor say, "You have a coughing disorder," and prescribe cough drops—without worrying
about whether you have lung cancer, strep throat, or tuber-
culosis? Or if you develop a swollen leg, should your doctor
diagnose it as "a lump," and give you an aspirin, without
determining whether that lump is a tumor, an insect bite, or
gangrene?

Of course not. Yet this is how doctors "diagnose" hyperactivity. Is your child overly active? Does he run around too
much? Does she fidget in class? Then your child is one of
two million hyperactive children and needs to take amphetamine-like drugs—possibly for life. Likewise, if your child
makes careless mistakes, doesn't seem to listen, doesn't finish
schoolwork, loses things, and is easily distracted and forgetful,
then he or she has attention deficit disorder and also needs
drugs. Yet just as hyperactivity is merely a symptom, so are
attention problems. The unanswered question, obviously, is,
"What is *causing* your child to be hyperactive?" Or, "What is
causing your child to have attention problems?"

It's a critical question. Children with early-stage brain
tumors can develop symptoms of hyperactivity or poor attention. So can lead- or pesticide-poisoned children. So
can children with early-onset diabetes, heart disease, worms,

viral or bacterial infections, malnutrition, head injuries, genetic disorders, allergies, mercury or manganese exposure, petit mal seizures, and hundreds—yes, *hundreds*—of other minor, major, or even life-threatening medical problems. Yet all of these children are labeled hyperactive or ADD.

Furthermore, hundreds of thousands of perfectly normal children are labeled hyperactive or attention disordered, even though there's *nothing at all* wrong with them. These children are lumped in with the truly ill children I mentioned above, and all are medicated willy-nilly with potent and potentially dangerous drugs.

In short, huge numbers of healthy children are being drugged for no reason—and huge numbers of sick children are taking Ritalin to cover up the symptoms of undiagnosed and untreated medical problems. The latter is particularly tragic in light of the fact that most truly hyperactive and attention-disordered children have treatable or even curable medical conditions. The subtle behavioral changes that underlie these conditions require equally subtle diagnostic techniques, not a checklist and a pill.

Of course, most doctors do acknowledge that "a few" cases of hyperactivity and attention disorder are caused by diagnosable medical disorders. In the course of the fifteen-minute evaluation most hyperactive or attention-disordered children receive, doctors generally do a cursory check for some of these causes—hearing and vision problems, for instance. But because they believe that hyperactivity itself is a diagnosis, few doctors rule out all of the medical problems that can cause a child to be hyper or inattentive.

Labeling a child hyperactive or ADD, without finding out the underlying causes of the hyperactivity, can have many consequences—almost all of them bad.

Warren: Hyper or Sick?

I met Warren* when he was eight. A previous doctor who labeled Warren hyperactive had started him on Ritalin, and his parents came to me for a second opinion.

Warren was a normal, sturdy boy. He looked healthy except for his pallor, which contrasted strikingly with his mother's rosy complexion. His medical reports offered few clues about the roots of his impulsiveness, restlessness, and inattention. He'd had some breathing problems, episodes of partial hearing loss during ear infections, and a heart murmur—all conditions considered benign by previous doctors—but his records contained no significant red flags.

According to Warren's mother, he was cranky and sniffly as a baby, but his symptoms cleared up as he aged. However, shortly after a move to a new house, Warren changed for the worse.

"I can't remember that he ever balked at going to school," his mother told me. "He brought home good report cards. He never had any trouble with his teachers. Now he's in trouble all the time."

I asked her what was happening at school.

"He's in squabbles and scrapes with kids who used to be his good friends. He pesters his teacher. And he isn't learning anything in school. He's even backsliding. His handwriting and his spelling were better last year than they are now."

Warren's teacher was the first to bring up the word "hyperactivity." Warren wasn't destructive, she told his mother, but he constantly disrupted the class. If he wasn't raising his hand dozens of times an hour to ask an endless stream of questions, he was bouncing out of his chair to sharpen pencils, get a drink, or just wander around. He forgot his homework assignments. He

---

* The names and identifying characteristics of all patients described have been changed to protect their privacy. None of the changes relates to any medical condition or diagnosis.

ground his teeth while doing class work. He squirmed. He had trouble doing math problems he'd mastered days earlier.

"She told us to take him to a specialist in hyperactivity," Warren's mother said. They did, and the doctor prescribed Ritalin. Warren's parents worried about the drug's possible side effects, but the doctor convinced them that Ritalin would solve their son's academic and behavioral problems.

"We thought, well, if it would do any good . . . but it didn't."

No surprise. After an extensive three-day workup, I was able to diagnose Warren's real problem. By day two, I'd unearthed several clues. First, Warren was color-blind. Second, his electroencephalogram (EEG) showed abnormal but nonspecific brain wave patterns. A test called an electronystagmography (ENG) also produced abnormal results. These test results, taken together, told me that something serious was wrong with Warren's brain, but they didn't tell me what the problem was.

The next day, I discovered the answer: A carbon monoxide assay revealed a blood saturation of this deadly gas at the dangerous 20 percent level. Carbon monoxide was displacing the oxygen in Warren's bloodstream, drastically reducing the supply of oxygen to his brain. His fidgeting, falling academic performance, and purposeless hyper behavior were all symptoms of low-level carbon monoxide poisoning.

Warren's parents immediately called the gas company and had their heating system overhauled. They also started driving Warren to school, rather than having him ride for several hours a week on an old school bus with a faulty exhaust system.

Repeat studies three weeks later showed that Warren's carbon monoxide level had dropped to 3 percent. Already, his teachers and his parents were seeing dramatic changes in his behavior. Within six months, Warren's EEG was normal, and his color blindness—not hereditary in his case but due to toxic exposure—was resolved.

It took three days of evaluation, and many studies, for me to identify Warren's problem and rule out the hundreds of other conditions that could have caused his symptoms. Was it worth it? Warren's parents certainly thought so. His previous doctor's "diagnosis" may have been faster, but it was wrong—and Ritalin certainly wasn't a cure for carbon monoxide poisoning.

Symptoms in Search of a Diagnosis

Do all hyperactive* children suffer from carbon monoxide poisoning? Of course not. As I've noted, hundreds of different disorders can cause the symptoms that doctors call hyperactivity or attention deficit disorder. Some are common, some are rare, and some happen only once in a blue moon. These disorders have different causes, different prognoses, and different treatments. And that's exactly my point.

If a hundred different disorders can cause fidgeting, academic problems, overactivity, sleep problems, and attention disorders, then how can doctors pretend to treat all hyperactive or attention-disordered children with a single drug? The approach is even more illogical when you consider that this drug, Ritalin, merely masks symptoms without addressing what's causing them.

An even more dangerous trend is letting elementary school teachers "diagnose" hyperactivity and ADD, a frighteningly common practice these days. Here's how it works. A teacher, frazzled by Johnny's disruptive behavior, calls Johnny's parents to a meeting. Flanked by a school psychologist or principal, the teacher advises the parents that Johnny needs to be taking Ritalin. The parents take Johnny to a doctor, who in essence rubber-stamps the teacher's "diagnosis," often without even conducting a physical examination.

I understand that teachers can be tremendously burdened by impulsive, overactive, disruptive students. Teaching these children can be a nerve-racking and frustrating experience. In effect, many of these children are completely unteachable, and Ritalin does restrain some of them to the point that they can sit and learn. But allowing teachers to "diagnose" hyperactivity and

---

* I use the term *hyperactive* throughout the book to refer to a symptom, not a diagnosis.

doctors simply to rubber-stamp the teachers' recommendations to put children on Ritalin is an extraordinarily risky situation.

To illustrate just how misguided this practice is, consider the following two scenarios.

Case I: James

At six years old, James is driving his adoptive parents crazy. He wets the bed. He bounces off the walls at home and at school. He's confrontational and destructive and has wild tantrums when he's crossed.

James also exhibits pica—that is, he eats nonfoods such as dirt and paste. He grinds his teeth. He's been placed in a special education class because he can't attend or behave well enough to keep up with other students. His teacher recommends Ritalin.

James is a classic case of hyperactivity. But Ritalin and counseling won't treat the medical conditions my evaluation reveals.

First, tests reveal toxic lead levels that are crippling James's brain cells. In addition, he suffers from fetal alcohol syndrome (FAS), a tragic consequence of prenatal alcohol exposure. Children with mild cases of FAS often show no obvious physical signs, and in James's case, there is only one subtle physical clue—abnormal epicanthal folds over his eyes. The real clue comes from his family history: James's biological mother had a long history of both drug and alcohol abuse.

James needs immediate treatment to lower his toxic lead levels, and his family needs to determine the source of the lead he's ingesting and remove it. James also needs a different special education class, with teachers knowledgeable about FAS children's disabilities.

Case 2: Debby

Debby, age five when I see her, is tiny and delicate. Her mother, however, describes her as a "mean little kid" who has temper tantrums and screaming fits. As a baby, she cried continuously, slept very little, did not nap, and banged her head on her crib. Now in school, she's run away from kindergarten twice. Her teacher despairs over her out-of-control behavior and recommends medication. Debby's first doctor agrees.

Fortunately, Debby's mother demands a second opinion. My examination leads me to call for a cardiac consultation, which uncovers a defective blood vessel between Debby's heart and lungs, preventing a normal flow of oxygenated blood to the brain. Surgery corrects this serious and potentially fatal condition. Almost immediately, Debby's behavior improves, her tantrums stop, and her teachers begin praising her academic achievement.

NOW ASK YOURSELF: DID DEBBY'S TEACHER AND JAMES'S teacher make correct diagnoses when they suggested that these children were hyperactive and needed Ritalin?

The answer obviously is no. Ritalin treatment wouldn't have corrected the lead poisoning that was continuing to damage James's already malfunctioning brain. And Ritalin would merely have masked symptoms of a disorder that could eventually have killed Debby.

The Problem That Doesn't Just Go Away

Once a teacher or doctor identifies a child as hyperactive or attention disordered, the next step is almost a forgone conclusion: a quickie medical evaluation and a prescription for Ritalin or similar drugs. When these drugs *do* work, they work in the extremely limited and temporary sense that children taking them tend to be calmer, more focused, and easier to live with, at least in the short term. But, as I explain later, these drugs are far from benign, and their benefits are questionable.

The real tragedy, however, is that masking children's symptoms merely allows their underlying disorders to continue and, in many cases, to become worse. Contrary to popular belief, hyperactive children don't simply outgrow their symptoms. Instead, many grow into troubled teens and adults.

About half of all children labeled hyperactive do well in adulthood. Many of them originally suffered from time-limited physical disorders in childhood (developmental seizures, for instance); when the disorders cleared up, so did their hyperactivity. Others were never hyper in the first place but merely normal, active children (see Chapter 8). The outlook for the other 50 percent of children labeled hyperactive, however, is grim.

Salvatore Mannuzza and colleagues, studying adults labeled hyperactive in childhood, found that they were far more likely than control subjects to hold low-paying jobs and to be high school dropouts, and that a large minority of them regularly committed irresponsible and violent acts.[2] Eric Taylor and colleagues found that hyperactivity—*even in children who showed no early evidence of serious behavioral problems*—was a risk factor for problems in late adolescence, frequently leading to violence, other antisocial behaviors, social problems, and school failure.[3] And H. R. Huessy and colleagues, following eighty-four hyperactive children for up to a decade, found that their rate of institutionalization for delinquency was *twenty times* that of the general population.[4] Numerous studies also show that children labeled as having both hyperactivity and conduct disorder—a fancy psychiatric term for stealing, lying, and acting out—are at extremely high risk of drug abuse, teenage pregnancy, and criminality in adolescence and adulthood.

Moreover, study after study shows that treating hyperactivity with Ritalin does nothing to change this dismal long-term prognosis. At one time, doctors optimistically thought that after a decade or so of Ritalin treatment, behavior-disordered kids would somehow snap out of it and turn into happy, well-adjusted adults. No such luck: In 1987, the Interagency Committee on Learning Disabilities reported to Congress:

> *A distressing finding in recent years is the increasing awareness of the limitations of psychopharmacological treatment in [ADHD]. . . . It was hoped that two to three years of*

early treatment would provide sufficient performance incre-
ments and enhancement of self-esteem to carry the child over
the pubertal transition. Data from a number of longitudinal
studies, however, have shown that this is often not the case.
Subsequent to discontinuation of drug therapy at approxi-
mately age 13, levels of social functioning and interpersonal
skills continue to be lower for [ADHD] adolescents and young
adults than for their age-matched normal peers. This finding
is especially true for that subgroup who displayed assaultive or
aggressive behavior in childhood. Adolescents and young adults
may carry over one, two, or three of the symptoms of
[ADHD], and those who carry over multiple symptoms seem
to be at higher risk for substance abuse.[5]

The textbook *Developmental Neuropsychiatry* notes that "clini-
cians treating large numbers of hyperactive children who were
receiving adequate amounts of stimulants and whose medication
was well monitored found that over the years, in spite of medication, many problems continued. By adolescence, these
stimulant-treated hyperactives were still failing in school and
continued to be behavior problems; many had developed antisocial behaviors, as well as experiencing social ostracism. . . .
[T]he children continued to be in various degrees of trouble,
and other methods of management as well as (or instead of)
stimulants were required."[6]

The poor outcome of children labeled hyperactive is not
surprising. Why? Because their underlying medical conditions
were never addressed—and because many medical conditions
that can cause hyperactivity also cause social problems, academic difficulties, and even criminality. To cite just a few examples:

- High lead levels, *even in the absence of clinical lead poisoning,*
  place children at great risk for both school failure and delinquency.
- High mercury levels can cause agitation and cognitive problems.
- Manganese toxicity is linked to aggression and criminality.

- Iron-deficiency anemia can lead to poor job performance, despondency, fatigue, and often aggression and irritability.
- B vitamin deficiencies, common in teens and young adults, can lead to symptoms of subclinical beriberi, including hostility and violent outbursts.
- Hyperthyroidism can cause fear, hostility, and demanding, hypercritical behavior, all of which can lead to job and social failure.
- Individuals with Tourette's syndrome, a genetic disorder that can cause hyperactivity, have high rates of antisocial or even criminal behavior.
- Temporal lobe seizures, sometimes almost continuous and often too subtle to be detected by eye, can cause violent outbursts, restless movements, and bizarre behavior.
- The fluctuating blood sugar levels seen in subclinical diabetes can cause fugue states, in which individuals commit unexplained and sometimes violent acts.
- Cardiac conditions can reduce the supply of blood, oxygen, and nutrients to the brain and, over time, can cause the death of brain cells. This results in impaired thinking and aberrant behavior.
- Some drugs, both prescription and illegal, can cause the brain to atrophy, leading to disturbed cognition and behavior.

Many of the hundreds of disorders that cause childhood hyperactivity and attention problems grow worse, not better, with age. Brain cysts, seizure disorders, metabolic disorders, genetic defects, and heart disorders, for instance, usually don't just go away. Instead, they cause more (and often more serious) symptoms in adulthood. Although some children have temporary conditions that can be cured by a move to a less toxic environment, recovery from an infection, or dietary changes, many others aren't so lucky.

Sometimes, the conditions plaguing these children worsen so dramatically that physicians finally detect them—for instance, when a previously undiagnosed brain tumor in a hyperactive child becomes life-threatening. More often, however, the unwell child simply becomes an unwell adult, his or her symptoms masked by a succession of prescription drugs (and often by illicit drugs and alcohol as well) while a smoldering disease continues to cause damage. Often, drug abuse becomes a secondary problem that increases the hyperactive individual's chances of job failure, social problems, and encounters with the law. The hyperactive person, having never felt truly "good," has no clue that he or she is chronically ill. All he or she knows is that a marijuana joint, a bottle of Scotch, or a snort of cocaine makes the symptoms go away—for a little while.

Why the Hyperactivity Label Is So Popular

You might ask, at this point, why doctors are content to label children hyperactive or ADD without evaluating them for all of the medical conditions that can cause hyperactivity, impulsiveness, and inattention. After all, the job of the doctor is to diagnose. Furthermore, in medical school, doctors learn about dozens of syndromes that can cause hyperactivity. And, in their daily practice, doctors see the results of simply labeling children hyperactive: chronic academic and social problems, troubles with the law, failure, and tragedy. Why are so many diagnoses being overlooked, in a population so desperately in need of help? There are, in my opinion, two reasons—and neither of them reflects well on the medical profession.

The Growth of Managed Care

Medicine isn't what it used to be. Twenty years ago, most doctors made medical decisions based on only one standard: what was best for the patient. With generous insurance policies underwriting virtually all medical treatment without much question, doctors were free to make diagnostic decisions with only their parents' interests in mind. And there was no question about where a doctor's allegiance lay: with the patient.

Today, however, with most doctors working under managed care plans, the questions are more complex and the ethics more murky. Doctors are now working for two masters, their patients and their managers, and the goals of those two groups are often in conflict. In fact, many if not most managed care programs are actually set up to punish doctors who offer careful and thorough care, and to reward those who skimp.

For instance, many managed care plans are capitated. This means that the doctor receives a set fee each year for treating a group of patients. If these patients have minor and easily diagnosed problems, the doctor will be sitting pretty at the end of the year, with money left in the bank and possibly a nice bonus from the bosses at the managed care program. But the doctor unlucky enough to get lots of patients with complex, expensive problems requiring extensive evaluations, testing, and consultations will be in trouble. This doctor, if he or she insists on providing the best of care for each patient, can actually wind up paying for patients' care. Furthermore, conscientious doctors can wind up being let go by managed care companies unhappy with patients receiving "too much" care.

As one doctor commented in *Medical Economics*, "It used to be that the harder you worked and the more care you provided, the more money you earned. Under capitation, it's the opposite. The more you limit, the more you're paid. You want to be the patient's advocate, but the system makes it awfully hard."[7]

An increasing number of Americans are subject to managed care plans. In 1973, when President Nixon signed the HMO Act, only a few thousand people were members of HMOs. "By the end of 1994," managed care consultant Thomas Garvey notes, "HMOs had 51.1 million members—about 20 percent of the population." And by the year 2000, Garvey predicts, "Managed care entities will boast more than 100 million members and will dominate health care services in the United States."[8] Already, when all forms of managed care (and not just traditional HMOs) are included, more than 70 percent of Americans with health insurance belong to managed care groups.[9]

As the HMO population grows exponentially, the number of children labeled as hyperactive and put on Ritalin is growing right along with it—from about 150,000 in 1970 to approximately 2 million today. In my opinion, it's no coincidence that the number of children labeled hyperactive or ADD started skyrocketing at about the same time managed care took over the medical industry. Under managed care, the pressure for doctors to treat patients quickly is intense. The ten-minute office visit is the gold standard, and many procedures must be approved by nonmedical business managers who frown on diligent and appropriate diagnostic efforts. This new system puts pressure on even the most conscientious doctors to cut corners.

What does this mean to a hyperactive patient? It means, realistically, that a family practitioner has about ten or fifteen minutes to diagnose the child. It also means that the doctor has disincentives, not incentives, for ordering tests or referring the child to specialists who could identify neurological, cardiac, metabolic, infectious, or genetic disorders. In short, it means that the odds of getting a careful differential diagnosis are slim.

A decade ago, when the managed care movement was still in its early years, a Georgia parent advocacy group found that of 102 children put on Ritalin, *only 2* received an evaluation that met even the cursory standards recommended by the manufacturers of the drug.[10] With managed care in full swing now, it's likely that the number of children getting thorough evaluations is even smaller.

An Obsession with Lumping

For centuries, doctors have obsessively sought the roots of disease, and this process of discovery continues. In recent years, for instance, researchers have discovered that Lyme disease causes some cases of arthritis, that bacteria cause many ulcers, and that heart valve defects are to blame for many anxiety attacks.

Learning the *causes* of the symptoms in these cases—not just continuing to label them arthritis or ulcers or anxiety—dramatically improves doctors' ability to help their patients. I call this type of medical progress "splitting," because it splits large, vague groups of symptoms into ever more accurate diagnostic categories. *And when you know what you're treating, you know how to treat it correctly.* For instance, patients with bacteria-caused ulcers are no longer put on useless bland diets, given years of medication, or referred to psychotherapy for stress. Because we now know what's wrong with these patients, we don't waste their time and money on worthless treatments.

Unfortunately, splitting is losing ground to a new and opposite trend in medicine. I call it "lumping," or the grouping of many symptoms together into handy but diagnostically worthless categories. (Some doctors call them "wastebasket diagnoses.") Lumping is particularly popular in modern psychiatry—not a surprising fact, since psychiatry has always been the least scientific of the medical specialties.

Thus, we have a "disease" called "depression," which in reality is a group of symptoms (sadness, loss of appetite, etc.) that can be caused by anything from thyroid disorders to brain tumors. Likewise, we have a "disease" called "anxiety disorder," which actually can result from a host of conditions ranging from inner-ear problems to medication errors. Lumping, which has spread quickly from psychiatry to other medical specialties, leads to one-size-fits-all treatments such as Prozac and tranquilizers, rather than to real diagnoses, real treatments, and real cures.

Hyperactivity and ADD, when spoken of as diagnoses rather than symptoms, are classic examples of lumping. Completely normal children can exhibit enough behaviors to earn a label of hyperactivity or attention deficit disorder and a prescription for Ritalin. So can children with pesticide poisoning, brain cysts, parathyroid disorders, or hundreds of other conditions. Do all of these children have the same "disease"? Hardly.

Attention deficit hyperactivity disorder, or ADHD, is actually the latest in a progression of meaningless labels tacked onto children with behavior disorders (or normal but active behavior). In the early 1900s, doctors did a good job of diagnosing such children, given the limitations of medical technology at the time. Then psychiatry took over, first lumping all of these children into the category of "minimal brain damage." When they couldn't identify what that damage might be, the psychiatrists switched to "minimal brain dysfunction." Next came "hyperkinetic reaction," followed by "attention deficit disorder with (or without) hyperactivity." Now, of course, the psychiatric profession has given us "attention deficit hyperactivity disorder," or ADHD. And when children aren't hyperactive enough to qualify as ADHD, doctors simply remove the "H" and label them as ADD. Gerald Coles commented in *The Learning Mystique*, "Rather than moving toward ever greater precision, they're constantly sweeping over the disasters of last year's conception."[11]

As Professor Richard Vatz notes, "Attention deficit disorder is no more a disease than is 'excitability.' It is a psychiatric, pseudomedical term." Yet the labels ADHD and ADD, invented by psychiatry and codified in its *Diagnostic and Statistical Manual of Mental Disorders* (DSM), are now almost universally accepted by neurologists, pediatricians, and general practitioners—not as starting points for diagnoses, but as diagnoses in and of themselves.

The current mantra of these physicians is that hyperactivity and ADD are distinct disorders, much like chicken pox or cancer, that can be identified using a cookbook list of symptoms originally concocted by the psychiatrists who authored the DSM. As you can see from the following checklist, the DSM has made "diagnosing" these purported disorders a cinch. Doctors simply need to choose from a Chinese menu list of symptoms—pick six from column A, and six from column B. And if a child doesn't quite fit the categories, many doctors are willing to label him or her a "borderline" case.

Thus, millions of children with hundreds of diseases, *or no diseases at all*, are lumped into a single category: hyperactivity. All get the same treatment: Ritalin or another drug. And all get the same diagnosis, which is to say, none at all.

A Quick Word About the DSM

Normally, I wouldn't bore you by talking about a tedious medical reference book. But unlike most medical books, the DSM—a huge (800-plus pages) book dubbed the "psychiatric

Criteria for 'Diagnosing' Attention Deficit Hyperactivity Disorder

(from *Diagnostic and Statistical Manual of Mental Disorders*, edition IV)

A. Either 1 or 2:

1. Six or more of the following symptoms of inattention have persisted for at least six months to a degree that is maladaptive and inconsistent with developmental level:

   a. Often fails to give close attention to details or makes careless mistakes in schoolwork, work, or other activities.

   b. Often has difficulty sustaining attention in tasks or play activities.

   c. Often does not seem to listen when spoken to directly.

   d. Often does not follow through on instructions and fails to finish schoolwork, chores, or duties in the workplace (not due to oppositional behavior or failure to understand instructions).

   e. Often has difficulty organizing tasks and activities.

   f. Often avoids, dislikes, or is reluctant to engage in tasks that require sustained mental effort (such as homework).

   g. Often loses things necessary for tasks or activities (toys, school assignments, pencils, books, or tools).

   h. Is often easily distracted by extraneous stimuli.

   i. Is often forgetful in daily activities.

2. Six or more of the following symptoms of hyperactivity-impulsivity have persisted for at least six months to a degree that is maladaptive and inconsistent with developmental level:

Hyperactivity:

   a. Often fidgets with hands or feet or squirms in seat.

   b. Often leaves seat in classroom or in other situations in which remaining seated is expected.

   c. Often runs about or climbs excessively in situations in which it is inappropriate (in adolescents or adults, may be limited to subjective feelings of restlessness).

   d. Often has difficulty playing or engaging in leisure activities quietly.

   e. Is often "on the go" or often acts as if "driven by a motor."

   f. Often talks excessively.

Impulsivity:

   g. Often blurts out answers before questions have been completed.

   h. Often has difficulty awaiting turn.

   i. Often interrupts or intrudes on others (e.g., butts into conversations or games).

B. Some hyperactive, impulsive, or inattentive symptoms that caused impairment were present before age 7 years.

C. Some impairment from the symptoms is present in two or more settings (such as in school or work and at home).

D. There must be clear evidence of clinically significant impairment in social, academic, or occupational functioning.

E. The symptoms do not occur exclusively during the course of a pervasive developmental disorder, schizophrenia, or another psychotic disorder and are not better accounted for by another mental disorder (such as a mood, anxiety, dissociative, or personality disorder).

Bible"—plays a major role in whether or not your child receives real treatment. It's a dangerous book, and you need to know about it.

The DSM is published by the American Psychiatric Association, and is revised every few years. Simply put, it's a guidebook to what psychiatry considers to be mental illnesses. It lists hundreds of labels for such illnesses, followed by lists of the symptoms needed for a patient to qualify for each label. These labels are now accepted as diagnoses by hospitals, medical journals, and insurance companies, as well as most physicians.

Many of the doctors your child is likely to see—not just psychiatrists but also general practitioners, pediatricians, and neurologists—rely almost exclusively on the DSM when determining what's wrong with your child. Most school psychologists also have well-thumbed copies of the DSM, which they use in making their own "diagnoses." These professionals rely on the DSM because most of them believe, naively, that the DSM is a well-supported, scientifically based work. However, nothing could be farther from the truth.

In fact, DSM is as much a political document as a medical document. New versions are compiled every few years by powerful psychiatrists who quibble over what constitutes a mental illness and what doesn't. "Diagnoses" are regularly voted in or out. (Homosexuality, for instance, was a disease in DSM-II but was voted out in DSM-III. Self-defeating personality disorder was a disease in DSM-III-Revised but deleted in DSM-IV. And narcissistic personality disorder was in, then out, then back in again!) Furthermore, the symptoms for virtually all DSM diseases change from revision to revision. Thus, your hyperactive child might be mentally ill according to one DSM and perfectly normal according to the next edition six or seven years later. Needless to say, this sort of thing doesn't happen with real diseases such as pneumonia or measles.

In addition to its political nature, DSM has two obvious and dangerous flaws. First, as I've said, it's the source of the pat labels doctors give patients in lieu of diagnoses. For instance, using DSM, I can label patients as having "impulse-control disorder not otherwise specified" or "oppositional defiant disorder" or "hypersomnia," prescribe a drug for each condition, and collect my fee—without ever examining these patients to find out *why* they're impulsive or aggressive or sleepy. This is, of course, exactly what is happening to children labeled hyperactive or attention disordered.

The other major flaw of DSM, related to the first, is that it labels virtually *everything* as some type of disorder. Thus, a child who sees a DSM-oriented doctor is almost assured of a psychiatric label and a prescription, even if the child is perfectly fine. In their book, *Making Us Crazy*, Herb Kutchins and Stuart A. Kirk note that under DSM, symptoms of mental disorder include—to name just a few—"frustration, anger, difficulty concentrating, restlessness, increased appetite, weight gain, often losing one's temper, being easily fatigued, muscle tension, . . . having extremely frightening dreams, being inappropriately sexually seductive, theatricality, showing arrogance, lacking empathy, being preoccupied with being criticized, and difficulty making everyday decisions." And individual DSM labels include so many vague criteria that almost anyone can qualify. Psychologist Paula Caplan noted that when a psychology professor gave students lists of DSM symptoms for several disorders, the students found that 75 percent of the class fit the criteria for "borderline personality disorder," and 100 percent of the *men* fit the criteria for "premenstrual dysphoric disorder"![12]

The result is no surprise: Researchers are concluding that almost everyone is crazy. The National Institute of Mental Health, using DSM criteria, announced in May 1996 that "24.1 percent of the population, or 48.2 million Americans, have some kind of mental disorder *within a 12-month period*." In short, according to DSM, a quarter of all people in America were crazy last year! And many of those people, according to psychiatrists, had hyperactivity or attention deficit disorders—disorders now said by their most zealous fans to affect *up to 33 percent* of all Americans.[13]

This willy-nilly labeling of virtually everyone as mentally ill is a serious danger to healthy children, because virtually all children have enough symptoms to get a DSM label and a drug. And, of course, DSM labeling is a danger to ill children, whose true diagnoses remain undiscovered and untreated.

Most important, however, DSM is dangerous because doctors are using the book as a substitute for clinical judgment and diagnostic skills. If a doctor tells you that your child has a "DSM diagnosis" of ADHD, ADD, conduct disorder, oppositional defiant disorder, depression, or anxiety, find another doctor who relies on real medical knowledge and evaluation rather than on this diagnostic cookbook.

The "Evidence" for Hyperactivity

Many doctors, as I've noted, will tell you that your child is hyperactive because the DSM says so. In addition to the DSM argument, however, there are four other arguments advanced by doctors who believe in these labels. If you've been to such a doctor, you've probably heard them. But let's take a look at whether they're valid.

Argument 1: Stimulant Drugs Treat All Cases of Hyperactivity and ADD.

Not true, as I explain further later on. A large number of children don't respond to Ritalin treatment, or they respond by becoming sick, depressed, or worse. Some children actually become psychotic. And many children who are considered better are behaving more quietly because they've become "Ritalin zombies."

Furthermore, the fact that many hyperactive children respond to Ritalin by becoming calmer doesn't mean that the drug is treating a disease. Most people respond to cocaine by becoming more alert and focused, but that doesn't mean that they're suffering from a disease treated by cocaine.

Consider, too, that half of hyperactive children continue to do poorly in life, in spite of medication treatment, and to grow into troubled teens and adults. Clearly, Ritalin isn't treating anything; it's merely covering up a variety of symptoms that continue to simmer. When untreated children have as many problems ten years later as treated children, it's a pretty good guess that doctors aren't identifying the real problem.

Argument 2: Brain Scans and Other Medical Tests Show Abnormalities in Hyperactive Children.

Of course they do, because hundreds of disorders cause brain scans to be abnormal. Since children with many different disorders are lumped together in studies of hyperactivity, lots of these children will show brain scan abnormalities. It's no wonder that researchers searching for a specific brain abnormality in hyperactivity come up empty-handed: what they're seeing is a variety of brain abnormalities due to a variety of medical disorders.

Here's an example of how misleading reports of brain defects linked to hyperactivity can be. A 1986 study using computerized tomography (CT) scanning found that compared to matched controls, adults with a history of hyperactivity were much more likely to exhibit underdevelopment of the cerebral cortex.[14] Many doctors said, "Aha! That's evidence that hyperactivity is caused by a specific brain abnormality." But it's not evidence of any such thing. Cerebral underdevelopment can occur when previously normal brain tissue atrophies, and this atrophy can be caused by a huge range of conditions that also cause hyperactivity. These conditions include head injuries, some parasitic infections, alcohol abuse or glue sniffing, steroids and other prescription drugs (possibly including, according to some very disturbing research, Ritalin—see Chapter 5), some viral or bacterial infections, strokes (yes, children sometimes have strokes), and carbon monoxide poisoning—to name just a sampling.

Similarly, biochemical tests argue against, not for, the concept of hyperactivity as a disease. One report that made headlines was the finding that 2 or 3 percent of hyperactive children exhibit a genetically influenced resistance to thyroid hormone. What does this mean? Not that hyperactive children have thyroid abnormalities, as many papers reported, but rather that we've isolated a cause of two or three out of every hundred cases of hyperactivity. That doesn't tell us what causes the other 97 or 98 cases.

As physician Warren Weinberg and colleagues recently put it, "A large number of biologic studies have been undertaken to characterize ADHD as a disease entity, but results have been inconsistent and not reproducible because the major features of ADHD are merely the symptoms of a variety of disorders."[15] And the Food and Drug Administration, which apparently has no problem with two million children taking Ritalin for ADHD, recently admitted in a letter to a physician, "We acknowledge . . . that as yet no distinct pathophysiology for [the] disorder has been delineated."[16]

Argument 3: Hyperactivity Runs in Families.

Indeed, hyperactive children often have hyperactive relatives. But that doesn't mean that hyperactivity is a genetic disease. It means that many genetic diseases can cause hyperactivity. (The genetic thyroid disorder I just mentioned, which affects a small percentage of hyperactive children, is a good example.) That's why I've included an extensive section in this book on genetic diseases.

However, familial hyperactivity sometimes stems from causes other than defective genes. In families with a high rate of alcoholism, for instance, each generation is likely to include some children who suffer from hyperactivity and other subtle effects of prenatal alcohol exposure. The alcoholism that runs in these children's families may be genetically influenced, but the children's alcohol-induced brain damage is not. And when several children in a single family are hyperactive, the cause is as likely to be a toxin such as lead or carbon monoxide as it is to be a bad gene.

Argument 4: Hyperactivity Is Primarily a Male Disease.

Here's a question skeptical doctors sometimes pose to me: If hundreds of different medical problems can lead to hyperactivity, shouldn't these disorders affect boys and girls equally? Yet many more males than females are identified as hyperactive. (For every girl with hyperactivity, there are at least four or five boys.) The sex disparity in hyperactivity does seem odd at first glance. However, there are two obvious reasons for it.

One reason, which I'll address at length later, is that hundreds of thousands of perfectly normal little boys who are labeled as hyperactive aren't really hyper at all. Little boys tend to be more active, aggressive, and annoying than little girls, and in the current pro-Ritalin culture, any little boy who squirms in his seat, gets into scuffles on the playground, or clowns around in class is a target for a hyperactivity label and a pill.

It's also true, however, that more boys than girls develop extreme symptoms of hyperactivity, attention disorder, and impulsiveness. There's a good explanation for this: Boys are more prone than girls to develop hyperactivity-causing medical conditions. They're much more likely to be victims of lead or pesticide or manganese poisoning, because they play in the dirt more often. They suffer far more head injuries from skateboarding, baseball, and other sports than girls do. They are more susceptible to worms and other parasites, because they're dirtier than little girls. They're more likely to experiment with smoking, alcohol, and drugs. They're more likely to pick up infections, because they're notoriously bad hand-washers, and they are much more likely to come in contact with other kids' spit, blood, and germs.

In addition, certain very common hyperactivity-causing genetic disorders, such as Tourette's syndrome and fragile X syndrome, strike boys more often than girls. And the brains of boys develop at a different rate than the brains of girls, making them more susceptible to brain damage and dysfunction in general.

The Sick Neuron

In summary, there is no evidence that hyperactivity is a single disorder with a single cause. Furthermore, there is no evidence that all hyperactive children should receive Ritalin or other psychiatric drugs, or that these drugs cure anything. There is, on the contrary, substantial evidence that doctors who treat hyperactive and attention-disordered children with Ritalin after quickie exams are covering up, rather than solving, a wide range of serious medical problems.

Why do all of these different diseases result in hyperactivity and attention problems? Simple: They all disrupt the functioning of neurons, the brain cells that think, feel, see, and hear for us. Behavior is the sum of neuronal activity, and disturbed behavior is the result of disturbed brain cells.

There are many ways to upset the brain's neurons. Some disorders, such as anemias, reduce oxygen to the brain. Others—metabolic disorders, for instance—reduce the brain's supply of glucose, the body's fuel. Some diseases rob the body of nutrients. Some poison the brain with toxins. Some alter levels of hormones or neurotransmitters, the chemicals that brain cells use to communicate with one another. Some cause seizures, short circuiting the brain's electrical system. Tumors, cysts, and head injuries alter the brain's structure. And viruses, parasites, and immune disorders can make a child feel "sick all over."

These disorders, although they frequently affect boys for reasons I've explained, can strike anyone, of either sex, at any age.

And whatever a patient's age or sex, hyperactivity is likely to persist—Ritalin or no Ritalin—until a doctor discovers and treats its real causes.

In later chapters, I take a look at some of the most common culprits responsible for hyperactivity, impulsiveness, and inattention. Then I look at how to obtain real treatment for these medical problems, rather than a label and a pill. First, however, let's take a closer look at why Ritalin and other drug treatments are misguided and potentially dangerous—and also look at the uses, limitations, and dangers of popular "alternative" treatments for attention problems and hyperactivity.

PART 2

Drugs and Alternative Therapies

CHAPTER 2

Ritalin and Other Pharmaceutical Cover-Ups

[We] have become the only country in the world where children are prescribed such a vast quantity of stimulants that share virtually the same properties as cocaine.
Gene R. Haislip, U.S. Drug Enforcement Administration

IT'S A STORY I HEAR ALL THE TIME. BUT THIS TROUBLED young man wasn't one of my patients. He was a major celebrity, and I watched his tragedy play out on the nightly news.

Born to a housewife and a mechanic, he was a creative, inquisitive child who loved art and music and had an imaginary friend named "Boda." He was so bright, his mother said, that he scared her. And he was active—so active that doctors labeled him hyperactive and prescribed Ritalin. The drug kept the boy awake all night, so doctors gave him a sedative as well.

As he grew older, the boy's behavior became more erratic. After his mother divorced his father, the child drew caricatures of his parents on his bedroom wall and scrawled, "I hate mom, I hate dad," under them. He grew so wild that his mother sent him to live with his father. The father in turn turned the boy over to a series of relatives, who also couldn't handle him.

The boy grew up and made good in his music career. His life, however, was another story. He suffered from chronic, severe stomach pains, saying, "It's burning, nauseous. I can it just being all raw and red. When I eat, the food sits in it and burns. It's probably the worst pain I've ever felt." Doctors couldn't find the cause. He also suffered from bronchitis, and from back pains, reportedly caused by scoliosis (curvature of the spine). He started coughing up blood. A marijuana smoker since high school, the young man worked his way up to hard drugs including heroin, which he took to relieve his abdominal pain. He injected opiates directly into his stomach. He drank heavily. He slept all day. "I'd sleep to get away from my stomach pain. Then I'd wake up and curse myself that I was still alive," he once said. His attempts at rehab all failed. He tried to commit suicide with an overdose of pills. In 1994, he took an overdose of heroin, added some Valium, and then put a gun to his head and shot himself to death.

The young man was Kurt Cobain, pop idol and lead singer of Nirvana.

I don't listen to rock music. But I was interested by Cobain's story, because, as I said, I hear it all the time.

Self-Medicating "Junkies"

Like Cobain, many of my adolescent patients are abusing drugs or alcohol—and many have escalated from "soft" drugs like marijuana to "hard" drugs like cocaine and heroin. When I evaluate one of these teens, I always ask, as part of my workup, what medications he or she has taken in the past. Almost every time, I get the same answer: Ritalin.

As it turns out, I'm not the only one who's spotted this pattern. A while ago, over lunch, I asked a friend of mine, a retired sheriff, "What percentage of your drug-abusing parolees have ever taken Ritalin?" His answer was, simply, "All of them."

Why would so many drug abusers have a history of Ritalin use? Not because Ritalin use automatically leads to drug addiction (although I believe, as I explain later, that it often sets the stage for serious drug abuse). Rather, it's because Ritalin isn't curing anything. It isn't even treating anything: unlike drugs such as insulin or thyroid hormones, Ritalin isn't correcting an identified neurochemical imbalance and thus making the body healthier. It's merely hiding a problem for a little while, without making the problem go away.

The purpose of Ritalin is to cover up symptoms, much like aspirin masks the pain of a broken leg. When a child stops taking Ritalin, usually in the late teens, the symptoms the drug has been concealing come back—but the chemical crutch, the daily dose of Ritalin, is gone. It's not surprising that many of these adolescents seek out a new crutch, *any* crutch.

Like Cobain, most of the drug-abusing Ritalin graduates I've seen aren't using drugs to get high or to be cool. They're using drugs to medicate their symptoms, just like they used Ritalin when they were children. Drugs and alcohol bring them down when they're hyper, calm them when they're anxious, help them stay alert when they're fatigued, or help them sleep when they're bothered by insomnia, headaches, dizziness, and other symptoms. It's not a great solution, but it's the only one they've ever known.

In 1997, I conducted a study with Andra Fisher and Dave Gaerin. We compared twenty young adult drug abusers to twenty nonabusers, matching our groups for age, sex, and social class. None of the nonabusers in our study had taken Ritalin in childhood, and none had suffered from chronic medical problems as kids. In contrast, 50 percent of the drug abusers had taken Ritalin as children. These subjects told us that the Ritalin they took as children, and the illegal drugs they were taking as adults, helped to ease symptoms including headaches, fatigue, and dizziness. Dave, a drug counselor, says the findings correlate with his clinical impression that "approximately 85 percent of adolescent drug abusers we counsel have a significant associated physical complaint."

A later survey we conducted, this time to get an idea as to how often Ritalin users later wind up abusing illegal drugs, led to an even more startling finding. Of fifteen consecutive childhood Ritalin users we identified, *all* later developed substance abuse problems. This was a small and informal survey, but the results still startled us—and they made us question the almost universal opinion among doctors that Ritalin use only rarely leads to substance abuse.

The "Ritalin Pattern"

The abusers we studied ranged from successful businessmen to unemployed high school dropouts. Some grew up in good families; others had abusive parents. Some were very bright, while others struggled intellectually. The only consistent pattern running through our subjects' lives was a history of childhood physical problems—and, often, medical problems in their family members as well.

Take Bob, one of our subjects, for example. A twenty-eight-year-old college dropout, Bob was an incorrigible child who ran away from school and got in trouble in his teen years for shoplifting, car theft, and other minor crimes. Labeled both hyperactive and antisocial, Bob got his first prescription for Ritalin at age ten and stayed on the drug until he was fifteen.

Numerous doctors saw Bob over the years, but none of them wondered what might underlie Bob's behavioral problems. That's a shame, because Bob undoubtedly had—and still has—diagnosable and treatable medical problems.

Our study did not include diagnostic workups, but I've referred Bob to a number of specialists who should be able to isolate the causes of his symptoms. From the data we collected, it's clear that Bob needs a careful evaluation by a neurologist, and endocrinologist, and possibly several other specialists. Among the red flags overlooked by all of Bob's doctors:

- At five, Bob suffered a severe head trauma when his head went through the windshield of the family car. Because many of his problems started around then, it's quite likely that he suffers from a post-traumatic subclinical seizure disorder.
- Although he's normally a pleasant man, Bob suffers from episodic temper explosions that frighten his family and friends.

These fits of temper seem to come out of the blue, and Bob himself can't explain them. A good doctor, however, probably could. Bizarre fits of temper often stem from temporal lobe seizures, which can be too subtle to detect without a twenty-four-hour electroencephalogram (EEG). The fact that Bob's temper outbursts usually follow a few drinks is interesting; there's a condition known as dyscontrol syndrome, first identified by Vernon Mark and Frank Ervin, in which even light drinking can lead to violent fits of temper.[1] Most of the men studied by Mark and Ervin showed signs of seizure disorders. But Bob's outbursts might not be caused by seizures. Episodic aggression can also stem from slow-growing tumors, cysts, or metabolic disorders that alter blood sugar levels.

- Bob's mother was placed in a mental institution when he was still a child. That means that Bob should be checked for hereditary causes of behavior problems (see Chapter 6).
- Bob's headaches and severe sleep problems, which started in early childhood, point to a wide range of other possible diagnoses, ranging from temporomandibular joint disorder to parasites.

But none of Bob's doctors ever checked him for these problems. Instead, they treated him with Ritalin during his childhood and then assumed that he'd outgrown his symptoms. When they took the drug away from him, he found two new ones: marijuana and alcohol. He drank and got high for twelve years, before realizing, to his credit, that the mind-altering substances that once eased his symptoms were making his life worse.

Bob has stopped drinking heavily, and he's back in junior college. But he's still fighting an uphill battle. To overcome his insomnia and restlessness, he plays basketball two hours every day, works three different jobs, and surfs. And he still suffers from episodic temper outbursts that get him into trouble.

Bob, however, is lucky. Many of the drug abusers who participated in our study haven't gotten their lives together. Some have spent time in jail, almost always for committing crimes to get drug money. Others have lost jobs or families. Many are tempted by Cobain's "ultimate solution" and contemplate suicide. Almost all think of themselves as losers. But should they shoulder the *entire* blame for their drug abuse? I don't think so.

Bob and the other drug abusers in our study told us that they had felt "sick," in a low-grade way, since they were kids. That's why they acted up in the first place. Chronically sick kids often misbehave: Their attention wanders, they can't focus, they get angry or irritable at the drop of a hat, and they wander aimlessly rather than sitting still and working. They lash out at authorities and act impulsively. They sleep badly and eat badly, compounding their health problems and making their behavior even worse.

These children can't put their finger on what ails them. They just know they "hurt," and that pain translates into behavior problems. In a 1997 study, Marja Mikkelsson and colleagues identified 124 schoolchildren who said they experienced chronic widespread pain and 108 children who reported chronic neck pain. When the researchers compared these children to a control group of children who did not report any chronic pains, the results weren't surprising: The children experiencing chronic pain were more depressed, more anxious, slept far more poorly, and had more social deficits and attention problems than the other children. Furthermore, the researchers say, "according to parents and teachers, both pain groups had more aggressive behavior problems than controls."[2]

Note, too, that these weren't children selected from clinical or hospital settings because of pain severe enough to require medical intervention. Their pains were identified only because researchers asked about them. Presumably, most of these children had been suffering in silence for years.

Children like these need help, but the hyperactive kids my own research evaluated later as adults didn't get that help. No one investigated their low-grade fatigue, aches, and other symptoms. Instead, doctors looked at their behavior problems, said "hyperactive," or "attention disordered," and prescribed Ritalin. The drug made these kids feel better, *for a while*. But when the kids became teenagers, and the prescriptions for Ritalin stopped, these individuals turned to other remedies for their pain. The obvious choices: alcohol and street drugs.

That's the path that Kurt Cobain followed. The first symptoms of the disorders that tormented him were present during his early years, although in a more subtle form. (According to one article, Cobain's chronic bronchitis began in infancy, and he was excused from gym classes in school due to burning stomach pains.) It's a good guess that these problems contributed to his hyper and antisocial behavior. His troubled childhood couldn't have helped, either. But what was Kurt taught as a child? That his problems, whether they stemmed from medical disabilities or a miserable home life, could be cured by a pill.

What was really wrong with Cobain? Without examining him, it's impossible to know. The problems he suffered from can result from a host of diseases and disorders, ranging from porphyria (a hereditary enzyme-deficiency disease) to temporal lobe seizures. Cobain's physicians no doubt included some excellent doctors who ruled out many possible causes of his ailments. In time, I'm sure, they could have uncovered the causes of his agony and offered help. But Cobain had already turned to another form of help: alcohol and hard-core narcotics.

Why did Cobain seek out heroin and booze when he was hurting? In part, because the doctors who initially put Cobain on Ritalin and sedatives gave him the message that drugs were the solution to his problems. It's the same message that more than two million children are getting right now. Many of these children, I fear, will fall into the "Ritalin pattern" I see so often, and graduate to hard drugs and alcohol.

The New Black Market Drug

Like Cobain, most of the former Ritalin users in our study later began abusing alcohol and marijuana. Often, they found temporary relief. Both of these substances, in addition to being effective short-term tranquilizers, can ease many symptoms of disease. (Marijuana's pain-relieving and antinausea properties, for instance, have made it a popular underground treatment for conditions as diverse as arthritis, cancer, AIDS, chronic back injuries, and postsurgery pain.)

When joints and drinks no longer soothed their symptoms, a significant minority of our study participants graduated to hard-core drugs such as heroin, cocaine, and speed, which were the most popular and readily available drugs when they were teens. The drugs eased their aches and pains, helped them sleep, kept them awake if they were fatigued, or, in some cases, just gave them enough of an artificial high to make them forget they felt bad.

These days, however, many teens in this same situation are discovering another drug: Ritalin itself. From their perspective, the drug has two big advantages over crack and speed. In the first place, it's incredibly easy to come by. (After all, two million children are getting it legally, and many don't mind sharing with friends.) Second, children don't think of Ritalin as a hard drug. Because it's handed out left and right by school nurses, children tend to think of Ritalin in the same light as cough syrup or Tylenol. After all, their school tells them to "Just Say No" to real drugs, doesn't it? And yet, the same school hands out dozens or even hundreds of doses of Ritalin every day at lunchtime. The schools' attitude is catching: One teen told CNN's Larry LaMotte, "It's not like somebody was asking me to do a line of cocaine or anything. It was like somebody asking me if I wanted an aspirin. Yeah. Give me an aspirin."[3]

But Ritalin (brand name for the generic drug methylphenidate), while often portrayed as nonaddictive, is not as harmless as its manufacturers, or the schools, or the students who use it like aspirin would like you to think. The drug was banned in Sweden several decades ago after an epidemic of Ritalin abuse there. In the 1970s, the United States reclassified Ritalin as a Schedule II controlled substance—that is, a substance that has a high potential for abuse and may cause severe psychic or physical dependence liability.*

---

* To put this in perspective, morphine is also a Schedule II drug, while Valium is only a Schedule IV substance.

That high potential for abuse is becoming a reality. The media, from TV shows to medical journals, are reporting an upsurge in the number of kids taking Ritalin to get high and in the number of students, teachers, and coaches getting rich selling the drug. The Canadian magazine *Maclean's* reported recently on a rash of home break-ins, in which only Ritalin was taken. "Teenagers on Ritalin may sell their pills [for] $10 to $20 a tablet," Patricia Chisholm reported. "Worse, younger children on the drug may be terrorized by teens looking for a hit."[4]

Most Ritalin abusers crush the tablets, dissolve them in water, and take them intravenously, a sometimes fatal act—particularly when Ritalin is mixed with downers. Other abusers snort the crushed tablets.[5] But William J. Bailey, Executive Director of the Indiana Prevention Resource Center at Indiana University, notes that "even when taken according to the prescription directions, there is a risk of developing dependence and tolerance to the drug."[6]

Ritalin abuse is a growing threat not just to older teens and adults but also to young children. According to reporter John Lang, writing in Florida's *Naples Daily News*, "In 1991 there were fewer than 25 emergency room mentions tracked nationwide for methylphenidate [Ritalin] abuse by children aged 10 to 14. In 1995 the number climbed above 400—about the same as for cocaine abusers in that age group."[7]

Many doctors who prescribe Ritalin say the media have overblown the issue of Ritalin abuse, but that's not what the experts are saying. The International Narcotics Control Board of the United Nations warned in 1995 that "the abuse of methylphenidate in the United States has increased and cases have been reported of serious damage to health as a result of such abuse." Concerned by the astonishing increase in both legal and illegal Ritalin use in the United States, the board has issued a stern lecture to U.S. authorities to prevent "medically unjustified treatment with methylphenidate and other stimulants."[8]

Another expert body, the U.S. Drug Enforcement Agency, recently stated that "the documentation . . . directly refutes the assertions that methylphenidate is a benign, mild stimulant that is not associated with abuse or serious side effects."[9] In October

1995, the DEA ranked Ritalin as one of the "top 10 most frequently reported controlled pharmaceuticals stolen from licensed handlers."

At a recent conference, DEA official Gene R. Haislip commented, "These drugs [Ritalin and other stimulants] have been over-promoted, over-marketed and over-sold, resulting in profits of some $450 million annually. This constitutes a potential health threat to many children and has also created a new source of drug abuse and illicit traffic."[10]

If you're still skeptical, listen to another kind of expert: a recovering Ritalin abuser. One Ritalin abuser told PBS, "It's like a speed, it's the same thing, except if someone has it and their parents are paying for it, it's a free high for everyone else." Another user told CNN's Larry LaMotte, "With Ritalin you're kinda more like humming, you're up there." And still another told LaMotte how "we'd just do it at our desk before we went to class . . . we'd just crush the pill and do a line."

LaMotte noted that thirteen-year-old Julia Solomon, for a statewide social science competition, surveyed 335 junior and senior high school students about Ritalin. She found, LaMotte reported, that "just under 10 percent said they are regular abusers of Ritalin" and that "26 percent said they have friends who use the drug."

We have to question the wisdom of giving a drug with this potential for misuse to behavior-disordered children who are already at a very high risk of becoming drug abusers. The drug isn't as addictive as cocaine or Valium—not by a long shot—but it's not harmless, either.

Furthermore, child psychiatrist Denis Donovan notes that early use of stimulant drugs makes the brain physically more receptive to other drugs such as cocaine. In short, Donovan says, we may be teaching young children's brains to develop a "taste" for stimulants. "When a child has taken Ritalin . . . from the third or sixth grade on," he commented, "that child no longer has a stimulant-naive brain. . . . Why would we want to be initiating all these brains into more efficient responsiveness to this whole class of licit and illicit stimulants?"[11]

Studies suggest that Donovan's concerns are justified. Susan Schenk, a psychopharmacologist, devised an experiment in which rats pressed a lever to give themselves cocaine. Rats who had taken amphetamine drugs for nine days were more likely to hit the cocaine-dispensing lever than rats receiving a placebo. And when Schenk and psychologist Nadine Lambert studied 5,000 hyperactive subjects to see if Ritalin promoted later drug use, they found that Ritalin users were significantly more likely to become smokers than children not taking Ritalin—and three times more likely than nonusers to try cocaine.[12]

Carol Whalen and Barbara Henker also are concerned about giving Ritalin to children at high risk of becoming drug abusers. They warn that "evidence of a familial tendency toward alcoholism in families with hyperactive children raises the possibility that hyperactive children may be particularly prone to drug dependence, and that the medical use of psychostimulants with these youngsters may potentiate substance abuse."[13]

Kids Who Hate Ritalin

It's puzzling but true: While some children are getting high on Ritalin and spending good allowance money to get their hands on the drug, many other youngsters hate it. Ritalin appears to affect this substantial group of children, to a milder degree, in much the same way as heavy psychotropic drugs affect severely mentally ill patients: It numbs them into behaving but makes them depressed, anxious, or emotionally "flat" in the process.

Many children say that Ritalin and similar drugs make them feel unhappy, sick, or "not myself," and pediatrician Esther Sleator, who studied a group of stimulant-medicated children, reported, "Above all else, we found a pervasive dislike among hyperactive children for taking stimulants." Sleator found that children frequently pretended to swallow their pills and then threw the drug away when no one was watching.[14]

This dislike of Ritalin is greatly underestimated by doctors, for the simple reason that most children want to please their doctors and parents. Children often say they like taking Ritalin when the opposite is true. Sleator tells of a ten-year-old who told his doctor that taking stimulants was helpful and denied trying to avoid taking his pills. But, Sleator reports, "this child was known to hate taking [his medicine], and his mother fought with him about it daily. The physician actually witnessed a scene during which the mother was trying to persuade the child to go back on medication and she alternately pleaded, begged, demanded, and threatened. Tears were shed and voices raised in the doctor's office." Such scenes are played out across the country every day, but few doctors witness them—and few children are brave enough to tell their doctors, "I hate this stuff!"

But many children *do* hate it: Sleator and colleagues found that "of the 52 subjects interviewed, 32 had specific complaints about taking medication." Moreover, the researchers found that the longer children took stimulant drugs, the more they objected to taking them. This hatred was intense enough, in some cases, that the researchers said, "One device we have used is to stop medication and agree not to restart as a goal (and reward) for continued satisfactory performance."

Ritalin's Effects and Side Effects

Ritalin is an amphetamine-like drug, much like speed. Chemically, it also resembles cocaine, another drug that helps users focus and increases performance. Both cocaine and Ritalin inhibit the reuptake of the chemical dopamine at the same receptors in the same brain areas, causing more dopamine (a mood-influencing brain chemical) to be available in the synapses between brain cells. The primary difference is that cocaine is cleared from the brain more quickly. In other words, Ritalin has much the same effect as cocaine on the brain, only it doesn't wear off as fast.[15] As Dr. Robert Morrow of Eastern Virginia Medical School says, "If we gave cocaine to hyperactive children, instead of Ritalin, we have every reason to believe they would improve on it, too."[16]

In fact, when listening to parents talk about how Ritalin helps their children become more focused and "normal," I'm reminded of Sigmund Freud, who told his friends and patients that cocaine's effect "consists of lasting euphoria which does not differ from normal euphoria of a healthy person." Like coke, Ritalin makes the user feel smarter and more alert and focused by creating an artificial chemical high. But it's just that—a chemical high, not a real treatment.

Interestingly, many kids recognize this themselves, even if their parents don't. Several years ago, PBS aired an in-depth and highly critical look at Ritalin, including interviews with a number of children taking the drug. Several of the children commented that they didn't like themselves when they were on the drug. They explained that "You're not you," and "It's a fake person that the medicine's creating."[17]

As psychologist Theodore LaVaque puts it, giving children Ritalin is "rather like giving steroids to an athlete."[18] The drug artificially enhances performance, at least in the short term, but does nothing to address the child's real problems.

And while Ritalin makes children sit still longer, obey authorities better, and complete their homework more neatly, it also robs many children of something much more important: their souls. Many of my patients who come to me on Ritalin feel as if they've been put in emotional straitjackets. One parent of such a child noted recently in the *Minnesota Parent*, "He feels he's not himself when he's on [Ritalin]. When he gets on medicine, he's so focused and he doesn't laugh or joke around very much at all. . . . [When he's off the medicine] he's so alive, he just shines. His eyes are dancing. He's cracking jokes. He's fun, he's exciting."[19]

This child's response to Ritalin is not unique. D. P. Cantwell and J. Swanson reported that a number of children respond to Ritalin by becoming isolated, withdrawn, and overfocused. These children can appear zombie-like, somber, quiet, and still, and spend increasing amounts of time alone.[20] If zombification, somberness, and social withdrawal are the price a child has to pay for sitting still, that price is too steep.

Despite its chemical resemblance to street drugs, and its ability to create zombies out of happy children, doctors will tell you that Ritalin is a "safe" drug. But take a look at the *Physician's Desk Reference (PDR)*, the manual provided by drug manufacturers themselves. According to the *PDR*, reported adverse reactions to Ritalin include nervousness, rashes, anorexia, nausea, dizziness, headaches, cardiac arrhythmia, blood pressure changes, angina, abdominal pain, and weight loss.

Another extremely common side effect is a pattern of sleeplessness, much like that experienced by cocaine users who can't stop their wired brains from racing. In the PBS interview, one child complained, "You're tired but you can't sleep. . . . Tired with hyperness . . . and you can't sleep because your mind is still awake."

Patients taking Ritalin have also reported experiencing anemia, transient depression, and hair loss. In some cases, Ritalin brings on symptoms of Tourette's syndrome, a tic disorder. (One recent study found that 9 percent of hyperactive and attention-disordered children treated with Ritalin or other stimulant medications developed tics or dyskinesias, which are abnormal muscle movements that stem from disrupted brain function.[21]) Ritalin can also cause "toxic psychosis," a syndrome that usually occurs in overdoses but has been reported in individuals taking standard doses.[22] Symptoms of toxic psychosis include hallucinations, delirium, and sometimes violent behavior. A recent report notes that Ritalin can interact with anesthesia in unexpected ways, possibly endangering children who need surgery.[23]

And those are just the short-term effects. As to its long-term effects, we don't really have a clue. *The long-term effects of Ritalin have never been thoroughly tested*, despite the fact that millions of children take the drug every day. Imagine using that many children as guinea pigs for a drug whose effects twenty, thirty, or forty years down the line are completely unknown!*

The danger of such shortsightedness was brought to light recently, when researchers reported preliminary evidence that Ri-

---

* Not only is there little research on Ritalin's actual effects, but some of the most influential research on the drug later proved to be an outright fraud. The

talin may be carcinogenic.[24] While studies indicate that the drug is probably only a weak carcinogen, increasing the future cancer risk of millions of children—even a little bit—is not something to be done lightly. Another recent report warns that Ritalin "may have persistent, cumulative effects on the myocardium" (the thick muscle layer that forms most of the heart wall).[25] In Chapter 5, I also look at frightening evidence that long-term Ritalin use may actually lead to brain shrinkage.

Incidentally, there's one more consequence—this one not a medical side effect but a "lifestyle side effect"—that parents should think about before allowing their children to be put on Ritalin. Currently, the U.S. military is not accepting recruits who have used Ritalin past the age of twelve. A Pentagon spokesman's position on the issue: "If they're using Ritalin after that, there's probably some underlying problems."

Other Drugs, Other Dangers

So far, I've discussed only Ritalin, which is by far the most popular treatment for hyperactivity. Other drugs, however, are also given to hyperactive children, particularly when Ritalin doesn't reduce symptoms or when it causes dangerous side effects. These drugs aren't any more effective than Ritalin, and several are potentially much more dangerous.

One of these drugs is desipramine (Norpramin), an antidepressant. Described several years ago as "the most popular medication for children among child psychiatrists," desipramine was, until recently, prescribed for everything from attention problems

initial Ritalin boom in the 1980s was fueled in part by positive data reported by Stephen Breuning, a researcher at the University of Pittsburgh. Breuning later became quite famous for this research, but not for the reasons you'd expect. Investigators at the National Institute of Mental Health discovered, in the mid-1980s, that Breuning had *not* actually conducted much of the research he was reporting. Billy Goodman notes in *The Scientist* (March 18, 1996) that "in 1988, Breuning became the first independent researcher in the United States to be indicted on research fraud, and ultimately pled guilty to two charges of filing false reports." Breuning also was involved in research on Dexedrine, another drug used to treat hyperactivity.

to bed-wetting. That was before the drug was linked to six cases of sudden death in children from cardiac arrest.[26] The *Physician's Desk Reference* notes that side effects reported in conjunction with the use of desipramine and chemically similar drugs include seizures, drowsiness, dizziness, weakness, fatigue, headaches, fever, potentially dangerous blood disorders, stroke, hallucinations, anxiety, agitation, insomnia, incoordination, tremors, and blurred vision. In addition, the *PDR* notes, "Norpramin (desipramine hydrochloride) is not recommended for use in children since safety and effectiveness in the pediatric age group have not been established."

Then there's pemoline (Cylert), which, like Ritalin, is a stimulant. Researchers recently reported a significant association between Cylert and the development of liver problems in children, including jaundice and actual destruction of liver tissue. At least three children have died after developing liver failure while taking the drug,[27] and a number of other children required liver transplants. As a result of evidence indicating that the rate of liver failure in patients taking Cylert is four to seventeen times greater than the rate in the general population, the drug's manufacturer modified its label in 1997 to include a warning that the drug not be considered as a first-line drug for hyperactivity. A recent FDA medical bulletin noted, moreover, that these frightening estimates of hepatic toxicity related to Cylert "may be conservative because of underreporting and because long latency may make it difficult to recognize the association between Cylert and hepatic failure."[28]

Other side effects of Cylert include seizures, precipitation of Tourette's syndrome, hallucinations, dyskinesias, abnormal eye movements, depression, dizziness, irritability, headaches, and drowsiness. And Cylert, like Ritalin, has the potential to be addictive.

Adderall, a mixture of dextro and levo amphetamine that is gaining popularity among drug-oriented doctors, is so new that little or nothing is known about its long-term effects. Its short-term effects, however, may include loss of appetite, weight loss, insomnia, headaches, tics, dizziness, irritability, stomach pain, increased heart rate, and hallucinations.

Another drug sometimes given to hyper kids is clonidine (Catapres), a blood pressure medication and antidepressant. The drug's side effects include drowsiness and low blood pressure. Far more alarming, however, is a report by physicians Michael Maloney and Jeffrey Schwam that when combined with Ritalin, clonidine may cause sudden death in children. Maloney and Schwam have identified two cases of sudden death in children taking this combination (and a third in a child taking clonidine and high doses of Prozac) and say that "a review of the literature shows that clonidine, even at low doses, has been associated with abnormal EKG findings."[29]

In some cases, hyperactive children are put on Dexedrine (dextroamphetamine), a once-popular drug that's now used less often. Dexedrine has side effects similar to Ritalin's, and also can be habit-forming. Once popular as a diet drug, Dexedrine fell out of favor when too many women hoping to lose a few pounds wound up "Dexie junkies" instead. Apparently, however, many doctors consider it okay to use this potent drug on children.

An increasing number of children who don't become less hyper while taking Ritalin or the other drugs I've mentioned are now being given fluoxetine (Prozac) a drug touted as a treatment for virtually every psychiatric ailment. Many other children are put on Prozac because doctors label them both hyperactive *and* depressed, an increasingly common practice. Doctors will tell you Prozac has a better "safety profile" than most psychiatric drugs (an example of damning with faint praise, given that most psychiatric drugs have potentially fatal side effects). But as more and more people take Prozac, we're learning that the drug isn't anywhere near as benign as its proponents would have you believe. Among Prozac's potential side effects:

- heat intolerance, sometimes leading to loss of consciousness or even permanent brain damage.[30]
- akathisia, or extreme restlessness, fidgeting, and sleeplessness. Children with akathisia may become extremely irritable, or even very violent.[31]

• tardive dyskinesia, a neurological disorder resulting in involuntary muscle movements. This side effect, while very rare in Prozac users, can interfere with eating and breathing—and it doesn't always stop when the drug is discontinued.[32]

A bigger concern about Prozac, however, is that its long-term side effects are completely unknown. The drug, and similar drugs known as selective serotonin reuptake inhibitors, or SSRIs, have been on the market only a short time and have been tested on children for only a few years. We have *no idea* what they might do to a developing child's brain or to other organs, although we're already seeing evidence that the drugs can cause a variety of side effects. As Michael Lemonick noted recently in *Time*, "So far, the tools used to manipulate serotonin in the human brain are more like pharmacological machetes than they are like scalpels—crudely effective but capable of doing plenty of collateral damage."[33]

In the face of our ignorance about the long-term effects of Prozac, one would expect doctors to be cautious about prescribing this drug to children. But they aren't being cautious at all; in fact, they're racing to prescribe the new, mint-flavored form of Prozac to thousands of American children now being described as "depressed," as well as to thousands of children labeled as ADD or ADHD. And a surprising number of parents are allowing their children to be used as guinea pigs in this massive experiment: the number of Prozac prescriptions written for American children between five and ten years of age jumped from 61,000 in 1992 to nearly a quarter million in 1994.[34]

THE DOCTORS PRESCRIBING PROZAC, RITALIN, AND OTHER psychiatric drugs for children are playing a dangerous game. Clearly, none of the drugs used to treat behavior-disordered children is harmless, and the side effects these drugs cause can often be far worse than the symptoms they're intended to treat. They're especially dangerous when combined into "medication cocktails," a common practice despite the fact that the effects of mixing these drugs are virtually unknown. Yet few parents are adequately warned, either by their children's doctors or by the many books recommending drug treatments, about how risky these drugs can be. In fact, books sometimes appear to downplay the risks, giving parents the incorrect idea that there's no need at all to worry. One popular book, for instance, mentions that "inflammation of the liver may occur in a small number of children" taking Cylert, but goes on to say that "liver changes are rare and reversible once the medication is stopped."[35] Tell that to the parents of the three children who died after taking this drug, or the parents whose children required transplants when Cylert destroyed their livers.

Obviously, these drugs are more dangerous than many doctors are letting on. The greatest harm that drugs do, however, is to cause complacency. By temporarily easing the symptoms of hyperactive or attention-disordered children, drugs convince parents and physicians that these children are fine. They *aren't* fine, and they won't be until someone diagnoses and treats the conditions that are making them hyper in the first place.

Any parent considering giving a child Ritalin, Cylert, clonidine, or other hyperactivity drugs should do a risk/benefit analysis. Is it worth the risk of potentially serious side effects, or even death, to achieve the questionable benefit of temporarily squelching inappropriate behaviors?

WARNING: If your child is taking any of these drugs, do not discontinue it without medical supervision. Children who stop taking Ritalin can suffer serious "rebound" effects, in which symptoms far worse than their original symptoms occur. Sudden discontinuation of any drug used to treat hyperactivity can cause serious harm. Consult a doctor on how to taper your child off drugs if you choose to do so.

Clues from Drugs

Although I'm not a fan of drug treatments for hyperactive or attention-disordered children, I always ask parents if their children's symptoms were ever reduced by Ritalin or other drugs.

Often, the fact that a child is a drug responder points toward a diagnosis.

This is *not*, as previously thought, because Ritalin magically affects hyperactive children differently from nonhyperactive children. Doctors once believed that this amphetamine-like drug calmed hyperactive children while making nonhyperactive children more active, a phenomenon called a paradoxical effect. But controlled studies show that, as a group, children who are hyperactive react to Ritalin in much the same way as children without this symptom. Thus, doctors who use Ritalin as a "diagnostic" tool—that is, doctors who administer Ritalin and then pronounce that *responders have ADHD simply because they responded to the drug*—are completely misguided.

The manner in which an *individual* child responds to drugs, however, can offer clues about that child's underlying problems. Ritalin, for example, can affect carbohydrate disorders, such as diabetes and neuroglycopenia (a condition in which insufficient sugar is reaching the brain cells). And it can alter the balance of calcium, phosphorus, and magnesium in the body, sometimes alleviating disease symptoms. Other drugs commonly given to hyperactive children also have a variety of effects on the brain and body; clonidine, for instance, affects the cardiac system, alters brain chemical levels, and acts as a potent pain reliever.

Although Ritalin, Cylert, Prozac, clonidine, or desipramine can reduce symptoms of a dozen or so common disorders, this doesn't mean that a child needs to take any of these drugs. It means, on the contrary, that a doctor should ask, "*Why* is this drug alleviating some of this child's symptoms?" A response to Ritalin or Cylert might point to carbohydrate disorders, while a response to Prozac, clonidine, or desipramine might point to entirely different diagnostic possibilities, including thyroid disorders, seizures, abnormal blood sugar levels, or sleep disorders. And finding these underlying diagnoses, and addressing them head-on, makes far more sense than hiding symptoms with drugs while allowing disease processes to continue.

Chemically Designing Children

Doctors who cover up disease symptoms with a "feel-good" amphetaminelike drug such as Ritalin, lulling families into believing that their children are being treated when they're merely being pacified by a mind-altering drug, are irresponsible. But an even more irresponsible act being committed by far too many doctors is the drugging of children with *no behavior problems at all*. Although I discuss this problem in depth later on, it deserves a brief mention here.

A few decades ago, boisterous little boys and girls were affectionately called scamps, rascals, and class pests. Now these children are called sick, and doctors are putting them on powerful medications for years or even decades. Doctors are increasingly labeling normal childhood moods and behaviors as hyperactivity and attention disorder and altering these moods and behaviors with potent drugs.

In effect, we are coming ever closer to chemically designing children who will be obedient, docile, and compliant—something that should be abhorrent to moral individuals. (It's chilling that on the Revised Conner's Questionnaire, a form often used to "diagnose" hyperactivity before prescribing Ritalin, two symptoms include being "sassy" and "wanting to run things." In adults, those characteristics might be called independence and assertiveness, and they probably wouldn't be drugged away.) As columnist Arianna Huffington recently said, commenting on the epidemic of psychoactive drug consumption by both adults and children, "Treating life as an illness is bad enough. But treating childhood as a disease is tragic."

It's also a good way to encourage normal young boys to develop drug or alcohol problems. We're not just telling this group of children that it's okay to take drugs to mask symptoms of disease. We're actually telling them it's okay to take drugs to treat perfectly normal moods and behaviors, such as restlessness or boredom. (Many of these normal, active children are simply bored out of their minds in school.) In short, we're entering the realm of "cosmetic drugs," used not to treat disease or even to mask symptoms but simply to eliminate any unpleasant or inconvenient feelings.

We're also using drugs, in these instances, to solve problems that aren't biological but social. For instance, a boisterous child in a class of fifteen students is easy to keep under control. A normal, boisterous boy in a classroom of thirty-four students is a real problem. It's not surprising that as class sizes get bigger and bigger, the number of children labeled hyperactive and put on Ritalin keeps increasing.

Evidence also suggests that that Ritalin is prescribed much more often for children of single mothers than for children in two-parent families. In part, this could stem from the fact that children in one-parent families are at higher risk for a number of health problems, including malnutrition and toxic exposure, which can lead to behavior problems. But it's also true that children from broken families act out frequently because they're scared and hurt. Too many doctors find it cheaper and easier to drug these children than to take the time to get to the roots of their problems.

What's still more frightening is the growing use of Ritalin to enhance normal children's performance, much in the way athletes use steroids to gain unfair advantage over competitors. The *Houston Chronicle*, for instance, recently told about a Little League coach demanding that a perfectly normal nine-year-old catcher be put on Ritalin during games to improve his performance. The newspaper article also told of one mother whose children get A's and B's, and score above average on tests. Despite their success, the mother was told by one teacher, "Look how much better they could do if they were on Ritalin."[36]

The mother refused the recommendation, but some people aren't so wise: Increasing numbers of college students are using Ritalin as a study aid during finals.[37] And David Kessler, former commissioner of the FDA, says, "Where I see enormous abuse is the high school student who wants to have it prescribed to do better on SATs."[38] Again, there is a parallel to cocaine users, who often use coke to achieve a boost in high-pressure situations.

The Ritalin Epidemic: Follow the Money

Ninety percent of Ritalin is consumed in the United States, and Ritalin use is growing by leaps and bounds: The annual U.S. production of the drug increased by 500 percent between 1990 and 1995.[39] The people most responsible for this astronomical growth in Ritalin prescribing are, of course, the physicians who are writing all those prescriptions. In general, these physicians honestly believe that Ritalin treats hyperactivity and that hyperactivity is a legitimate disease rather than a symptom in search of a diagnosis. But many of these doctors are also being influenced, either knowingly or unwittingly, by financial pressures.

Managed care programs, as I mentioned in Chapter 1, apply most of this pressure. These plans are far more interested in profit margins than in patients' health, and they can be ruthless to doctors who spend "excessive" time seeing patients, or who order expensive consultations. Even the most dedicated doctors find it hard to resist subtle (and often not-so-subtle) demands to cut down on patient care.

I don't believe, however, that this pressure alone is behind the Ritalin epidemic. The doctors I know still want to provide good patient care. But other factors affect doctors' decisions—among them, the influence of drug companies, which are all too adept at convincing physicians that good patient care comes in a bottle.

Doctors are exposed to a tremendous amount of self-serving information from drug companies, from advertising in prestigious medical journals to pharmaceutical-company-sponsored seminars touting drugs. Like everyone else, doctors are only human, and they tend to accept this often biased input far less critically than they should. In addition, medical journals, just like newspapers and magazines, want news, and studies are newsworthy only if they report dramatic findings. Only about 50 percent of research studies are accepted by journals, and studies reporting no benefits from a drug treatment are often among the first to be rejected.

Thus, doctors are unlikely to get a balanced view of a drug's benefits and risks. In general, they're inundated with ads, articles, and conferences promoting a given drug, and have to search much harder to learn about its drawbacks. This makes drug therapy seem not only simple and cost-effective but also beneficial for their patients. It's a combination doctors are hard-pressed to resist.

Of course, companies that manufacture the drugs used to treat hyperactivity don't *want* doctors to resist the use of drugs. Their goal, needless to say, is continually to expand their market. In fact, they have increased their sales exponentially in recent years by recommending the use of drugs for "adult hyperactives," a move that has added millions of new customers. (Like their younger counterparts, "adult hyperactives" actually suffer not from ADHD but rather from a wide range of undiagnosed and untreated medical disorders—or, quite often, from no real problems at all.)

Fighting the Ritalin Pressure

Where does the current "label-and-drug" fad leave parents who don't want a quick Ritalin fix for their behavior-disordered children but instead want a real diagnosis? Many of these parents are learning that their doctors, once their advocates when the system got in the way of proper care, now have their hands tied by HMO review panels and red tape. And many others are finding that their doctors, convinced that Ritalin is the correct—indeed, the only—treatment for hyperactive, behavior-disordered kids, are completely unsympathetic.

If you're in this situation, the best advice I can give you is to stick by your guns. After reading this book, I hope you'll be convinced that there are far better options for your child than a Ritalin "Band-Aid." If your doctors don't agree, seek out more knowledgeable doctors (see Chapter 10). No matter how much pressure is placed on you, the decision to accept or reject Ritalin treatment is *your* decision, not a doctor's or a teacher's.

A Final Note

One last caution, before we leave the subject of Ritalin—this one a warning about guilt trips. Numerous parents have agreed to put their children on Ritalin after doctors hit them this with classic guilt-provoking line: "Depriving your child of Ritalin is like depriving your child of insulin." I've heard this approach so often that I'm starting to suspect that it's being taught in medical school. But I don't care if a hundred doctors try this speech on you—*don't fall for it.*

Diabetic children need insulin because their bodies don't produce enough of this necessary hormone. But, as therapist Billie Jay Sahley once said, "Nobody is suffering from a Ritalin deficiency."

Think about it.

CHAPTER 3

Nondrug Therapies: What They Can and Can't Do

There are no cure-alls for all the conditions
classified under the term "hyperactivity."
There is no universal drug, no universal diet, that will cure it.
W. Harding leRiche, A Chemical Feast

PARENTS WHO RIGHTLY WORRY ABOUT GIVING THEIR HY-
peractive kids stimulant drugs are turning to a wide range of
alternative therapies, ranging from special diets to neurofeedback and behavior modification.

Do these therapies work? Some do and some don't.

Do I recommend them? Yes—and no.

The problem is that too many parents put the cart before
the horse by trying alternative therapies willy-nilly *before*
knowing what's really wrong with their children. Before you
consider any of these therapies, remember rule number one:
You can't treat what you don't know.

Like Ritalin, alternative therapies (with one or two excep-
tions I'll note) don't cure anything. They merely ameliorate
symptoms. You still need to find out what's *causing* the symptoms; otherwise, you're just sticking on more Band-Aids.

Dietary therapies, behavior modification, and other approaches may make your child behave better. But a diet won't
treat toxin-induced brain dysfunction. Behavior modification
won't cure hyperthyroidism. Vitamins won't eliminate a brain
cyst, and neurofeedback won't correct anemia. *To effectively*

treat a disease, you have to know what that disease is. So before you turn to a diet, a vitamin, or a behavioral therapy, find out what's causing your child to be hyperactive or behavior disordered.

Once you know what's wrong with your child, however, there are times when it's a very good idea to try alternative therapies. Sometimes, dietary approaches can actually *cure* behavior problems (although these cases are the exception, rather than the rule). In other cases, diets or other nondrug treatments can at least reduce the symptoms of disorders that medical science can't yet cure.

Moreover, most nondrug therapies are at worst harmless, and I'd certainly try them instead of Ritalin. Keep this principle in mind: When selecting a treatment, always start with the most benign, and then move on to less benign treatments only if needed. Don't use a sledgehammer to pound in a thumbtack—and don't use a drug when a nondrug approach can be just as effective.

That said, let's take a look at some of the most common alternatives to stimulant drugs, and what they can—and can't—do for your child.

Diets

Special diets are second only to Ritalin as popular treatments for hyperactivity and other childhood behavior problems. Depending on a doctor's orientation, he or she might want to place your child on an allergy diet, a diet low in food colorings and additives, an anti-*Candida* diet, or a diet that includes nutritional supplements.

Will these diets help your child? It's impossible to say because the answer depends on what's ailing your child in the first place. Here are some examples.

The Candida Controversy

One infectious condition often blamed for causing hyperactivity is monilia, or an overgrowth of *Candida albicans*. According to some doctors, hyperactive children are infested with *Candida albicans*, the same common fungus that causes oral thrush and most vaginal "yeast" infections. The treatment these doctors recommend includes a special diet low in yeasts and yeast-promoting foods, along with antifungal drugs such as Nystatin.

Are the *Candida* doctors right? Up to a point. Many hyperactive children do have chronic *Candida* infections, and I often spot *Candida* growth on their eardrums. Frequently, teenage girls with hyperactivity report a long history of vaginal infections. Moreover, the *Candida* treatment makes a number of these children feel and behave better.

But—and this is critically important—doctors who believe in *Candida*-caused hyperactivity are making the same mistake as doctors who prescribe Ritalin. *Candida* drugs *will* ameliorate *Candida* infestation, a symptom common in hyperactive children, but they won't answer the question, "What *causes* this group of hyperactive children to be so susceptible to *Candida* in the first place?"

Candida, after all, isn't some rare, scary pathogen. It's as common as dirt. Everyone is exposed daily to *Candida albicans*, but hardly anyone develops chronic infestations. The people who *do* suffer from *Candida* infestations have some underlying problem—frequently an immune disorder, or a disorder affecting carbohydrate metabolism and thus altering sugar levels—that makes their bodies a fertile environment for this normally unaggressive, relatively harmless little fungus. And guess what: The same disorders that often lead to *Candida* infection can cause the symptoms of hyperactivity as well. Take immune disorders, for instance. Treat an immune-disordered child's hyperactivity with Ritalin, and treat the child's *Candida* infection with Nystatin, and your patient still has an undiagnosed immune disorder.

Candida susceptibility can also stem from overtreatment with some antibiotics, from the use of birth control pills, and from liver, thyroid, or adrenal gland abnormalities. It can even stem from poor hygiene, because dirty kids carry around lots of natural "potting soil" in which *Candida* can take root.

Frequently a child's *Candida* infestation is caused by the same underlying medical problem as his or her hyperactivity. Sometimes, it's completely unrelated. In either case, drugs and special diets only cover up the symptom without uncovering its true cause. In short, *Candida* often is a clue pointing to what's causing hyperactivity. It's not, however, a diagnosis.

The Allergy Question

Some physicians report success in reducing hyperactivity and attention disorders in children through diets that remove allergens—commonly milk, chocolate, and grains, but often other foods as well. I've seen children whose symptoms did stem, in large part, from allergies. For such children, an allergy diet specifically designed to remove the foods that are truly causing symptoms can alleviate hyperactivity, fatigue, migraines, and even bed-wetting.

In most cases, however, hyperactivity stems from causes other than allergies. And in many cases where allergies *are* a factor, they're only one piece of the puzzle.

This is true even for children who appear to have "classic" allergy features: eyelid wrinkles, black circles under their eyes, puffiness around the eyes, wrinkles at the bridge of the nose, drippy noses, and a pale, dull, apathetic look. Often, allergy-oriented doctors immediately "diagnose" these children as having allergy-induced hyperactivity, based on appearance alone. Headaches and sleep problems, too, are often considered as part of the "allergy pattern."

This is a dangerous assumption. That's because the symptoms that sometimes point to allergies often point to other disorders entirely. Pallor and apathy, for instance, can stem from anemia, heart problems, or even Ritalin use. Children poisoned by pesticides often have rashes, swollen eyes, scratchy throats, indigestion, and other symptoms commonly attributed to allergies. A chronically runny nose can stem from allergies, *or* it can be a sign of cerebral spinal fluid escaping through a rip in the dura mater, the membrane that envelops the brain. Headaches, considered a classic symptom of allergies, can indeed result from eating chocolate or other allergenic foods—or they can result from tumors, calcium deficits, sinus troubles, blood vessel dilation or constriction, collagen disease, vertebral problems, carbon monoxide poisoning, or temporomandibular joint disorder. Clearly, it's a mistake to write off all pale, sniffly, headachy children as simply having allergies.

If you think your child has food allergies, go to a qualified physician and find out for sure. Otherwise, you'll be removing many nutritious and tasty foods from your child's diet for no reason. And when I say a "qualified" physician, I mean one who does a complete physical examination and rules out *other* causes of hyperactivity before declaring that your child's problems are allergy-induced.

Additive-Free Diets

How about diets that reduce food additives and food colorings? There is, indeed, evidence that certain food additives can sometimes cause or exacerbate behavior problems. In a 1994 placebo-controlled study, Katherine and Kenneth Rowe reported in *The Journal of Pediatrics* that some hyperactive children react adversely to tartrazine (yellow dye #5). When challenged with the dye, reactive children cried more often, had more tantrums, were more irritable and restless, slept badly, and were disruptive, "aimlessly active," and "lacking self-control."[1] In another placebo-controlled study, Bonnie Kaplan and colleagues found that hyperactive boys who ate meals free of additives, artificial colors and flavors, preservatives, chocolate, and caffeine had significantly fewer behavior problems than when they ate standard meals.[2]

These and several other studies suggest that an additive-free diet can help some hyperactive children feel and behave better. In addition, it's a risk-free approach, because nobody *needs* to be eating tartrazine or MSG. Furthermore, a diet free of additives is, by its very nature, high in unrefined carbohydrates, fresh fruits and vegetables, and other healthful foods. Thus it's probably more healthful than your child's current diet.

(One possible exception is the Feingold diet, which—in its first stage—prohibits salicylates. To avoid eating these natural substances, your child will have to give up many healthful foods, including apples, apricots, tomatoes, green peppers, nectarines, oranges, peaches, corn, and berries. Unless you see some remarkable improvement when you remove salicylates from your child's diet, the loss of nutrients from fresh fruits and vegetables far outweighs the benefits.)

There's no reason not to try cutting additives out of your child's diet. But, again, *an additive-free diet is not a cure*. I have yet to read a credible case of a hyperactive child becoming completely normal simply through the use of the Feingold diet or other approaches that limit additives. At most, children improve slightly or moderately when additives are taken out of their diets. That's progress, but it's not good enough. Many (if not most) hyperactive children have two or three problems, and solving one doesn't absolve doctors and parents of the responsibility of looking for others.

One of my latest patients, for instance, had some evidence of allergies—but he also had elevated lead levels and evidence of strep-related neurological dysfunction. Putting him on an allergy diet would have made him feel a little better, but it wouldn't have cured his hyperactivity.

Furthermore, I'm concerned about the Feingold Association's promotional materials, which include checklists of symptoms that parents are told to use in determining if the Feingold diet is appropriate for their children. While noting that "the following symptoms are not to be considered abnormal," the association says that "a truly chemically-sensitive person will display more of them more frequently and to more of an extreme than the average person." What are these possible symptoms of "chemical sensitivity," according to the Feingold list? They include headaches, hives, asthma, stomachaches and leg aches, sleep problems, compulsions, impulsiveness, screaming, overreaction to touch, abdominal bloating, constipation, diarrhea, low blood sugar, excessive thirst, excessive sweating, swollen lips, poor coordination, eye disorders, seizures, anxiety, and pica—to name just some. Now, some children with symptoms included on this list are actually sensitive to food additives. But the vast majority of children who suffer chronically from these symptoms have other medical conditions, some life-threatening. Sweating, excessive thirst, and blood sugar fluctuations, for instance, suggest diabetes. Pica, poor coordination, and seizures suggest that a child is being poisoned by lead or some other toxin. Head-aches, screaming, and seizures can be caused by tumors. I could suggest a few hundred other diseases that can cause symptoms on this list, but you get the idea.

So try an additive-free diet if you want, and continue it if it helps—as long as it doesn't unduly restrict your child's access to fruits, vegetables, and other healthful foods. But don't stop your efforts to find a real diagnosis, and treatment based on that diagnosis, for your child.

A Word About Hypoglycemia

Mainstream doctors are terrified of the very word "hypogly-cemia" these days because the term was so abused during the 1960s and 1970s, when nearly everyone in America claimed to be suffering from the condition. Holistic doctors, on the other hand, love hypoglycemia and label many of their patients hy-poglycemic, putting them on diets low in refined sugars and carbohydrates.

Sometimes these diets make children feel much better. But does that mean the doctors have correctly diagnosed and treated these children?

No.

Hypoglycemia, you see, isn't a *disease*. Like hyperactivity, it's a *symptom*. Hypoglycemia, which simply means low blood sugar, can stem from thyroid disorders, liver or pancreatic problems, or adrenal gland abnormalities. More commonly, it stems from the high insulin levels that occur during the early stages of di-abetes. Some of the causes of hypoglycemia are minor, while others are potentially very dangerous.

Thus, a diet may control a symptom—hypoglycemia—but the odds are that it's not treating the cause of that symptom. And that means that a hypoglycemia diet, although it often makes children feel better for a while (and is harmless and healthful in and of itself) can be dangerous if it stops doctors from looking for the real culprits causing a child to have low blood sugar.

If a Diet Works, Do You Know Why?

Obviously, the same rule of thumb applies for all dietary approaches to hyperactivity: Find out what's causing your child's hyperactivity and then use special diets only if they address the real problem. Of course, a good basic diet, with plenty of fruits and vegetables, unrefined carbohydrates, and protein, and low in sugar, processed foods, caffeine, and added fats, is important no matter what's causing your child's disorder. Most other "hyperactivity diets," however, aren't likely to address the real conditions making your child behave badly.

That doesn't mean you need to discontinue a dietary intervention if it appears to be helping a little. In fact, if there's clear evidence that any dietary intervention changes your child's symptoms, let your child's doctors know. The foods a child responds to, positively or negatively, may provide valuable clues about his or her real health problems. But those clues might surprise you!

Consider nutritional supplements, for instance. If a vitamin/mineral supplement improves your child's health, then perhaps your child needed extra nutrients. But—and this is crucial—*why did your child need these extra nutrients in the first place?* It may be because an intestinal parasite is stealing nutrients from your child's digestive system. Keep feeding your child extra supplements, and your child will be healthier—but so, most likely, will the parasite. In this case, the cure involves getting rid of the hitchhiking critter rather than merely improving its food supply.

Children who respond to supplements may also be suffering from anemias, lead toxicity, or diseases that cause the intestines to absorb food inefficiently—and all of these disorders can and should be diagnosed.

Pycnogenol, a nutritional supplement, also is being recommended for children with behavior problems. From what we know about this substance it does indeed appear to be safer than the drugs currently used to treat hyperactive children (although, to my knowledge, no one has conducted any scientifically controlled, long-term studies to evaluate its safety). According to one preliminary study, Pycnogenol, extracted from the bark of the French maritime pine tree, may help protect blood vessels from damage by oxidants (destructive substances linked to cardiovascular damage).[3] There also is some evidence that Pycnogenol increases the activity of certain "killer" cells in the immune system.[4]

Again, however, it's critical to ask: *Why* would this substance improve the behavior of a hyperactive child? Two obvious answers that come immediately to my mind are (1) the child is suffering from a condition that damages blood vessels in the brain, or (2) the child is suffering from a disorder that affects the immune system. Although Pycnogenol may possibly reduce the damage being done by such disorders, *the disorders are still there*. Again, it's a case of masking symptoms rather than getting to their roots. And masking heart disease, or diseases that cause immune system defects, is a dangerous practice.

Other dietary interventions also can reduce hyperactivity for a variety of reasons. For instance, parents often remove milk from children's diets on the assumption that it's an allergen. But reducing a child's calcium intake can also reduce symptoms of hyperparathyroidism, a disorder that can cause behavior problems. So are you treating allergies or a parathyroid disorder when you take away milk? Maybe neither. Some children suffer from iron deficiency brought on by filling up on iron-poor foods such as milk and skimping on iron-rich foods such as meat, raisins, and nuts. Take away their dairy products, and they'll often eat other foods that increase their iron intake. So the child who responds to a milk-free diet may be suffering from borderline iron deficiency brought on by a low-iron diet.

Obviously, the diet/behavior connection is complex. In my opinion, doctors who believe that hyperactivity can be addressed by crude, hit-or-miss, same-size-fits-all diets, in the absence of any real diagnosis, are sadly lacking in nutritional training.

Once your child receives a real diagnosis, however, the picture changes radically. At this stage, dietary measures can often make a huge difference. For instance, attention problems stemming from developmental seizures can often be treated by controlling the seizures with a special nutritional intervention called a ketogenic diet. It's not a diet you're likely to hear about as a hyperactivity treatment—it's actually a very odd diet, high in certain fats and low in carbohydrates. But *when prescribed for the right children*, it works wonders. Likewise, a child whose behavior problems stem from caffeine overconsumption (see Chapter 7) will respond to a diet free of chocolate and sodas. A child sensitive to salicylates may need to eat fewer tomatoes and other salicylate-rich foods; a child whose hyperactivity is due to iron deficiency, on the other hand, can benefit from eating *more* tomatoes, because foods high in vitamin C promote iron absorption. A child with celiac disease needs to avoid wheat and many other grains, while a child with prediabetic blood sugar swings needs to *add* whole grains.

The message here, obviously, is that treating all hyperactive children with one type of diet doesn't make much more sense than treating all of these children with a single pill. There's no magic bullet, dietary or pharmaceutical, that will cure all (or even most) hyperactive children. *Find out what's really wrong before you try to treat your child*, either with food or with a drug. And if you do find a dietary intervention that helps, don't stop there. Ask your doctor, "How and why does it work?" And make sure he or she gives you a logical answer.

One more word of caution on the subject of diets and supplements. A healthful, nutrient-rich diet benefits virtually *every* child, and especially a hyperactive child. Supplementing a child's diet with a well-designed vitamin and mineral formula won't hurt either. But if you venture into more unusual dietary interventions, remember that you can sometimes do real harm.

One seven-year-old I saw years ago had learning problems due to mixed brain dominance—that is, neither the right nor the left side of her brain was dominant. It's a fairly common cause of learning problems and relatively easy to treat through educational means. But mixed dominance didn't explain this little girl's temper tantrums, random activity, and inability to follow directions. Biochemical tests, however, did explain these behaviors: The child had a massive excess of vitamin A in her system. Her stepmother, a not-too-well-informed amateur nutritionist, had been dosing her with high-potency vitamin A supplements combined with cod liver oil.

If you opt to try supplements, don't make this same mistake. Remember, in particular, that vitamins A, D, E, and K are toxic when taken in very large amounts. These vitamins are fat soluble rather than water soluble, meaning that they can accumulate in body fat. Many minerals, too, can be toxic if taken in excess. (Iron is a good example of a mineral that has a fairly narrow margin of safety.) Be wary of teas and herbal treatments, too, unless you've researched the effects of the ingredients they contain. Above all, remember that *you can't possibly know how to supplement you child's diet correctly until you know what, if anything, is wrong with your child.*

Behavior Modification

I'm not an expert in behavior modification techniques, but a good friend of mine, psychologist Bernard Rimland, is an authority on the subject. "Behavior mod sounds almost too simple to work," he says, "but in fact it's one of the most powerful behavior-changing tools ever developed."

Basically, behavior modification teaches appropriate behaviors by rewarding them, and discourages inappropriate behaviors by ignoring them or exacting consequences. For instance, a hyperactive child who behaves well for an entire day might get a small present or extra TV time, while a child who acts up or refuses to do his or her homework might lose TV privileges. Another valuable behavior modification technique, called self-monitoring, teaches hyperactive children to spot their own behavior problems, control them, and reward themselves when they succeed. And still other techniques can help children learn to stretch the amount of time they're able to sit still and pay attention.

A psychologist skilled in behavior modification can help you design a program tailored for your child. If you can't afford professional help, your local library may have a good collection of books specifically on the topic of behavior modification techniques for children with attention and behavior problems. (One good book is *Parents Are Teachers*, by Wesley Becker. It's an older book but still in print.) You may be surprised at how effective such techniques can be, *if* you use them consistently and correctly.

Behavior modification won't work instantly, and it may take some time to tailor a program that works for your child. On the other hand, it won't *hurt* your child, as medications certainly can. And, in the right circumstances, it can help enormously. As behavior modification expert Betsy Hoza of Purdue University says, "taking a pill is only a three-hour solution to [a] problem. Teaching children to control their behavior might be expected to make more of an impact on their lives."

California researcher James Swanson, profiled a few years ago in *Time* magazine, is making behavior modification work for an entire school full of hyperactive and behavior-disordered students. At the Child Development Center in Irvine, California, students earn points and praise for good behavior, and special privileges at the end of successful days. In addition, Swanson and colleagues drill students in managing their own behavior. The result, according to *Time*: "Only 35% of the kids at the center are on stimulant drugs, less than half the national rate for ADHD kids."[5]

Although behavior modification can reduce behavior problems, it can't eliminate underlying medical problems. If your child's problem is simply a lack of discipline or structure, behavior modification might be all you need. But if your child suffers from a medical condition that's causing true pathological hyperactivity, behavior modification isn't going to solve his or her problems. It's infinitely safer than Ritalin, but it's merely a tool that helps compensate for disabilities without correcting them.

As Rimland says, "All educational programs—even the best ones—are merely Band-Aids if the problem is basically biological. Finding a good educational program is important, but it is more important to attack behavior problems at their roots."

Neurofeedback

In my own practice, I've studied biofeedback, a method in which patients can actually learn to regulate their own temperatures, blood pressure, and other "involuntary" processes. These days, a relatively new form of biofeedback, called neurofeedback, is gaining popularity as a treatment for hyperactivity. Its goal is to teach children how to increase the types of brain activity associated with paying attention, while decreasing the brain activity associated with distraction.

Some parents report remarkable results from neurofeedback. Juanita DeJesus, for instance, said recently that her eight-year-old grandson Ricardo used to fight other children, tear up bathrooms, and hide from teachers. After neurofeedback, the boy became calmer, less aggressive, and more cooperative. "I can finally see the real Ricardo," DeJesus said.[6]

We're beginning to get some study data on neurofeedback as well, and preliminary studies tend to be encouraging. Thomas Rossiter and Theodore La Vaque reported in 1995 that "a treatment program with EEG biofeedback as the major component led to significant reduction in both cognitive and behavioral symptoms of ADHD after 20 treatment sessions completed over a period of four to seven weeks." The neurofeedback group, the researchers reported, showed "improvement in attention, impulse control, speed of information processing and consistency of attention," and mothers of the children noted significant declines in pathological behaviors. "This confirms," the researchers say, "that improvement was not limited to . . . test scores but had generalized beyond the clinic and was observed as symptom reduction in the patients' daily lives." According to their data, the researchers said, neurofeedback is "a viable alternative to the use of psychostimulant medication."[7]

A number of studies have reported similar results. Unfortunately, most are hampered by weak study designs, small numbers of subjects, and a lack of placebo controls. Because we don't have data from large-scale, well-controlled studies of neurofeedback, it's difficult to say how useful the approach will prove to be.

Should you consider neurofeedback for your hyperactive or attention-disordered child? Before deciding, consider this list of pros and cons.

Pros

- Preliminary data suggest that neurofeedback can reduce behavior problems and improve attention in some children.
- There is some evidence that the effects of neurofeedback can be long-lasting. (A follow-up study suggested that the benefits of neurofeedback on ADHD were still evident up to ten years after treatment.)
- There is no evidence at all that neurofeedback can harm your child.

Cons

- Neurofeedback has not been subjected to rigorous, large-scale testing to prove its usefulness.
- Neurofeedback is expensive—about $50 per session, and requires twenty or more sessions.

My opinion? *If* your child has already received a thorough differential diagnosis, *if* you've exhausted all treatment avenues, and *if* you can afford an expensive therapy, neurofeedback therapy won't hurt and might help. Anecdotal evidence certainly suggests that some children behave and attend far better after they receive the treatment. But go into it knowing that the technique hasn't yet been subjected to the test of time. Clearly, however, it's safer than Ritalin and other drugs.

THERE ARE A SLEW OF OTHER ALTERNATIVE THERAPIES FOR hyperactivity, ranging from crawling exercises to herbal enemas to exorcism (no kidding). There isn't room (or reason) to discuss all of them, but I do have room for some all-purpose advice: Do your research and avoid any therapies that aren't backed by research published in legitimate medical or educational journals. Check on the potential dangers as well as the potential benefits of any therapy you're considering trying. And use the same common sense you'd apply to other situations. If a treatment sounds too good to be true, it probably is. One more suggestion: Look for articles both *supporting* and *criticizing* any approach, so you'll have the full story.

Above all, avoid any therapies that claim to be "the" cure for hyperactivity, because there is no single cure for a symptom with hundreds of causes. In the next four chapters I look at some of those causes and show why a "one size fits all" treatment can't work for hyperactive children.

PART 3

The Many Causes of Hyperactive Behavior

CHAPTER 4

The Invaders: Pests and Poisons

[Humans are] some of the most interesting real estate in the world.
Roger M. Knutson, Furtive Fauna

LIVING INSIDE AND ON OUR BODIES ARE MILLIONS OF UN-
invited guests: bacteria, viruses, parasites, and other micro-
scopic creatures. Most of these hitchhikers are harmless or
even beneficial, But some can make us downright miserable,
and a surprising number can make our children hyperactive,
irritable, spacey, or even violent.

Fortunately, some of the most common causes of infection-
linked hyperactivity are simple to diagnose, easy to treat, and
completely curable. That doesn't mean, however, that doctors
always (or even usually) diagnose these disorders correctly.

Laura: Incorrigible or Infested?

Seven-year-old Laura was brought to me after her teacher complained that the cute little redhead was a "demon."

I wasn't Laura's first doctor. A previous physician had put her
on Ritalin, which did nothing except cause her to develop facial
tics. Another doctor had recommended a strict additive-free diet
that, although improving Laura's eating habits, didn't curb her
hyperactivity, jittery behavior, or foul temper.

Laura's mother told me Laura fidgeted all day and rarely slept
through the night. She often had nightmares and frequently got

up to go to the bathroom or get a drink of water. In the mornings, she was grumpy and tired.

Until a few years earlier, Laura had been a happy, pleasant child. Her family's medical history provided few clues about the cause of her problems, and when I examined her, I found her to be a well developed child with no clear-cut neurological problems. A few of her symptoms, however, gave me diagnostic leads to pursue.

To narrow down the list of disorders from which Laura might be suffering, I ordered several tests. The results of one of these tests indicated either an allergy or the possibility of parasites. We used an old-fashioned, low-tech technique to check for parasites: Scotch Tape placed on the anal area at night revealed the presence of multiple pinworm ova.

Laura's hyperactivity, in short, stemmed from chronic fatigue caused by pinworm infestation. Pinworms lay their eggs in the anal area, causing tickling and itching, which are most bothersome at night. Laura probably hadn't had a good night's sleep in years. Think of how irritable, impulsive, and unmotivated you are after missing a night of sleep, and it's easy to understand why Laura was difficult in school!

I treated Laura and her entire family with Povan, a drug that rids the body of pinworms. Within days, she began sleeping normally. Within weeks, her daytime behavior was back to normal as well.

LAURA'S CASE IS A CLASSIC EXAMPLE OF HOW DOCTORS BENT on labeling children as hyperactive and prescribing Ritalin can overlook even the simplest diagnosis. Pinworm infestations are common, especially during the preschool and kindergarten years—just the time when Laura started showing symptoms. When an otherwise healthy child is wiggly, can't sleep, and suffers from chronic itching, pinworms should be on any doctor's top-ten list of suspected diagnoses. If Laura's first doctor had taken a few minutes to question her mother about Laura's sleeping habits, he'd have gathered enough clues to warrant a number of tests, including a Scotch Tape test. That simple test could have saved Laura from years of Ritalin treatment.

Quite simply, there's no excuse for a doctor missing such a simple diagnosis, especially when as many as one in ten children is infested with pinworms at any given time. The rate among preschool children may be even higher, because day care centers are heaven for pinworms: One child, scratching and getting a fingerful of eggs, and then touching crayons, tables, toys, and doorknobs, can infect dozens of other children *and* their teachers.

Although pinworms have only a short life span, children in infested houses can keep reinfecting themselves, and their family members, for years. Minor infestations cause few or no symptoms, but heavy infestations like Laura's can drive kids nuts.

Pinworms, however, aren't the only worms linked to childhood behavior problems. If you own a puppy, your child can pick up canine roundworms simply by wandering barefoot across a lawn. These worms can cause transient fevers, sleep disturbances, abdominal pain, headaches, and behavioral disturbances. Hookworms and tapeworms tend to make children sluggish and dull, often leading to labels of depression, learning disability, or attention deficit disorder.

Children are the most common victims of worms, for obvious reasons: Their toileting skills are primitive, they tend to put their fingers in their mouths, and they participate in a lot of hands-on activities with other kids and with pets. Children who have lived overseas are at particular risk, because worms are far more common in non-Western countries than in the United States.

While pinworms make children miserable on the outside, by causing anal itching, other worms cause hyperactive behavior, learning problems, depression, or attention deficits by making children miserable on the inside. These worms attach themselves to the wall of the intestines and eat their victim's blood, causing carriers to lose iron and other nutrients. (Iron deficiency, in particular, often leads to childhood misbehavior and learning problems.) The worms also wiggle around, causing physical discomfort. And they cause children to lose their appetites and pick at their food, increasing the risk of nutrient deficiencies.

Worms are sometimes seen in children with cyclical hyperactivity, because these parasites are fairly quiet at some stages and quite aggressive at others. But even when the worms are "lying low," the chronic stress of a low-grade parasitic infection saps the body's resources, leading to a general feeling of irritability and malaise.

All doctors should be familiar with the common, garden-variety worms endemic to the United States. A really savvy doctor, however, can sometimes spot a more exotic pest that is causing behavioral disorders. In *Guess What Came to Dinner*,[1] Ann Louise Gittleman tells the story of a little boy in Arizona who fell prey to one of these unusual parasites.

The hero of Gittleman's story is a doctor who refused merely to prescribe Ritalin for this nine-year-old patient's hyperactivity and serious behavior problems. Instead, the doctor gave the boy a complete exam, including tests for parasites. One of these tests uncovered schistosomiasis, a fluke seldom seen in children in developed countries. "After the proper treatment [for schistosomiasis] was administered," Gittleman says, "the child's hyperactivity diminished and his behavior became normal."

Where this little boy picked up his infection, by the way, is a mystery: He hadn't traveled to Egypt, where the infection is endemic, or to other countries where schistosomiasis is common. And, although the boy liked to play with snails, a common host of schistosomiasis, snails in the United States don't carry this fluke. In general, it's impossible to pick up schistosomiasis if you haven't traveled outside the United States, and the infection is generally seen only in people who've emigrated from Northern Africa, South America, and Asian countries where these parasites are common.

Parasites in general, however, aren't rare at all. In my own practice, I've seen half a dozen children whose behavior problems stemmed directly from infestation by these unpleasant little invaders. The good news is that worm infestations and other parasitic infections are easy to diagnose and (depending on the parasite) usually fairly easy to treat. If your child has a parasitic infection, treatment will generally lead quickly to a dramatic improvement in behavior, appetite, and sleep patterns. Thus, ruling out parasites should be at the top of any diagnostician's list when a parent reports that a child is hyperactive or irritable.

This simple step, however, is rarely taken by doctors. It would be interesting to know how many children are taking Ritalin for parasitic infections. My guess, and I think it's conservative, is thousands.

The "Hyperactivity Bugs"

Worms aren't the only infectious agents that can cause the symptoms that doctors dub hyperactivity. A more aggressive and often more dangerous group of invaders—viruses and bacteria— also can leave their mark.

In the early 1900s, doctors learned this the hard way. Between 1917 and 1926, a bizarre and terrifying epidemic of a brain inflammation called encephalitis lethargica swept the world, affecting millions of people. To this day, researchers don't know what caused the outbreak, although it was almost certainly a virus. The epidemic vanished as mysteriously as it started, and only sporadic cases have been reported since.

Although the epidemic went away, the victims who survived an attack—which often began with hiccups and progressed to comalike stupor—were far from out of the woods. Many got well, only to come down later with peculiar and frightening symptoms. Even mild cases often led later to severe symptoms, which sometimes appeared years or even decades after the initial infection.

Older adults frequently developed Parkinson's-like movement disorders. But in children, the disease attacked in a different way. The children became mean, angry, and hostile. They were hyperactive and developed tics, obsessions, and compulsions. Some teenagers and young adults (both men and women) became promiscuous or turned into exhibitionists. In severe cases, patients became psychotic; in milder cases, they showed the symptoms that doctors today would call hyperactivity and conduct disorder.

Physicians Sarah Cheyette and Jeffrey Cummings, who have studied the encephalitis lethargica epidemic extensively, describe typical young victims: "They became disobedient and quarrelsome, often leading to expulsion from school. Emotional lability [changeability], irritability, and temper tantrums were common. Many children committed destructive and harmful acts on people or animals; self-destructive behavior was also common. Kleptomania, pyromania, coprolalia [swearing], sexual precocity, exhibitionism, sexual aggression, and paraphilias [fetishism, sadism, voyeurism, etc.] were manifestations of the behavioral disorder. Many children felt compelled to perform these acts even though they recognized them as 'bad' behavior. . . . The children were hyperactive and impulsive, and they appeared to lack empathy; they were often called 'moral imbeciles.' "[2]

The encephalitis lethargica epidemic passed into history long ago, and these days viral encephalitis is a relatively uncommon cause of childhood behavior disorders. But the epidemic taught us an important lesson: "Psychiatric" symptoms, *including hyperactivity and conduct problems*, can stem from an infection, even one that's been "cured."

In the years since, we've discovered that other infections, some of them common, can cause behavior changes both during *and* after the initial illness. Acute bacterial meningitis, for instance, afflicts thousands of children each year, many of them under the age of three. A survey of eighty pediatric bacterial meningitis cases found that nearly 5 percent of patients developed long-term hyperactivity following infection, and more than 12 percent had learning problems.[3] Encephalitis, a brain inflammation caused by viruses or bacteria, can cause long-term behavior problems, as can prenatal infections such as cytomegalovirus.

Unfortunately, there's generally little or nothing doctors can do to ameliorate the behavior problems caused by viral infections, or by bacterial infections severe enough to cause permanent brain damage. But a number of chronic bacterial infections *can* be treated, and treatment can greatly reduce symptoms. And even in the case of viral infections that can't be treated, proper diagnosis can avoid unnecessary or harmful treatments.

One of the most important and most commonly overlooked infections linked to hyperactivity is group A beta-hemolytic streptococcus, better known as "strep." Although these bacteria are most commonly thought of as the cause of strep throat, they sometimes do more than give your child a sore throat. Left untreated, strep can cause rheumatic fever and a movement disorder called Sydenham's chorea. Moreover, recurrent infections can lead, in susceptible children, to a group of symptoms collectively known as PANDAS (for "pediatric autoimmune neuropsychiatric disorders"). Symptoms of PANDAS include obsessive-compulsive behavior, Tourette's syndrome, hyperactivity, and cognitive problems. Physician Susan Swedo says that the young PANDAS patients she has studied "exhibited a peculiar 'squirminess' in which the children tried very hard to sit still but constantly wriggled and fidgeted in their chairs."[4]

Swedo, the researcher at the National Institute of Mental Health who first identified the strep-PANDAS link, believes that PANDAS occur when the immune system, reacting abnormally to a strep infection, begins attacking basal ganglia cells in the brain. Symptoms of PANDAS subside after the initial strep infection, but reoccur during later strep infections (or, sometimes, during other infections). Swedo and colleagues, who are testing immune system therapies on children with PANDAS, report that the children they have treated improved dramatically, showing 40 to 50 percent decreases in abnormal movements. The researchers are also using penicillin, with good results.

How many children are suffering from strep-linked psychiatric disorders? There's no way of knowing, because most children with symptoms similar to PANDAS are currently labeled as having ADHD, ADD, or Tourette's syndrome. However, it's a good guess that thousands of children have strep-linked hyperactivity, because just in my own practice I've treated dozens of children with behavioral and physical symptoms linked to recurrent strep infections. Identifying and treating these children is critical for two reasons. First, proper treatment can dramatically decrease their symptoms. And second, these children are at risk for strep-linked cardiac problems (which can be fatal) and for debilitating movement disorders if their strep infections go untreated.

The recurrent bacterial ear infections that thousands of

children suffer in infancy and early childhood also are strongly linked to hyperactivity, attention problems, and learning difficulties in the early school years. Sometimes these infections can be cleared up with standard antibiotic therapy. Unfortunately, recent reports suggest that antibiotics and another common treatment, drainage tubes, are not as effective as previously believed. However, there's another step parents can take to help prevent ear infections, or to lessen their impact when they occur. Preliminary data reported in the *British Medical Journal* indicate that simply having children chew gum sweetened with xylitol can reduce the risk of ear infections by nearly half.[5] Apparently xylitol inhibits the growth of *Streptococcus pneumoniae*, which causes a large percentage of acute otitis media attacks. Although this study needs to be confirmed, it appears that giving ear-infection-prone children a few sticks of xylitol-sweetened gum each day may drastically cut down on ear infections *and* their behavioral effects.

One common viral infection that can alter behavior and hurt academic performance is mononucleosis, fondly known as the "kissing disease." This infection is most common in 15- to 25-year-olds, and infects 1 to 3 percent of all college students each year, but it strikes preteens, too—and yes, it's often spread by kisses. Caused by the Epstein Barr virus or cytomegalovirus, mono usually causes extreme fatigue, but it can also cause irritability, anxiety, emotionality, and attention problems. Although most cases clear up in a few months, some last long enough for zealous doctors to label them as attention deficit disorder and prescribe Ritalin. Identifying a mono infection is critical, because parents need to know why a child is misbehaving or failing in school, and they need to know that rest and a good diet, not Ritalin, are the treatments of choice.

Toxic Hyperactivity

So far I've looked at the living pests that can make children's brains malfunction, but there's another category of invaders that can poison brain cells and make children nuts. These are brain-altering pollutants, and in particular solvents, pesticides, and heavy metals including lead, manganese, cadmium, and mercury.

Children are far more vulnerable to these toxins than adults, for whom standards for exposure have been calculated. That means that even at "safe" dosages, children may be exposed to toxic levels of these substances. Furthermore, as researcher Herbert Needleman points out, "Children eat, drink, and breathe more for their body weights than adults do, so they get bigger proportional doses of whatever is out there."

Sadly, it's the littlest of these children who are in the most danger of suffering from toxic exposure. Infants and toddlers spend their time on the ground, so when they're outdoors, they're getting a maximal dose of lead, gasoline fumes, herbicides, and highway pollutants. And the indoors, if anything, is *less* safe. A recent article by Wayne Ott and John Roberts in *Scientific American* points out that the American carpet is one of the most dangerous spots in the country. The researchers noted that "if truckloads of dust with the same concentration of toxic chemicals as is found in most carpets were deposited outside, these locations would be considered hazardous-waste dumps." Among the substances Ott and Roberts found in high amounts in carpets: cadmium, lead, PCBs, pesticides, and the highly toxic chemical benzo(a)pyrene. This toxic house dust, Ott and Roberts note, "can be a particular menace to small children, who play on floors, crawl on carpets, and regularly place their hands in their mouths."[6]

When children are exposed to toxic substances, their brains and nervous systems are often affected, even at doses too low to cause overt physical symptoms. These "silent poisonings" often go unnoticed, labeled as low intelligence or ADHD, and the victims wind up being placed on Ritalin or other powerful drugs—in effect, adding more chemicals to their contaminated brains.

In my practice, I've seen dozens of children with hyperactivity and behavioral problems due to elevated levels of lead or other toxins. Sometimes, these toxins are the sole cause of hyperactivity, attention deficits, irritability, and learning disabilities. Other times, the toxins exacerbate other disorders such as heart problems or seizure disorders. That was the case with Tommy, a teenage patient of mine whose attention problems stemmed from a part-time job that cost him far more than the minimum wage he was earning.

High-Octane Hyperactivity

I'd seen Tommy years earlier and had diagnosed and treated a mild seizure disorder that we easily got under control. Tommy had what are known as developmental seizures, which usually become milder with time. So I was surprised when his mother brought him in, saying that his seizures were back. He was having staring spells again, and his teachers noted that he was "spacing out" and acting oddly in class.

I knew that Tommy's seizures had been well controlled for years. Moreover, they should have been getting less, not more, common as he got older. Some new culprit had to be lowering his seizure threshold. But what?

The answer lay in Tommy's part-time job as a gas station attendant. This was back in the days when few people pumped their own gas, and Tommy was responsible for filling up dozens of customers' gas tanks every day. Frequently he'd been contaminated by gas spilling from the tanks.

I measured Tommy's lead levels, thinking that exposure to leaded gas might be harming his brain (even though leaded gas had recently been banned). But Tommy's lead levels were normal. When I tested for other toxins, I got a big surprise: Tommy's levels of manganese, an additive supposedly not allowed in gasoline at that time, were very high. I pursued the matter and got still another surprise: The gasoline company supplying Tommy's station appeared to be enriching their gasoline with manganese.

Tommy's manganese levels weren't high enough to require therapy. I simply told him to find another job, and his seizures and behavior abnormalities soon stopped.

At the time I saw Tommy, his case was a rarity. It's possible, however, that more and more cases of manganese toxicity will be popping up in the medical literature. Why? Because, over the protests of thirty-seven different medical and environmental groups, U.S. gas companies are now being allowed to add MMT, a manganese-based additive, to their gasoline. That means that manganese overexposure, once a problem primarily for manganese miners, may become more widespread, particularly among teens like Tommy, who are exposed to large amounts of gasoline through jobs at gas stations or car repair shops.

The Ethyl Corporation, which manufactures MMT, says that the substance is harmless, in spite of evidence that manganese miners suffer high rates of psychosis, neurological disease, and even premature death.[7] But then, the Ethyl Corporation is the same company that told us that lead was harmless when it first began selling leaded gasoline. That "harmless" substance, now banned in gasoline, is still causing thousands of cases of brain dysfunction being labeled as hyperactivity, attention deficit, or retardation.

Lead: Enemy #1

Research shows conclusively that children with even mildly elevated lead levels suffer from reduced IQs, attention deficits, and poor school performance. In addition, they are seven times as likely as other children to fail to graduate from school. And a new study by Herbert Needleman strongly links lead exposure—again, at levels well below the level at which lead is considered toxic—to delinquency and aggressive behavior.

Unfortunately, despite the ban on leaded gas, millions of American children are still exposed to excess levels of this toxic metal. In 1991, Joel Schwartz of the Environmental Protection Agency reported that one out of nine children under age six has a high enough blood lead level to place him or her at risk.[8] And don't think your child is home free if you're a middle-class or upper-class family. I've diagnosed lead poisoning in rich kids as well as poor kids, and in both rural and urban children. Furthermore, although we associate lead with leaded gasoline and leaded paints, toxic levels of lead show up in surprising places. For instance:

- High lead levels often show up in children whose parents work in radiator shops, at gun firing ranges, in stained-glass window design, in the manufacture of ceramic tile and pottery, or in demolition. In a typical case, reported by *Child Health Alert* in 1997, a six-year-old boy with a poor attention span, restlessness, and school problems was diagnosed with lead poisoning. The boy's father worked in a battery reprocessing plant and was bringing home enough lead on his clothes to heavily contaminate both his child and his wife.
- After a two-year-old boy who chewed on pool cue chalk was diagnosed with elevated lead levels, researchers investigated further and discovered that some brands of the chalk were laced with high levels of lead.
- In California, a group of Pakistani girls using eye cosmetics imported from their native land were found to have lead levels three times as high as Pakistani children not using the products. The cosmetics, it turned out, contained high amounts of lead.
- The restoration of old homes, a favorite hobby of upscale young adults, can be hazardous to their children's health and behavior. Up to 7 percent of cases of lead toxicity may stem from home renovation projects, particularly the sanding of old paint from walls.
- At least twenty-five million vinyl miniblinds imported from China, Taiwan, Mexico, and Indonesia contain potentially dangerous levels of lead. As the plastic in the blinds deteriorates, lead dust forms on their surfaces. Children who touch the blinds and then put their hands in their mouths can pick up enough lead to be at risk.

High lead levels have been found in everything from pottery to imported candy wrappers to beverages served in leaded crystal glasses. The moral: If your child is hyperactive or has other behavior problems, get him or her tested, because *any* child, rich or poor, can be a victim of lead poisoning.

As a neurologist, I've seen what lead can do to a developing child's brain. I also know that if lead is allowed to accumulate in a child's brain for too long, there's no way to repair the damage. One of my most tragic cases was a boy who, as an infant, chewed on his mother's leaded-paint tubes and paint rags. He was misdiagnosed by several doctors as simply being "slow," and by the time I saw him, he was irrevocably retarded.

Caught early, on the other hand, lead toxicity can be treated, lead-depressed IQ levels can rise, and behavior problems can vanish. Here's a case in point.

Greg: A Three-Year-Old Terror

Greg's foster mother brought him to my office. Dragged him to my office would be a more accurate, because keeping Greg going in one direction was a superhuman task. In fact, the foster mother had to bring along a caseworker to help her control the cute little blond.

"He's a perpetual motion machine," the foster mother told me. "He gets up at five A.M. and doesn't go to sleep until after ten. He chews up the neighborhood kids' toys. And he's completely uncontrollable." The caseworker, too, was beside herself. If this foster placement didn't pan out, finding a new home for Greg would be next to impossible.

Greg had been treated with Ritalin (despite the fact that the drug is not approved for children under six), but the drug reduced only his appetite, not his activity level. While the drug caused him to pick at normal foods, he continued to eat nonfoods including dirt, crayons, and toys.

I evaluated Greg carefully, paying special attention to his pica, his sleep disturbance, and his random, distracted behavior. Many children with lead poisoning exhibit pica, so I ordered, among many evaluations, an EEG (because lead poisoning alters brainwaves) and a lead level test. The EEG showed abnormal brain wave patterns, and the lead level test showed lead toxicity.

I treated Greg with a single dose of penicillamine, an agent that binds to lead and removes it from the body. I also treated him temporarily with an anticonvulsant to stabilize his cortical activity. And, with the help of his foster mother, I isolated the source of Greg's toxic lead levels—old, lead-based paint that was peeling off the walls in his room. It didn't take long for Greg's behavior, sleep patterns, and eating habits to normalize to the point where his foster mother reported that he was "a great kid."

More Brain Poisons

Lead is the leading culprit in toxin-caused hyperactivity, but children are routinely exposed to dozens of other brain-altering substances. Among the worst are solvents, which can severely disrupt the function of brain cells or even destroy neurons altogether. Children who sniff glue and other solvents to get high are at the highest risk, but kids who often help refinish furniture, glue model airplanes, or clean guns can breathe in enough solvent fumes to cause brain dysfunction (particularly when these jobs are done in poorly ventilated rooms).

Many children also are chronically exposed to pesticides, which can cause nervousness, poor coordination, irritability, memory problems, and depression, as well as lowering seizure thresholds. If you frequently spray your yard or house, or you live close to farms, or you often spray your pets for fleas or ticks, your child could be breathing in enough pesticides to be affected. (I discuss this at length in Chapter 9.)

Then, as I noted in Chapter 1, there's carbon monoxide. According to the National Center for Health Statistics, in 1994—the most recent year for which I could find statistics—nearly 1,900 children under age six were exposed to toxic levels of this gas.[9] Sources include gas heaters and other gas appliances such as fireplaces, dryers, and water heaters. Although CO poisonings are more common in older, substandard housing, they can happen anywhere. Acute, low-grade CO poisoning symptoms tend to resemble the flu, but long-term, low-grade exposure causes memory loss, hyperactivity, attention deficits, and personality changes.

Another substance that sometimes turns out to be the culprit in hyperactive behavior or learning disabilities is cadmium, a dangerous heavy metal found in some batteries and older art supplies. R. O. Pihl and M. Parkes, comparing learning-disabled and nondisabled students, found that cadmium was closely associated with learning disabilities.[10]

Last but not least, mercury amalgam dental fillings deserve a mention. This issue is highly controversial, with the American Dental Association claiming that doctors who worry about mercury fillings are alarmists. On the contrary, however, evidence continues to mount that a relatively small but significant number of people are adversely affected by the mercury in their dental fillings. It's not that fillings cause mercury "poisoning." Rather, in children or adults who grind their teeth, minute amounts of mercury are constantly released into the system, sometimes causing mercury sensitivity leading to headaches, restless behavior, and irritability. As many as 15 percent of people with amalgam fillings—often called "silver fillings"—show signs of sensitivity to mercury.

That's not surprising, given that mercury is a highly toxic substance, and one that doesn't "stay put." Research in the 1970s revealed that mercury vapor is released from silver fillings and that mercury levels in the blood and urine increase with the number of fillings. In the 1980s, researchers gave sheep dental fillings; one of the researchers, Dr. Murray Vimy, said, "We showed that mercury migrated from the teeth into nearly all of the tissue, especially the brain, kidney and liver. We also showed it crossed the placenta into the fetus."[11]

Vimy also studied the effect of mercury fillings on human patients. "When I first measured mercury coming off a filling in a human mouth," he says, "that was the day I threw all that stuff out of my office. Every time you eat or chew, every time you brush or grind your teeth, you absorb it."[12]

While American dental associations are defensive on the subject of mercury fillings, European countries are taking action. A 1990 study by researchers at the National Board of Occupational Safety and Health in Sweden concluded, "From a toxicological point of view, amalgam is an unsuitable material for dental restorations." Sweden has reacted to this and similar studies by recommending that dentists discontinue the use of mercury amalgam fillings until the issue is clarified. Austria is banning the fillings as of the year 2000, and Germany is phasing out their use.

Are these countries' researchers being alarmist? Having

treated both children and adults with behavioral disorders exacerbated by mercury sensitivity, I don't think so. And neither are parents of hyperactive children who want to know if their children have elevated mercury levels.

If your hyperactive child has fillings, and grinds his or her teeth, a doctor should consider mercury sensitivity as one possible diagnosis and should order a serum mercury level test. If your child's doctor pooh-poohs the notion, find another doctor.

Better Safe Than Sorry

Toxins are a common cause of hyperactivity. They're dangerous and can lead to long-term damage—but many can be easily eliminated from the body if they're spotted early enough.

Therefore, it's obvious that children with *any* evidence of overexposure to lead, mercury, cadmium, pesticides, solvents, or other toxic substances need to be carefully evaluated, *even if other hyperactivity-causing medical conditions have already been diagnosed.* Furthermore, if a doctor tests your child for exposure to lead or other heavy metals and reports that the test results are "within normal range," that's not good enough. Children should have virtually *no* trace of most of these toxins in their bodies, so if they're at the high end of the "normal" range—or, for that matter, in the middle—they're being exposed to too much of that toxin.

Why? Because even slightly elevated levels of heavy metals and other toxins place a burden on a child's brain cells. Also, the normal and abnormal values laboratory tests are based on are generalizations, and what's normal for one child's brain might be toxic to another, more vulnerable child.

Furthermore, acceptable levels of these dangerous substances are constantly being revised downward, as researchers discover that levels formerly considered safe are actually damaging children's brains. Additionally—and this is important—if a test shows moderate levels of toxins, there's no way of knowing if these levels are going *down* or *up*. That moderate level might, in a few weeks or months, rise to a dangerously high level.

Children Most at Risk for Toxic Exposure

Infants and toddlers

Infants' organs are still developing. Infants and young children frequently put their dirty hands in their mouths, and small children spend more time near the floor or ground where pollution is highest. Small children get far higher doses of pollutants per pound of body weight than larger children or adults.

Children whose hobbies include shooting, model building, painting, or woodworking

These hobbies put children in contact with dangerous solvents and/or paints.

Children whose parents work for pesticide companies, in auto repair shops, in gas stations, or in other jobs where there is routine exposure to dangerous chemicals

These children are often exposed to dangerously high levels of lead, pesticides, cadmium, and other poisons carried in on their parents' shoes and clothing.

Children living in older or recently renovated housing

These children are at high risk of lead poisoning from older leaded paint and old plumbing systems. Children in homes with aging heating systems are at high risk of carbon monoxide poisoning.

Children involved with gangs or counterculture friends

These children may be experimenting with glue sniffing and gasoline sniffing, which can cause severe brain dysfunction and, eventually, irreversible brain damage.

Teens working in gas stations or in industrial jobs

These children are often at higher risk than adults in similar jobs, because teens tend to be more lax about hand washing and other precautions against toxic exposure.

Children who bite their nails or exhibit pica (the eating of nonfoods such as dirt and paste)
These children are exposed to high levels of lead and other toxins from the dirty substances they ingest.

The bottom line: When it comes to lead poisoning or other toxic exposure, it's far better to be safe than sorry. If your family doctor hasn't checked your child thoroughly and ruled out toxins as a culprit, find a doctor who will do so. If your child does prove to have toxic levels of any substance in his or her system, ask your doctor to help you identify the sources of that exposure so they can be eliminated. Insist on a follow-up evaluation after several months, to guarantee that levels of the toxin are dropping. And don't waste any time, because symptoms caused by toxic exposure usually are reversible—but *only* if the toxin is eliminated before it's too late.

The Body Against Itself: Genetic, Metabolic, and Endocrine Diseases That Can Make Children Hyper

No family is free of actual or potential genetic misfortune.
Daniel L. Hartl, Our Uncertain Heritage

LIKE A BOX OF TINKERTOYS, YOUR BODY COMES WITH A SET of instructions included. Only your instructions aren't printed on paper. Rather, they're encoded in hundreds of thousands of genes.

What do these genes do? Each codes for a protein whose job is to build your body or keep it running. Some proteins build skin, bones, blood, and organs. Others form hormones and enzymes. And many enlist in your internal army as antibodies, defending against germs and other foreign invaders. Working together, these proteins manufacture and maintain the most complex creation on Earth: the human body.

It's a remarkable system—when it works. If even one of these tiny genes is defective, however, the system breaks down. Your body produces too much of a protein, or too little, or none at all. Sometimes, the resulting genetic disorder is so mild it's almost invisible. Other times, the disease is devastating.

When we think of genetic diseases, we tend to think of muscular dystrophy, cystic fibrosis, and other crippling disorders. Most of these disorders are diagnosed fairly easily, because their symptoms are obvious and often life-threatening.

Of the thousands of genetic diseases, however, a large number are relatively mild. Often these diseases initially make their presence known through subtle or cognitive behavioral changes, including hyperactivity, attention disorders, or learning disabilities.

Take, for example, mild cases of Turner's syndrome, a rare genetic disorder that occurs in females who are missing (either partially or completely) one of their two X chromosomes. "Full blown" cases of Turner's syndrome are generally diagnosed at birth or shortly afterward, because the clinical abnormalities seen in these children—including extreme shortness, webbed necks, kidney and cardiac problems, significant hearing loss, and facial abnormalities—are easy to spot. In quite a few Turner's syndrome cases, however, symptoms are far subtler. This is particularly true of girls with "mosaic" Turner's, in which some of the body's cells are normal and some are not.

Mildly affected girls with Turner's syndrome often have few externally obvious physical signs other than short stature. However, a significant minority have attention problems, minor hearing problems, and difficulties with math—all of which can combine to cause school problems that make the girls candidates for an ADD label. Because these girls often receive only cursory evaluations, many aren't diagnosed as having Turner's syndrome until they're fourteen, fifteen, or even older. (That's when one of the disease's most obvious symptoms—ovarian failure leading to a lack of sexual development—makes the diagnosis almost impossible to overlook.) That's too bad, because doctors have a wide range of medical treatments to help girls with Turner's syndrome—treatments that girls labeled as ADD aren't receiving.

Unfortunately, as I'll explain in this chapter, Turner's syndrome is only one of many genetic disorders overlooked by doctors hooked on ADD, ADHD, and other nondiagnostic labels. As a result, children with genetic disorders often receive no treatment other than Ritalin for the label of hyperactivity or ADD. Such oversights can hurt not only the children themselves but their families as well—and future generations.

Charlie: A Case of "Bad Blood"

Charlie was a little boy in serious trouble. But he had a powerful ally: a very smart dad who knew Charlie wasn't bad or attention disordered, but sick. Luckily, Charlie's dad worked for an airline and could travel inexpensively across the country. By the time Charlie reached my office in California, his dad had taken him to half a dozen doctors, in different states, looking for help. The doctors he'd consulted included several well-known experts at the department of neurology in a prestigious southern teaching hospital.

On the advice of these experts, Charlie was taking Ritalin for attention deficit disorder when I saw him. However, it hadn't fixed any of his problems. He was irritable, threw tantrums every day, and couldn't pay attention for more than a few minutes at a time in class. He was the slowest kid at school, too. In races, he quit halfway and sat on the sidelines while other kids, not even winded, dashed by. He had trouble sleeping. His legs hurt. He had a history of nosebleeds. He wet the bed. His previous doctors, unperturbed, said all of this was "normal enough." What wasn't normal, they said, was Charlie's behavior. Sometimes he was restless, aimless, and uncontrollable; other times he was tired and listless.

Charlie was a seven-year-old African-American with a shy smile and beautiful, long fingers. He was very slender, with eyes that seemed too large for his face. But what caught my attention right away was the shape of his head. One glance told me Charlie's previous doctors had been grossly negligent in giving Charlie Ritalin instead of evaluating him for genetic disease.

Charlie's skull was elongated and dome-shaped in front, with slight bulges at the sides of the forehead—an abnormality physicians call "tower skull." In Charlie's case, the abnormality was subtle, but it should have triggered any competent physician's curiosity, especially in an African-American child. Why? Because it's a physical sign often seen in sickle-cell anemia, a disorder that affects one in four hundred African-Americans, as well as a smaller number of Hispanics and people of Mediterranean descent. Most cases of sickle-cell anemia are correctly diagnosed early on, but subtle cases like Charlie's can be missed by doctors who focus exclusively on behavioral symptoms.

After evaluating Charlie carefully to rule out other possible diagnoses, I ordered tests that showed that he indeed suffered from sickle-cell anemia. This genetic disease, in which the body makes an abnormal form of hemoglobin, causes the red blood cells to form into sickle shapes. Sickled cells are fragile and die off too quickly for the bone marrow to replace them, leaving patients without enough red blood cells to carry sufficient oxygen to the lungs, brain, and other organs. In addition, sickled cells often become trapped in blood vessels, cutting off circulation. The disease causes fatigue, shortness of breath, and often agonizing pain crises when sickled cells block blood vessels and damage organs.

Charlie was lucky, because his sickle-cell anemia was quite mild and not life threatening. He'd never had a pain crisis, at least not one severe enough to be identified. But he had other symptoms common in sickle-cell disease, including delayed growth, lack of energy, and a frequent low-grade "achy" feeling. He also caught every illness that went around his school. In addition, he had bone deformities that would grow worse in his teen years.

I could diagnose Charlie's sickle-cell anemia, but I couldn't cure him. So what good did his diagnosis do? First, I was able to give his father crucial information about how to minimize Charlie's symptoms. Charlie needed to avoid strenuous exercise, high altitudes, dehydration, stress, and nutritional deficiencies, and he needed to be protected as much as possible from infectious disease. Because Charlie's disease was mild, these steps alone made a big difference in how he felt—and, in turn, in how he behaved.

Second, I referred Charlie's family to a genetic counselor who explained to them their risk, as carriers of the sickle-cell trait, of having additional children with sickle-cell anemia. And they found support groups of other parents dealing with this disease, who were able to offer practical advice and moral support.

Third, I told Charlie's dad to gradually wean him off Ritalin. By suppressing Charlie's appetite, and probably suppressing his growth as well, the drug was undoubtedly exacerbating his symptoms. Charlie's behavior problems stemmed from brain malfunction due to lack of oxygen, and possibly from small "silent" strokes that often occur in patients with sickle cell—conditions Ritalin certainly doesn't treat.

Consequences That Can Last a Lifetime— and Beyond

Charlie's story illustrates the dangers of overlooking genetic disease in hyperactive children. It's also a good example of how a careless physician who misses a genetic disorder can harm not just one child but the child's entire family as well. When I saw him, Charlie was young, and his parents were thinking of having several more children. Taking care of *one* child with a chronic and dangerous genetic disease is a tremendous burden for a family. But taking care of two, three, or four children with such a disability can break the strongest of families, both financially and emotionally.

Maybe Charlie's first doctor saved himself some time by giving Charlie a quick exam and a prescription. But was it worth it, if Charlie's family, unaware that they were carrying a genetic time bomb, had other children with the same disorder? Maybe they would have chosen to have more children, after evaluating their risk factors. Maybe they would have decided to stop at one child. Maybe they would have adopted. Whatever their choice, they desperately needed to know the truth about Charlie's condition.

In short, diagnosing a genetic disorder is important both to the patient and to the patient's entire family—and that can include aunts, uncles, cousins, nieces, and nephews, and generations to come. That's especially true of genetic disorders that affect some victims mildly and others severely, because these genetic defects often spread widely throughout a family tree before they're identified. Here's why:

Some genetic disorders get worse with each generation. Fragile X syndrome, a leading cause of mental retardation, is a good example. In its full-blown form, fragile X causes retardation, hyperactivity, speech delay, autistic behaviors, and unusual features including a prominent jaw, large ears, large testicles, flat feet, and loose joints. A few males with fragile X, however, aren't retarded and have only mildly unusual features. Occasionally, a rushed physician labels such children learning disabled or hyperactive.

That's unfortunate, not only for the misdiagnosed child but for his entire family. Why? Because the abnormal chromosome area that causes fragile X tends to grow longer in each generation, a process called amplification. Thus, future generations in the mildly affected child's family may inherit a far more devastating form of the disorder.

A genetic disorder can affect carriers (those who have only one defective gene) to a slight degree, while affecting the unlucky owners of two defective genes much more severely. Again, fragile X syndrome is a good example. Women who carry the fragile X gene defect usually are unaffected, because the normal gene on their other X chromosome protects them. But some female fragile X carriers have learning disabilities (particularly in math) and emotional symptoms such as anxiety or depression. If a mildly affected female fragile X carrier is labeled as learning disabled or attention disordered or anxious or depressed, her parents won't have a clue about the genetic risk to any later male children. They probably won't find out unless their next child is a boy who inherits the fragile X defect, or until their daughter grows up and has a retarded son.

Cases like these demonstrate how important it is for doctors to take careful family histories. A significant family history of retardation, hyperactivity, learning disabilities, or psychosis should raise a good doctor's index of suspicion, *even if a patient shows no obvious signs and symptoms of genetic disease.*

A family history of *any* disease, for that matter, should interest a doctor examining a hyperactive child. That's because some of the most common genetically influenced disorders—even those you'd least suspect—can make children act crazy.

Dana: Demonic or Diseased?

"It's like living with two different children," nine-year-old Dana's mother told me. "There's the sweet little girl, and then, a few hours later, there's the demon."

When Dana's bad moods struck, her mother told me, she would tear up her schoolbooks, hit her brother, and slam the door so hard the pictures fell off the wall. At least once or twice a week, Dana ended up in the principal's office, usually for starting fights. Her family didn't know whether to be angry or scared by her behavior. They did know, however, that the "diagnoses" her pediatrician offered when her symptoms first started—hyperactivity and oppositional defiant disorder—didn't ring true.

Once a mellow little girl, Dana had changed after her eighth birthday. At first, Dana's mom thought the girl was acting out because she'd started at a new school. But efforts by Dana's parents, the school's guidance counselor, and a sympathetic teacher all failed to change Dana's out-of-control mood swings. In fact, her behavior grew worse.

Dana didn't look good, either. The picture her mother showed me of Dana at age seven showed a slightly chubby, pink-skinned, healthy child. The child in my office, however, was thin, pale, and fragile-looking. She was also cranky and burst into tears when I asked her how she felt.

Clearly, something was making Dana sickly. And that same something was making her sleep badly, wet the bed, lose her appetite, and feel just miserable. That something, it turned out, was the beginning phase of diabetes.

Dana was in the first stages of insulin-dependent diabetes. In time her blood sugar levels would become dangerously high, unless she took insulin daily. But diabetes begins with the body producing too *much* insulin, which makes blood sugar drop. Eventually, the body's immune system responds by making cells resistant to insulin. During this process, as prediabetes turns into diabetes, blood sugar levels can swing wildly.

At the time I saw her, Dana was at the mercy of her blood sugar peaks and valleys. When her blood sugar dropped, she suffered from neuroglycopenia. That means, simply, that not enough "food," in the form of blood sugar, was reaching her brain. The result was violent mood swings, fatigue, and bad behavior.

"I don't know why I didn't think of diabetes," Dana's mother told me. "My husband's mother and sister are both diabetics." But it wasn't Dana's job to know that early-stage diabetes can cause hyperactivity. It was Dana's pediatrician's job, and he didn't do it.

It isn't as though diabetes is an uncommon disease. The disorder affects millions of Americans, more than 100,000 of them under the age of twenty. However, Dana's doctor wasn't the only one to miss this diagnosis; the Centers for Disease Control estimates that more than five million Americans have undiagnosed diabetes.

I've diagnosed early-stage diabetes in a half dozen behavior-disordered children, and in even more adults who came to me with "psychiatric" symptoms including aggression, depression, and anxiety. I always consider it as a possibility in hyperactive children who, like Dana, have family histories of diabetes.

I sent Dana to an endocrinologist, who taught her family how to control her diet and manage her disease. I haven't seen her since, because she no longer needs a psychiatrist or a neurologist. And she doesn't need Ritalin.

Hyper Hormones

Other metabolic or hormonal disorders that can make kids hyperactive—some genetically influenced, and some not—include abnormalities of the liver, adrenal glands, or thyroid. Many of these disorders quickly turn virulent, causing retardation or fatal illness, so doctors don't miss these diagnoses for long. But some—in particular, thyroid problems—can be subtle and reveal themselves only in a child's behavior.

The link between thyroid problems and hyperactivity has been in the news lately, with newspaper and TV reports trumpeting that hyperactivity is caused by a genetic thyroid problem. This is true only in part. Studies indeed suggest that a small but significant percentage of hyperactive children have a genetic condition called resistance to thyroid hormone, in which the body's response to its own thyroid hormones is blunted. But you'll notice that I said a *small* number of kids have this problem. And a small number of hyperactive or ADD children have other types of thyroid disorders. Thyroid disorders aren't *the* cause of hyperactivity, but they're one of hundreds of different causes.

Because thyroid problems affect a significant minority of behavior-disordered children, a savvy doctor will look carefully for signs of thyroid dysfunction, or for a family history of thyroid disorder, in any child with hyperactive behavior. Few doctors do this, however. In *No More Ritalin*, Dr. Mary Ann Block notes, "Last year I diagnosed four children with hyperthyroidism in four months. All of the children had been diagnosed as ADHD. When the thyroid problem was addressed, the symptoms (which had been called ADHD) resolved. How sad it is to see children drugged while their underlying health problems go untreated."[1]

Thyroid disorders generally are treatable—not with Ritalin, of course, but with hormones. Preliminary evidence suggests, for example, that hyperactive children with resistance to thyroid hormone respond well to the thyroid hormone liothyronine (L-T3), although the hormone does not benefit hyperactive children *without* thyroid abnormalities and may even make their symptoms worse.[2] (This is yet another example of the benefits of splitting hyperactivity into correct diagnoses, rather than lumping all hyper children together into the grab bag label of ADHD!)

One of the most common thyroid problems that causes hyperactivity, incidentally, is not a genetic disease but an autoimmune disease, one in which the body, mistaking its own cells for invaders, attacks itself. The autoimmune disease I'm talking about is called Graves' disease, and it received considerable attention a few years back when First Lady Barbara Bush was diagnosed with the condition. But it's not just a grown-up disease; in fact, about 5 percent of cases are diagnosed in children. A recent report by endocrinologist Andrea Eberle noted that 87 percent of the twenty-one children with Graves' disease whom she's seen in her practice were hyperactive, and that poor grades and dramatic drops in school performance were almost universal in these children. In addition, she notes, "There were mood swings in 53%, 47% had difficulty concentrating, and 40% were irritable or easily angered."

Although Graves' disease is one of the most easily diagnosed thyroid disorders, Eberle noted that two of the children she saw were taking Ritalin for a "diagnosis" of ADHD, a treatment that can actually exacerbate behavior problems in these children.[3]

Another gland disorder, this one genetically influenced and more rare but also much more dangerous than Graves' disease, is a tumor called a pheochromocytoma. Early symptoms of this tumor, which arises in the adrenal glands, can include anxiety, restlessness, headaches, and heart palpitations—all symptoms that can lead to a child being labeled hyperactive or attention disordered. Needless to say, mistaking these symptoms for symptoms of ADHD can be disastrous. When pheochromocytomas are benign, they're virtually 100 percent curable. When they're malignant, almost half of patients can still be saved. In either case, obviously, an ADHD label and Ritalin won't help.

The Surprise Diagnoses

There's no excuse for a doctor to miss a diagnosis of early-stage diabetes in a patient, because all doctors study this disease, and all doctors know that it can cause wild mood swings and behavioral problems. Likewise, the link between thyroid disorders and behavior problems is commonly known. Even pheochromocytomas, although they're rare, are recognized to be associated with hyperactivity.

Other stealthy genetic diseases, however, aren't commonly linked to hyperactivity or behavior disorders. But, again, *almost any genetic disease can cause behavior problems—even those that don't directly affect the brain.* And the routes by which these diseases act can be varied.

To prove this point, let's look at a disorder called Marfan's syndrome. You've probably heard of Marfan's syndrome because it killed Olympic volleyball star Flo Hyman and occasionally causes fatal ruptures of the aorta in basketball players and other athletes. It's *not* a disorder linked to hyperactivity, and I've never met a Marfan patient with behavior problems. In fact, I'll be surprised if I ever do. But let's look at why Marfan's syndrome, in spite of the fact that it's not a behavioral disorder, makes some children hyperactive.

Marfan's syndrome is a disease of the connective tissue, and it affects the skeleton, circulatory system, and eyes. People with Marfan's syndrome are usually very tall, slender, long-legged, and limber. Those who don't suffer from scoliosis, lung problems, or visual impairment are naturals at sports requiring height and litheness. In fact, the only obvious symptoms in some Marfan cases (particularly during early childhood years) are height and thinness, so the diagnosis of Marfan's syndrome can be missed for years or even decades.

Marfan's syndrome is thought of as a physical rather than a mental disease, and most individuals with the disorder have no intellectual or behavioral problems. But every patient is a statistic of one—and while Marfan patients *as a group* aren't abnormal behaviorally, some individuals with the disease are. Studies indicate that children with Marfan's syndrome have a somewhat elevated risk for learning disabilities, hyperactivity, and attention deficit disorder.[4]

Why are a relatively small number of children with Marfan's syndrome hyper? One reason is that about half of all people with the disorder have eye lenses that are dislocated or off center. Some children with this problem may have trouble learning and reading as a result, and may react by being pests in class. In these cases, hyperactivity is a secondary symptom stemming from frustration. A more likely culprit in most cases of Marfan-linked hyperactivity, however, is insufficient blood supply to the brain, due to heart and circulatory problems. But there are still other ways in which Marfan's syndrome can change behavior. It can cause sleep apnea (sudden cessation of breathing), for instance, or chronic headaches. And it can cause mitral valve prolapse, a heart condition that can lead to anxiety and heart palpitations—symptoms that can make a child act a little crazy.

Many children with Marfan's syndrome don't look unusual enough to fail a pediatrician's brisk physical evaluation, so these abnormalities are frequently missed. Thus, like almost all the other kids with hyperactivity, behavior-disordered children with subclinical Marfan's syndrome get a prescription for Ritalin. (Unfortunately, Ritalin is the wrong treatment for a child with Marfan's syndrome, because it's a stimulant, and stimulants make the heart work harder.) What they don't get is counseling on how to reduce their chances of sudden death (by avoiding heavy exercise) or referrals for surgery to correct their heart and aortal defects.

Now, your child almost undoubtedly *doesn't* have Marfan's syndrome. It's a fairly rare disease. The point is that *there are hundreds of similar, fairly rare genetic diseases that, through one pathway or another, can make your child hyper—even though these diseases aren't normally associated with hyperactivity.* That's why a doctor who doesn't take careful family histories and thoroughly examine children for signs of genetic defects isn't doing his or her job. And a doctor who simply prescribes Ritalin can sometimes—as in the case of Marfan's syndrome patients—risk endangering a child's life.

The Genetics/Environment Connection

Genes aren't always destiny, and altering a child's environment can alleviate many symptoms of genetic disease—but only if you know what disease you're dealing with and use the right interventions. Dana, for instance, needed to be eating a diet that would minimize her blood glucose swings. While the diet didn't cure her diabetes, it made her feel a lot better, and it helped slow the disease's progress. In the case of Charlie, the child with sickle-cell anemia, avoiding stress, high altitude, and infections was crucial to both his physical health and his brain functioning.

In some cases, environmental influences can actually be as critical as genes in determining whether a child with a genetic disorder develops hyperactivity. Take asthma, for instance.

Children with asthma, a disorder that's genetically influenced, are more prone to cognitive and behavioral problems than are non-asthmatic children. One reason is obvious: Children whose lungs aren't working efficiently sometimes can't think right because their brains aren't getting enough oxygen. But occasionally medications, and not the effects of asthma itself, are to blame. At excessive doses, the asthma drug theophylline can cause symptoms of brain dysfunction including restlessness, irritability, anxiety, confusion, or even delirium.[5] Even at standard doses, the drug can sometimes cause behavioral symptoms—particularly if it's combined with caffeine or some over-the-counter drugs. So the doctor of a behavior-disordered asthmatic child needs to carefully evaluate the child's medications to make sure the dosages are not too high and the drugs are being administered correctly.

You'll note that asthma can cause aberrant behavior *directly*, by reducing oxygen to the brain, or *indirectly*, when the drugs used to treat the disorder lead to behavioral symptoms. The purported link between asthma and behavioral problems, as you can see, isn't as simple as some doctors suggest.

Another interesting example of the gene/environment interaction, *and* of the problems medications can cause, is Tourette's syndrome, a mysterious disorder that affects thousands of children and is frequently linked to hyperactivity. Although Tourette's syndrome has genetic roots, we don't know exactly how it's passed down from parent to child. We don't know what causes its symptoms, which can include obsessions and compulsions, inattention, impulsivity, restlessness, learning disabilities, phobias, and anxiety. And we don't know what causes Tourette's syndrome patients to have chronic tics that can include twitching, grimacing, blinking, kicking, shrugging, throat clearing, barking, hissing, or cursing.

What we're starting to discover, however, is that although Tourette's syndrome is a genetic disorder, environmental factors can sometimes bring on symptoms—or, in other cases, make symptoms go away. Many doctors, in fact, believe that children inherit a *vulnerability* to Tourette's syndrome but not the disease per se.

In Chapter 4, I discussed how strep throat infections may bring on tics in vulnerable children. In addition, certain medications can unmask Tourette's syndrome in children who previously had no symptoms of the disorder. High on the list of these medications are Ritalin and other stimulant drugs; in fact, T. L. Lowe and colleagues believe that "the widespread use of stimulants may be increasing substantially the number of cases [of Tourette's syndrome] requiring clinical diagnosis and intervention."[6] Thus, if your child is placed on Ritalin for symptoms of hyperactivity, you may wind up with a child who also has symptoms of Tourette's—a good example of why throwing drugs at a symptom often makes a child's problem worse rather than better.

The Message for Parents

I've mentioned diabetes, fragile X syndrome, and Tourette's syndrome in this chapter, because they're fairly common causes of hyperactive behavior. But the bottom line, as I said in discussing Marfan's syndrome, is that *almost any genetic disorder* can cause hyperactivity or other behavior problems, even if the disorder isn't normally linked to such problems.

Many genetic diseases disrupt brain function (and thus, behavior) directly, through a variety of paths. Fragile X syndrome, for instance, probably changes the actual structure of the brain. Sickle-cell anemia can directly change the function of an otherwise normal brain, when it causes small strokes that damage brain areas. Sickle-cell and other anemias also harm the brain by reducing its supply of oxygen, as do heart problems that reduce blood flow to the brain. Metabolic disorders, on the other hand, affect the brain by altering brain levels of glucose. Still other genetic disorders cause brain dysfunction by disrupting levels of hormones, brain messenger chemicals, calcium, phosphorus, magnesium, sodium, potassium, and/or chloride.

But even disorders that don't directly or indirectly harm the brain can make a child restless, irritable, attention disordered, aggressive, angry, hostile, whiny, hyper, and otherwise a pain. That's because genetic disorders *make people feel bad*. When an adult feels bad, he or she often can pinpoint the cause: fatigue, an aching head, light-headedness, indigestion, etc. But when a child feels sick, especially when it's a chronic, low-grade sickness, the child tends to think that's normal. After all, how would a child who's been mildly ill for years even know what normal feels like anymore? But these kids *don't* feel normal, and, as I've said before, a kid who feels bad often acts badly as well. So whether a genetic disorder affects the lungs, the heart, the muscles, the nerves, or the digestive system, it's likely to have an impact on a child's behavior.

This doesn't mean, of course, that every hyperactive child needs to be tested for genetic diseases. I don't order such tests unless a child's appearance, symptoms, or family history raises my index of suspicion. But parents should insist on a genetic consultation if there is a strong family history of genetic disorders—either mental or physical. Also be forceful about requesting a consultation with a geneticist if your child has minor physical anomalies such as oddly placed ears, abnormally long or short fingers, webbing between fingers or toes, widely or narrowly spaced eyes, or an unusual body shape (for instance, breast development in a male). In addition, doctors should take a close look at children whose appearance is markedly different from that of their parents or other family members. And, of course, any family history of consanguinity (marriage between close biological relatives) is a major red flag, because it greatly increases the chances of a child inheriting two copies of a defective gene.

If your child doesn't have physical anomalies, a family history of genetic problems, or a family history of intermarriage, or any signs or symptoms (even subtle ones) suggesting genetic disease, then your doctor isn't being negligent in forgoing a genetic evaluation. But if there's *any* doubt about whether your child's hyperactivity could have genetic roots, your doctor should err on the side of caution. As I've said, it's not just your child's health that's at stake. It's the health of your entire family, both current and future.

CHAPTER 6

The Injured Brain: Structural Defects That Can Cause Hyperactive Behavior

> From the brain, and from the brain only, arise our pleasures, joys,
> laughter and jests, as well as our sorrows, pains, griefs, and fears.
> Through it, in particular, we think, see, hear, and distinguish the
> ugly from the beautiful, the bad from the good, the pleasant from
> the unpleasant. . . . It is the same thing which makes us mad or
> delirious, inspires us with dread and fear, whether by night or by
> day, brings sleeplessness, inopportune mistakes, aimless anxieties,
> absentmindedness, and acts that are contrary to habit.
>
> *Hippocrates*

BACK IN THE 1940s AND 1950s, PARENTS OF HYPERACTIVE children often heard the frightening verdict, "He's brain damaged."

Until the late 1900s, doctors thought that hyperactivity stemmed from some mysterious form of "minimal brain damage." This idea fell out of favor when doctors admitted that they hadn't a clue about what or where that damage might be. Since that time, doctors using everything from EEGs to MRIs to PET scans have failed to find any consistent brain lesions in hyperactive children (with an exception I discuss below). This is no surprise, of course, since so many different insults cause hyperactivity.

Of course, some hyperactive children *do* have permanent brain injuries due to fetal alcohol syndrome, prenatal infections, serious genetic defects, or severe head injuries. Usually, these children's symptoms are so severe that doctors diagnose them quickly and correctly. (An exception is mild cases of fetal alcohol damage, which I discuss a bit later.)

Many other children, however, are suffering from *treatable* structural brain abnormalities that are often overlooked by doctors—or, at least, overlooked until symptoms become severe. This category includes everything from minor cysts to brain atrophy to dangerous but curable tumors.

It's critical that children suffering from these brain disorders get real diagnoses, because some brain lesions can kill or cripple if not treated correctly. Furthermore, Ritalin treatment can exacerbate symptoms of brain defects and make children even sicker. And there's some evidence that *Ritalin itself may possibly be causing or contributing to the damage.*

Cortical Atrophy and Some Speculation About Ritalin

As I mention in Chapter 1, several medical studies now link hyperactivity to defects of the frontal lobes of the brain. Basically, MRI scans show that areas of the frontal lobes of the brain are too small in a significant number of hyperactive children. PET scans also show that glucose supply to these brain areas (a measure of how hard the areas are working) is lower than in nondisabled subjects.

This, of course, has been seen by many as evidence of a specific brain abnormality in ADHD. But I disagree. I believe it's strong evidence that many hyperactive children are suffering from cortical atrophy *due to a wide range of biological insults.*

What is cortical atrophy? It's a widening of the "valleys" and narrowing of the "hills" on the brain's surface. Although it *appears* that the white matter on the surface of the brain is atrophying, it's the gray matter underneath—that is, the neurons that do the thinking—that's actually shrinking. (Picture an apple wrinkling up more and more as it shrivels up and gets smaller. The white matter of the brain, like the peel of the apple, wrinkles and shrivels because the matter underneath—in the brain's case, the gray matter—isn't taking up as much space as it once did.)

Why is the gray matter shrinking? Sometimes, it's because the brain is dehydrated. In other cases, it's because the blood vessels aren't getting enough oxygen or glucose to brain cells, which literally are starving.

Cortical atrophy is a profound finding, one often associated with dementia. But it's often reversible in hyperactive children, because most of the causes of cortical atrophy can be treated. In early stages, atrophy most often involves the shrinking of neurons, not actual cell death. Eliminate the cause of the shrinkage, and the neurons will plump up and once again work normally.

Of course, doctors who simply assume that ADHD is a permanent condition, and that small and poorly functioning frontal lobes are part of this condition, won't do anything to treat cortical atrophy. Such doctors routinely miss common and obvious causes of frontal lobe shrinkage, including:

- Lead toxicity.
- Carbon monoxide poisoning.
- Head injuries.
- Prescription or nonprescription steroids, which cause a loss of water, leading to cell shrinkage.
- Chronic exposure to solvents.
- Parasites. One CT study of twenty-five patients infected with schistosomiasis showed that more than one-third had cortical atrophy.[1]
- Any conditions that reduce oxygen or glucose to the brain, including heart or lung defects; anemias; heavy metal toxicity; hyperinsulinism; prediabetes; pancreatic tumors; liver, thyroid, or adrenal disorders; and infections.

It's frightening that many doctors don't consider this multitude of possible diagnoses when they see smaller-than-normal frontal lobes on a child's MRI. But let me tell you something even more frightening.

One cause of cortical atrophy is a condition called amphetamine brain, seen in many drug abusers. It occurs when amphetamines cause the blood vessels in the brain to shrink, reducing oxygen and glucose supply to neurons. The vessels become irritated, further cutting down on the essential nutrients reaching brain cells. First, the cells shrink and begin functioning at less-than-optimal levels. If a patient continues to abuse amphetamines, however, neurons actually begin to die.

The original drugs used to treat hyperactive children, of course, were amphetamines. Now, however, doctors use Ritalin—which is called an amphetamine-like drug because, although its molecular structure differs from that of an amphetamine, many of its effects are similar.

Does this mean that Ritalin itself may be causing many of the cases of small frontal lobes being reported by researchers? One study, way back in 1986, suggested that this may be the case. Henry A. Nasrallah and colleagues performed CT scans on twenty-four young men who had been treated for hyperactivity since childhood, and found "a significantly greater frequency of cerebral atrophy" in the hyperactive group than in controls. Noting that all of the hyperactive patients had been treated with psychostimulants, the researchers suggested that "cortical atrophy may be a long-term adverse effect of this treatment."[2]

This study alarmed me, particularly since I've seen the tragic effects of amphetamine brain, which can include dementia. So I set out to see if later research implicated Ritalin in brain shrinkage. But I've found no follow-up research, except for one 1994 study by G. J. Wang and colleagues.

Remember what I said a few paragraphs ago about how amphetamine brain begins with constriction of the blood vessels that feed the brain cells? Wang and coworkers studied the effects of Ritalin on the cerebral blood flow of five healthy males and reported that "decrements in cerebral blood flow were homogenous throughout the brain (regional decrements 23–30 percent) and probably reflect the vasoactive properties of methylphenidate." In plain English, Ritalin appears to cause blood vessels in the brain to constrict significantly. The researchers concluded that Ritalin's effects on the brain's blood supply need to be considered when giving the drug to any patient with evidence of existing cerebrovascular disease, or "when prescribing this drug chronically." In short, they're concerned about the effects of giving this medication to people for five, ten, or fifteen years. And so am I.[3]

In looking over the studies showing cerebral underdevelopment in a high percentage of hyperactive subjects,[4] I'm struck by the fact that virtually *all* of the subjects in these studies have been taking Ritalin or other stimulant drugs. I spoke recently with F. Xavier Castellanos, a coauthor of several of these studies, who agrees that future research must address the question of whether the defects the researchers are seeing are caused by innate biological abnormalities, or by chronic use of stimulant drugs. The researchers have just begun a five-year study on Ritalin-free children, which may give us some answers.

It amazes me that, in spite of the fact that amphetamine brain is a well-known condition, and Ritalin is an amphetamine-like drug, so few researchers are investigating the possibility that Ritalin treatment may cause brain atrophy in children who take the drug for many years. This is incomprehensible to me. If there's a possibility that Ritalin could be causing brain shrinkage in children, then there's a distinct possibility that it also could contribute to the development of presenile dementia in older, chronically exposed adults. Are we setting up a number of children for early dementia, by giving them Ritalin for years or even decades? We don't know. Given what we *do* know about how amphetamines can damage or even kill neurons, it's inconceivable to me that more researchers aren't interested in finding out.

As I've noted, however, drugs are only one possible cause of cortical atrophy. If your child's doctor orders an MRI that shows abnormal frontal lobe structure, or a PET scan that shows reduced frontal lobe functioning, it's imperative that you find out *why* this is happening. Don't accept the explanation that this is merely a symptom of ADHD. It isn't. It's often a symptom of brain cells starving for water, oxygen, or glucose. And, in many cases, it's a reversible condition—if its causes are diagnosed and corrected in time.

*   *   *

ALTHOUGH CORTICAL ATROPHY CAN STEM FROM A VARIETY of insults to the brain, other problems are linked directly to head injury. Sometimes, for instance, a child's behavior problems start shortly after a concussion. Even in this situation, however, a doctor has to be cautious and not make a "curbside diagnosis." Let me explain why.

Head Injuries and Postconcussion Syndrome

A serious head injury can cause long-term brain damage, leading to hyperactivity, cognitive problems, and marked personality changes. If your child's hyperactivity began after a major head trauma, then the behavior's cause is probably no mystery. Doctors should be able to determine the extent of your child's injury and make some predictions as to whether your child's symptoms will clear up.

The vast majority of head injuries, however, aren't what we consider serious. In this category are the football quarterback who takes a hard hit and sees stars, the child who falls off a bike and gets a mild concussion, or the youngster who falls off the monkey bars and gets a goose egg. Children usually recover quickly from such lumps and bumps, and within a few days they're forgotten.

The brain is surprisingly forgiving, even when head bumps are severe enough to cause a concussion. (And a concussion, incidentally, doesn't necessarily involve unconsciousness. A person who sees stars is suffering from a concussion, even if he or she remains fully aware.) It's remarkable that a quarterback like Troy Aikman, or a boxer like Evander Holyfield, can take hit after hit and show little damage. Although decades of such punishment can lead to severe neurological damage, such as the dementia pugilistica that many boxers develop, most athletes don't suffer any obvious ill effects from repeated head bumps.

Surprisingly, however, a significant minority of people appear to suffer long-term effects from minor concussions. We call this postconcussion syndrome, and it's the subject of much interest in the medical community. One of the most puzzling features of postconcussion syndrome is that, often, the milder the head injury, the more serious the long-term symptoms. Sometimes a patient who's suffered only a minor concussion, with a few minutes of altered consciousness, suffers for months or even years afterward from attention problems, behavior problems, or personality changes. Common symptoms of postconcussion syndrome include:

- irritability
- emotionality
- memory problems
- depression
- headache
- light-headedness
- tinnitus (ringing ears)
- vertigo
- sleep problems

I've examined many patients with postconcussion syndrome, including several whose symptoms could easily be labeled attention deficit disorder or hyperactivity. They weren't suffering from either ADD or ADHD. In reality, they weren't even suffering primarily from a head injury. It turned out that the explanation for their out-of-proportion symptoms was simple. In every case, I found that the patients were suffering, even *before* their injuries, from other, undiagnosed medical conditions such as subclinical diabetes, heart problems, or chronic infections.

What do these seemingly unrelated medical conditions have to do with a concussion injury? Simple. A concussion disrupts brain functioning. It alters the output of neurons, and the connections between neurons, and the delicate balance of chemicals in the brain. In short, it disrupts the brain's status quo. In a healthy individual, the body immediately begins to correct this situation. Receiving a steady supply of glucose, oxygen, and other nutrients from the body, the brain is able to readjust its settings, so to speak. Damage is repaired, levels of brain chemicals go back to normal, and within a short time, the brain is back in balance.

But what happens if the rest of the body can't do its job in this repair process? What happens if the digestive system can't process carbohydrates adequately? What happens if the heart can't pump a sufficient supply of blood? What if there is too little iron in the blood, or too little glucose, or nutrient deficiencies due to parasites or intestinal malabsorption? Then the brain doesn't get the materials it needs to repair itself. In fact, it's barely getting the materials it requires to keep functioning at all.

Here's an analogy. Suppose your living room is flooded. If you have enough money, energy, and time, you can repair the damage in a few weeks. But if you're broke, ill, or overworked, your living room might be a mess for years. Similarly, the brain of a child suffering from postconcussion syndrome doesn't get fixed because the rest of the body can't pitch in and do its job.

One of my young patients, a classic case of postconcussion syndrome, suffered for years from behavioral and academic problems that began after a mild concussion. One doctor prescribed Ritalin, and another recommended counseling for posttraumatic stress disorder. (Doctors often dismiss postconcussion symptoms as "all in your head.") The boy didn't get better, however, until I diagnosed the problems that kept his brain from healing: high lead levels and a chronic parasitic infection.

If your child's hyperactive behavior, attention disorders, or learning problems began or grew worse shortly after a mild concussion, he or she could be suffering from postconcussion syndrome. If so, you need to find out *why* your child's brain hasn't healed from this minor insult. The problem almost assuredly isn't the head injury itself. Rather, your child's system is probably compromised by other illnesses and can't summon the resources needed to restore the brain to normal functioning.

SO FAR, I'VE LOOKED PRIMARILY AT DAMAGE DONE TO THE brain from outside—cortical atrophy due to toxins or drugs, concussions due to head injuries, etc. But some injuries arise within the brain. You're no doubt familiar with the most frightening of these problems—cancerous brain tumors. Fortunately, these tumors are fairly uncommon in children. Furthermore, cancerous tumors generally progress far too quickly to be the cause of long-term, chronic behavior problems. It's far more common for such behaviors to stem from milder problems such as benign tumors or cysts. Here's an example:

Hyperactivity and Headaches: More Than Just ADHD

Neurologist J. Gordon Millichap recently wrote about a nine-year-old boy labeled as having ADHD because of "inattention, distractibility, and homework organizational problems." The boy also suffered from headaches and was struggling through his classes.

Millichap noted that the boy had brief right-hand tremors and experienced episodes of confusion that suggested seizures. In addition, the boy's head was slightly enlarged, and he had trouble performing rapidly alternating movements with his right forearm. Millichap sent the boy for an EEG, which showed abnormal brain waves. The cause of the abnormal brain waves showed up on an MRI scan, which revealed a large cyst, called an arachnoid cyst, in the temporal lobe of the boy's brain.[5]

In some cases, surgery on such cysts can improve verbal and memory skills as well as behavior. In other cases, such as this boy's, doctors prefer simply to keep an eye on the cyst and make sure it doesn't get bigger and cause additional symptoms. In either case, diagnosis of brain cysts is important, and a simplistic label and Ritalin treatment can be harmful. That's because stimulant drugs, such as Ritalin, can make the symptoms of cysts—particularly headaches—much worse, and the drugs generally don't do a thing to reduce hyperactivity in these cases.

Millichap vetoed the use of stimulants for his patient and instead recommended a revised educational program and extra help with homework. And he'll keep an eye on the cyst, so that it can be quickly handled if it becomes dangerous.

Arachnoid cysts are a relatively rare cause of hyperactive behavior, but they're probably more common than doctors think. Millichap, for instance, has seen at least three patients with such cysts and hyperactive behavior, and he's only one of thousands of neurologists in the United States. The moral is that while cysts and benign tumors occur in only a few thousand children a year, doctors need to consider them as diagnostic possibilities. Statistically, these diagnoses may not be important—but to individual families, they assuredly are.

Seizures: The "Brain Damage" Myth

Thousands of hyperactive children have seizures, although these seizures often are so subtle that they go undetected by observers (and by doctors). These seizures can occur hundreds of times a day, causing symptoms including inattention, peculiar repetitive behaviors, mood changes, and in some cases even aggression.

Such seizures sometimes result from irreversible damage to the brain. Even though the damage can't be corrected in these cases, it's important to diagnose the seizures. Often, anticonvulsants can control both the seizures and the behavior problems they cause.

For every child whose seizures stem from a brain lesion, however, there are a dozen whose seizures stem from brain *dysfunction* that can be diagnosed, treated, and cured. These children shouldn't be labeled ADD or ADHD, and they shouldn't be labeled epileptic either.

Many people are surprised when I say this, because they've been led to believe that the brains of individuals who have seizures are somehow different from other people's brains. But seizures can happen to anyone. There's no such thing as an "epileptic" person or a "nonepileptic" person. I could have a seizure tomorrow at breakfast. You could have one today at the office. *Anyone, anywhere, at any time*, can have a seizure.

Why? Because seizures have hundreds of causes. They can result from medication errors, lead toxicity, heart conditions, or infections. Many seizures are treatable or even curable. Moreover, some "seizures" aren't really seizures at all but a condition called syncope (a fancy term for "fainting") that often goes undiagnosed.

Finding the causes of seizures or seizure-like spells takes time, effort, and sometimes many tests. Many patients, however, don't get a thorough diagnostic evaluation. What they get is a basic EEG (if they're lucky) and a prescription for anticonvulsants. There are, of course, cases where anticonvulsants are the only help we can offer patients. But I've seen hundreds of children who didn't need to be taking seizure drugs, because their seizures had obvious causes and simple cures.

One of my patients, Todd, is a good example of how hyperactivity can stem from seizures—and seizures, in turn, can stem from a medical condition having nothing to do with brain damage.

The Sleepwalking Paste Eater

I first saw Todd when he was eight, but he'd been a "problem child" since preschool. A doctor put him on Ritalin in the second grade, when teachers said he couldn't learn and wouldn't sit still.

Todd, like many children I see, was a paradox: He was hyper but also fatigued much of the time. In fact, his mother told me, "When I go shopping, I still have to put him in the cart. He says he just can't walk that far, and he's not being lazy. When I make him walk, he gets pale and has to sit down." When I asked Todd how he felt, he told me, "My elbows and knees hurt."

Todd slept poorly, ground his teeth during the night, and sometimes wet the bed. Occasionally his mother found him sleepwalking. And even though he was long past the toddler stage, he still ate paste, dirt, and other nonfoods.

I ordered a twenty-four-hour EEG for Todd, which revealed petit mal seizures. (Incidentally, you should always insist on a twenty-four-hour EEG rather than the quickie EEG most children are given. The percentage of "normal" EEGs in children with seizures is astronomical, because it's only lucky coincidence when a child has a seizure during a half-hour EEG. A twenty-four-hour EEG, on the other hand, is highly likely to catch seizure activity as well as to offer possible clues about the seizures' causes.)

I could have declared my job done when Todd's EEG revealed seizures, prescribing an anticonvulsant and telling Todd's mom, "Maybe he'll outgrow his epilepsy." Instead, I looked for the cause of his seizures—and I found it.

Todd's laboratory tests revealed toxic levels of lead, which was not surprising because most children with pica have elevated lead levels. Pica is a *cause* of lead poisoning (since dirt and other nonfoods often contain large amounts of lead), but it's also frequently a *reaction* to toxic lead levels. Why other doctors hadn't checked Todd's lead levels is beyond me, because many of his other symptoms—including fatigue, tooth grinding, and hyperactivity—also are classic signs of low-grade lead poisoning.

I also asked a specialist to check Todd for heart problems, because of the boy's chronic fatigue, but he passed the cardiology exam. However, he flunked another test: a screening for poststreptococcal sensitivity. That sensitivity explained Todd's joint pains and also the nosebleeds he frequently suffered. And he had mixed dominance, in which neither the left nor the right side of the brain is in control, so he needed educational interventions designed to overcome his learning problems.

Clearly, labeling Todd hyperactive without detecting his seizures was irresponsible on his original doctor's part. And I would have been irresponsible, too, if I'd discovered the seizures and simply labeled them epilepsy without uncovering their multiple causes.

Labeling everyone who has seizures epileptic harms many of them—as it would have harmed Todd—and kills some of them. A case in point: A recent article in the *Journal of the American Medical Association* reported on twelve "epileptic" patients whose symptoms actually stemmed from cardiac disorders, some of them life-threatening. *All but one of these patients* had been treated or were recommended for treatment with anticonvulsants. Such misdiagnoses, the reporting doctors said, may explain the high rate of sudden deaths among "epileptics."[6] No doubt!

If your child shows any evidence of seizures, or if a physician tells you that your child's behavior problems are caused by epilepsy, I can't overemphasize the importance of finding out *why* the seizures are happening. It may be a costly mission, because most managed care plans are quite happy to settle for a neurologist's label of epilepsy and balk at referrals to additional doctors. If you need to, pay for such referrals with your own money. Trust me—it'll be worth it.

Fetal Alcohol Effects (FAE): The Hidden Disability

I said earlier that most children with significant, permanent brain injuries are diagnosed early in life and then given appropriate schooling and medical help. But there's one glaring exception to this rule.

You've probably heard of fetal alcohol syndrome (FAS), a name that doctors use to describe the damage done to children's brains and bodies when their mothers drink heavily during pregnancy. FAS is the leading known cause of mental retardation, surpassing even Down syndrome and spina bifida. Although doctors often missed this diagnosis in the past, they're fairly good at spotting children with FAS now. These children usually are retarded (or at least slow) and have unusual facial features.

Prenatal alcohol impairment, however, also comes in a milder form called fetal alcohol effects, or FAE. Children with FAE often don't look disabled, and they tend to score in the low-normal or even normal range of intelligence. But these children aren't normal. Their maldeveloped brains cause them to exhibit a wide range of behavior problems, including hyperactivity, attention problems, learning disorders, and "ethical" disorders such as stealing, lying, and cheating. They tend to be impulsive and make bad judgments. And they're at extremely high risk for developing alcohol problems themselves, thus continuing the tragic cycle of FAS and FAE.

I saw one of these children not too long ago. Albert's foster parents, two gay men who had volunteered to take a "special needs" child, were baffled when the good home life and extra academic help they gave Albert didn't have much effect on his violent tantrums or his academic problems. Albert's doctors merely put the boy on clonidine (Catapres) and said he was hyperactive, but these two dedicated foster parents wanted better answers.

Later on, I discuss the importance of parents spotting diagnostic clues. These men had done some homework and provided me with information about Albert's biological mother, who was an alcoholic and used amphetamines during pregnancy. They also mentioned a bizarre behavior they'd both spotted: The little boy slept with his eyes open!

The maternal history, of course, alerted me to the possibility of FAE. So did Albert's minor physical abnormalities, including mildly misshapen eyelid folds. Also, a twenty-four-hour EEG showed abnormal brain activity occurring when the boy acted out. Albert's open-eyed sleeping was another clue, because people with weak facial muscle control—one symptom that can occur in alcohol-impaired children—sometimes have difficulty keeping their eyes closed during sleep. All of these clues pointed to FAE, in spite of the boy's relatively normal appearance and IQ.

With this diagnosis, the men were able to arrange for a special education placement for Albert. They also were alerted to the possibility that Albert's little brother, for whom they also were caring, might be alcohol-impaired.

In a way, it's unfortunate that children with FAE don't have clearly unusual facial features. Because they often look normal, thousands of them go undiagnosed, usually labeled as having hyperactivity, ADD, conduct disorder, or oppositional defiant disorder. Many of these children are adopted, and their adoptive families have no clue about the terrible biological legacy of the children's birth mothers. FAE children and their parents often spend years (and a great deal of money) in counseling, trying to find and conquer early life traumas that therapists blame for the children's behavior problems. But no amount of therapy, and no amount of stimulant drugs, can undo the damage caused by a mother who drank during pregnancy.

While heavy drinking often causes severe damage to the fetus, *even moderate social drinking* during pregnancy appears to cause significant harm to a baby. The most alarming aspect of fetal alcohol exposure, according to the National Institute on Alcohol Abuse and Alcoholism, is that studies to determine how much alcohol was safe to drink during pregnancy found that *"an effect occurred at even the lowest reported levels of alcohol intake, so that a clear threshold . . . could not be defined."*[7] Ann Streissguth, the leading researcher on alcohol's effects on the fetus, says population-based studies of social drinkers reveal "subtle offspring effects, including IQ and achievement decrements (especially arithmetic), attentional and memory problems, and learning problems, but of a smaller magnitude than those reported in patients with FAS."[8] One study by Streissguth found that children of mothers who engaged in social drinking during pregnancy were more likely than other children to perform poorly on arithmetic and reading tests, to be rated by their parents and teachers as having behaviors suggestive of learning disabilities, and to be placed in remedial classes at school.[9]

Clearly, if your hyperactive child is adopted, and you have reason to believe that the birth mother drank during pregnancy, you need to find a doctor competent to diagnose either FAS or FAE. We can't do much to treat either condition medically, but diagnosed children are eligible for a number of specialized educational and vocational services. And, according to one parent of an adopted child with FAE, "Just understanding *why* my child can't behave was a gift. At last, I knew it wasn't something I'd done wrong."

Alcohol is the best-known toxin that harms the developing fetus's brain, but there are many others. Heavy metal or pesticide poisoning in utero can cause permanent damage. So can many prescription drugs. And new evidence points to cigarette smoking during pregnancy as a cause of hyperactive and defiant behavior in children. If your hyperactive child is adopted, see what you can learn about the biological parents' medical histories and, in particular, any history of substance abuse.

IN THIS CHAPTER, I'VE LOOKED AT A VARIETY OF BEHAVIOR-altering conditions arising in the brain itself. But structural defects in other organs can lead, indirectly, to brain dysfunction. That's because the brain needs an adequate supply of oxygen, glucose, and nutrients in order to do its job. Cut down on any of this brain food, and you'll get symptoms ranging from fatigue and irritability to hyperactivity, attention problems, confusion, and learning disorders.

One of the quickest ways to interfere with the brain's food supply, of course, is to cut down on circulation. Even a perfectly normal neuron can't function normally without food, and defects of the heart or circulatory system literally starve brain cells. Corrected early enough, the damage is often temporary; but chronic hypoxia (lack of oxygen) eventually kills brain cells, causing permanent learning and behavior problems. That's why doctors who put young children on Ritalin for behavior problems, without doing thorough examinations to rule out cardiac defects, are negligent.

Contrary to what some doctors think, cardiac problems aren't all that rare in children. About one in one hundred children is born with a heart defect, and for reasons we don't yet understand, the numbers appear to be rising. In addition, some children who begin life with healthy hearts develop cardiac problems later in life, as a consequence of infections such as strep. Furthermore, doctors who think they can rule out heart disease by giving patients a quick once-over are wrong. Heart defects are often subtle, and children show few symptoms other than pallor, irritability and attention problems, lack of appetite, sweatiness, or slightly bluish fingers, lips, and toes. In many of these cases, only a careful evaluation by a cardiologist will uncover a defect and determine its seriousness.

While I'm on the subject of cardiac disorders, a word about heart murmurs is in order. Many heart murmurs in children are innocuous, and as many as nine out of ten people may exhibit heart murmurs at some time during their lives. But many heart murmurs *aren't* innocent—and doctors who think they can tell the difference between a harmless murmur and a serious murmur aren't always right. A study published in the *Journal of the American Medical Association* last year reported that younger physicians don't know how to use stethoscopes correctly, and fail to identify a large percentage of dangerous heart sounds. The physicians were asked to spot twelve heart problems by listening through a stethoscope to cardiac rhythms played on tape. "On average," study co-author Salvatore Mangione, M.D., said, "they were wrong four out of five times"—a lack of proficiency Mangione terms "disturbing."[10] The moral: If your hyperactive child's doctor says a heart murmur is "nothing to worry about," consider having a cardiologist check it out anyway.

Brain and heart defects aren't the only structural problems a careful physician will rule out when evaluating a hyperactive child. Deformities of the lungs, digestive system, or other organs can also cause a child to be "hyper," have poor concentration, or behave badly. It takes all of the body's organs, functioning at full power, to provide the brain with optimal levels of food, oxygen, hormones, and neurotransmitters. Damage virtually any organ of the body, and you wind up handicapping the brain.

That goes for the sensory organs, as well. Clearly, a brain that isn't getting correct input from a child's ears or eyes isn't going to perceive the universe the way other children's brains do. Unfortunately, hearing and vision defects often go unnoticed for years, even when children are routinely seen by their family doctors. Stephen Garber and colleagues, for instance, tell about an eight-year-old girl referred to them for evaluation of attention and learning problems. "During testing," they say, "we noticed that she positioned her paper and held her head in an unusual way as she wrote. After an eye examination by a specialist, she was found to be farsighted and almost legally blind in one eye." The girl's parents "were horrified to learn that she had such significant undiagnosed vision problems."[11] So, while it sounds basic, make sure your doctor checks your child's hearing and vision.

And remember that even if real structural damage is causing your child's hyperactive behavior—whether it's brain damage, heart damage, or vision or hearing defects—there's usually a treatment and there may be a cure. Brain cysts can sometimes be removed. Cortical atrophy can often be reversed. Surgeons can repair holes in hearts, eye doctors can prescribe glasses, and hearing aids can help children with partial deafness. So don't be scared away from seeking a real diagnosis by the fear that your child's doctor might find a brain lesion, heart defect, or vision or hearing problem. It's far more sensible to worry that a careless doctor might *miss* such problems and thus deny your child a real diagnosis, real treatment, and the possibility of a real cure.

CHAPTER 7

Self-Inflicted Wounds:
Cases of "Lifestyle Hyperactivity"

We have met the enemy, and he is us.
Pogo

SOMETIMES WE ARE INDEED OUR OWN WORST ENEMIES—
and that's especially true when it comes to hyperactivity. In
many cases, the hyperactive behavior we see in children stems
directly from the chemicals we expose them to, the diet we
feed them, the medications we give them, or the lifestyle
we're asking them to live.

In this chapter, I look at a wide range of lifestyle "mistakes"
that can lead to behavioral changes, including hyperactivity
and attention deficits. Some of these mistakes—for instance,
a poor diet or improper sleeping habits—are easy to spot and
easy to correct. Others are trickier to detect, but an observant
parent or doctor can still identify them. Here are some examples of both obvious health culprits and surprising causes
of self-inflicted hyperactivity.

James: Hyperactive or Legally "Wired"?

I like just about all of my patients. However, James, an eighteen-
year-old college student, was an exception. After James had been
in my office only ten minutes, I was wishing he'd found another
doctor.

A college sophomore planning on getting a law degree, James came to me because he was feeling terrible and couldn't concentrate on his studies. Even though he'd sought me out, he was irritable, angry, rude, and hyper. "There's nothing you can do for me," he told me shortly. "I've been to a dozen doctors, and none of you know what you're doing." I watched, interested, as he tapped his foot, jiggled his keys, and looked at the clock in an exasperated manner while I went through a long list of questions.

One of those questions was, "How much coffee do you drink every day?" I wasn't really surprised when James answered, "Seven or eight cups." In addition, he told me, he drank one or two cola sodas each day and sometimes had iced tea at lunch. When he got headaches, several times a week, he took Excedrin.

I quickly toted up James's daily caffeine consumption. In all, he was downing around 1,000 milligrams of caffeine every day.

My diagnosis was easy: James was suffering from "caffeinism." At doses as low as 250 milligrams per day—a level many American children easily exceed—caffeine can cause rambling speech, attention and concentration problems, agitation, heart palpitations, insomnia, and hyperactive behavior. Moreover, children or adults who become habituated to high levels of caffeine experience symptoms when they're deprived of their "fix" for even a few hours. These withdrawal symptoms can include irritability, fatigue, and headaches like the ones James suffered. (Ironically, it wasn't the painkiller in the Excedrin that eased his headaches, but the caffeine.)

Caffeinism is a common problem, and it's almost as likely to occur in children or teens as in adults. If you think your child's behavior problems may be caused or exacerbated by excess caffeine consumption, tally up his or her intake of these foods, drinks, and drugs:

- Iced tea or hot tea   50 milligrams per cup
- Coffee   100 milligrams per cup
- Colas, Mountain Dew,   40 to 50 milligrams
  Dr Pepper, and other
  caffeinated sodas

- Cocoa mix   3 to 15 mg
- Homemade cocoa (1 cup)   10 to 50 mg
- Chocolate   15 to 30 mg per bar
- No-Doz   100 to 200 mg
- Anacin   32 mg
- Excedrin   65 mg
- Vivarin   100 to 200 mg
- Midol   32 mg

If your child's daily consumption of caffeine is over 300 milligrams (less for elementary-school-aged or younger children), it's a good bet that caffeine is a culprit in his or her behavior problems. If so, cut down on high-caffeine drinks and foods—but do it very gradually, or the withdrawal symptoms will be as bad as the caffeine-induced behavior problems.

Caffeinism, in addition to causing problems in and of itself, can lead to other health problems that affect behavior. By causing insomnia, it leads to sleep deprivation, which makes a child cranky and inattentive. Additionally, too much caffeine consumption can contribute to iron-deficiency anemia. And James developed an interesting secondary problem stemming from his caffeinism: His high caffeine level led him to grind his teeth at night, and he ground off enough of his dental fillings to have an elevated mercury level (another health problem contributing to his irritability and hyper behavior).

You've probably heard that coffee calms hyperactive children. In some cases, it's true that coffee seems to make hyperactive children calmer and better behaved. One reason is that caffeine, like Ritalin or cocaine or speed, is a stimulant—and stimulants often make people feel better, at least temporarily. Also, the chemicals in coffee and tea act as diuretics, stimulate the respiratory system, cause the heart to pump more blood with less effort, and affect the body's breakdown of carbohydrates. Thus, coffee—like drugs—may help to mask the symptoms of cardiac, respiratory, and metabolic disorders. In the long term, of course, masking these symptoms does more harm than good.

Bedtime Follies

Many disorders, including caffeinism, can disrupt a child's sleep. Sometimes, however, lack of sleep *is itself* the sole cause of a child's hyperactivity or attention problems. Plenty of American kids with no medical reason for sleeplessness are dragging off to school after six, five, or even fewer hours of sleep. These children pay for their sleepless nights by being inattentive and glassy-eyed in class, being irritable and aggressive, or even dozing off. But these children aren't sick. They just have bad lifestyles.

Many of these kids are television junkies and stay up late watching TV in their rooms (a phenomenon we didn't see a few decades ago, when most families had one TV in the living room). I'm amazed at the number of eight- and nine-year-olds who watch *David Letterman*! Then there are joint-custody children, who sleep at one house on Monday and another house on Friday, often sharing a room with a new step-brother or step-sister. This game of musical bedrooms can lead to disturbed sleep and create grouchy, restless children who can't concentrate.

These problems can be fairly easy to solve. If your child is a late-night TV addict, take the TV out of his or her bedroom. Set a strict lights-out time and stick to it. Create a relaxing environment in your house during the hour or two before bedtime by turning off your own TV shows, putting on some mellow music, and dimming the lights. Having your child take a warm bath right before bedtime is helpful, too. Be sure, also, to ban late-night caffeine drinks. (In fact, it's a good idea to limit even non-caffeinated drinks in the evening, to cut down on middle-of-the-night bathroom runs that disrupt a child's sleep.) If your child is young enough, start a bedtime story ritual; it's much more relaxing than a shoot-'em-up cop show right before bedtime.

If you're sharing custody with another parent, ask your child if the sleeping accommodations at either house are uncomfortable. You may find out that an arrangement that's working fine for you is leaving your child feeling like a refugee, shuttled between two households and not feeling at home in either. If your child's arrangements include sleeping on the couch, or sharing a room with a squalling step-sister at the ex-spouse's house, work out something better. And if a child is sleeping in the same room with adults who are (to put it politely) being intimate during the night, insist that this arrangement stop immediately. A child awakened by adult sexual activity is likely to be traumatized *and* to lose sleep.

One more tip: Try to make your child's bedtimes consistent. Our bodies operate on a circadian rhythm, a biological clock that tells us when to be active, when to eat, and when to sleep. If your child is going to bed at nine one night and midnight the next, this internal clock can't adjust. As a result, your child, like a jet-lagged airline passenger, may experience sleep difficulties, fatigue, memory problems, and irritability.

If you cut down on the caffeine in your child's diet, set up a consistent schedule, and provide a good bedtime atmosphere, and your child still has significant sleep problems, then an in-depth evaluation is needed. A small but significant number of young children suffer from obstructive sleep apnea, which can often be treated with a minor surgical procedure. As mentioned earlier, many other problems, ranging from parasites to seizures, can prevent children from getting a good night's sleep.

One medical approach I *don't* recommend is giving children medications to help them sleep. Drugs that induce sleep unnaturally will generally backfire, eventually causing more problems than they solve. And above all, don't agree to a prescription of Ritalin if your child's poor sleep leads to behavior problems. Insomnia is a major side effect of the drug, so you'll simply be exacerbating the problem.

You Are What You Eat

From the Feingold diet to the *Candida* regimen, there are dozens of nutritional approaches recommended for hyperactive children.

Often, however, we overlook the obvious: that these children need a plain, old-fashioned, *healthful* diet.

Child psychologist William VanOrnum recently told the story of a fidgety, restless little boy who, according to his teachers, was out of control and needed to be on Ritalin. VanOrnum, however, thought the boy looked hungry, not hyperactive. "We gave him some oatmeal," VanOrnum said. "The oatmeal had this 'magical' effect."[1] The little boy didn't need a lifetime of medication; he needed a good breakfast.

Obviously, if you care enough to read this book, you're not sending your child off to school half starved. However, that doesn't rule out the possibility that your son or daughter is suffering from deficiencies of important nutrients. How much impact can these deficiencies have on your child's behavior and academic performance? Consider these studies:

- Ann Bruner and colleagues recently investigated the effects of iron supplementation on seventy-three high school girls who were only marginally deficient in iron. Thirty-seven of the girls took iron supplements, while thirty-six took placebos. When the girls' cognitive skills were tested eight weeks later, the researchers reported that girls who received supplements "performed better on verbal learning and memory tasks than the girls who had not taken iron supplements."[2]
- A 1994 study by Jun-Bi Tu and colleagues found that correcting iron deficiency can lead to remarkable improvements in the behavior of conduct-disordered teens. One of the researchers' subjects, a fifteen-year-old girl, was irritable, hyperactive, anxious, and disruptive and had a history of aggressive outbursts, sexual acting out, lying, and stealing. Within two months after the girl's iron levels normalized, the researchers say, "remarkable improvement was noted by staff and school teacher." The girl became less moody, her social adjustment improved, she had fewer temper tantrums, and she became more interested in academics.[3]
- Studying South African schoolchildren with a variety of nutrient deficiencies, L. M. Richter and colleagues assessed the behavior of fifty-five of these children and then fed them

healthy school breakfasts for six weeks. The researchers say the children were markedly less hyperactive following the six weeks of good breakfasts than they were at the start of the study. "The children showed a decline in both the occurrence and duration of off-task and out-of-seat behavior," the researchers said, "and an increase in active participation in class and positive peer interaction."[4]

- In the course of evaluating seriously troubled adolescents, D. Lonsdale and R. Shamberger identified twenty teens whose hostility, irritability, impulsiveness, and aggression stemmed from borderline deficiencies of the B vitamin thiamin.[5] When these children's diets were supplemented, their behavior improved markedly. "These teenagers," physician Joseph Beasley notes in *The Betrayal of Health*, "showed the typically American pattern of skipping breakfast, snacking on junk foods, and drinking many cans of soda a day.... [Yet] neither the teenagers nor their parents ever thought that the symptoms might be related to their diet."

It's important to note that Lonsdale's and Shamberger's subjects, as well as Bruner's, were suffering from *marginal* deficiencies. They weren't keeling over from starvation; in fact, they probably considered themselves well fed. Most were probably eating a typical American diet. The problem is that the "typical" American diet isn't particularly healthful, especially when it comes to children and teens.

Recently, the National Cancer Institute asked 3,307 American children to fill out three-day diet diaries. The results were startling: *Only 1 percent* of children between the ages of two and nineteen were meeting experts' recommendations for grains, vegetables, fruits, meats, and dairy foods, and 16 percent didn't meet *any* of the recommendations. In addition, the researchers found that America's children are getting 40 percent of their calories from fats and sugars added to foods.

"Nutrition research surveys in the last two decades have shown that Americans are eating anything but balanced diets, and also uncovered three startling facts," according to Beasley. "One, there is clear-cut malnutrition in America among certain groups. Two, there are widespread deficiencies in several nutrients among the population at large. And three, these deficiencies are affecting our health, disease resistance, and performance—including school behavior and achievement." Beasley notes that symptoms of subclinical deficiencies include concentration problems, loss of appetite, hysteria, headaches, lethargy, irritability, depression, fatigue, and insomnia.

Many hyperactive children suffer from such subclinical nutritional deficiencies, particularly of iron. Others, however, exhibit what I call "situational hyperactivity." This occurs when a child skips breakfast three or four mornings a week, or when a teenager, trying to save a few extra bucks, pockets his or her lunch money day after day instead of spending it in on food. In these cases, hyper behavior, irritability, attention problems, or fatigue occur when the child is hungry and blood sugar levels are dropping; they magically disappear when the child gets a good meal. If your child's teachers report behavior problems, but you aren't seeing them at home, ask your child what he or she is eating for lunch—and insist on a good breakfast before your child leaves home. Also, if you suspect that your child's lunch money is being spent on something other than food, consider packing sack lunches.

Illicit Drugs

If your formerly well-behaved child begins exhibiting attention problems, hyperactivity, depression, or other behavioral symptoms, you need to consider the possibility that he or she is experimenting with drugs or alcohol. Be especially concerned if your child's grades start slipping, he or she becomes moody and distant, money "disappears" from your purse or wallet, episodes of truancy increase, and your child's nice friends are replaced by a not-so-nice crowd.

Of all street drugs, the most dangerous are cocaine and glue or solvents. Sniffing glue or doing coke can lead to permanent brain damage or death. But all drug abuse can cause both short-term and long-term behavioral, learning, and attention problems. Even marijuana, considered by many people to be harmless, significantly impairs attention and short-term memory for up to twenty-four hours—and there's at least some evidence that it causes long-term impairment of attention.[6]

If you think your child is "using," get help immediately. Bear in mind, however, that substance abuse may itself be a symptom. Many drug abusers and alcoholics are self-medicating health problems (see Chapter 2), and their addictions can't be handled without addressing their underlying ailments.

Going "Buggy"

As I noted earlier, researchers are finding that the pollutants you intentionally introduce inside your home are as dangerous as the environmental pollutants you can't control. Among these pollutants are pesticides, which of all the toxins are the most likely to be "self-inflicted." While you may not be able to control the amount of lead in your drinking water, or the levels of cadmium in your air or soil, you *can* control the chemicals you use around your home and yard.

Each year we spray thousands of pounds of insecticides and herbicides around our houses, inside our schools, and on our lawns. Furthermore, on the mistaken assumption that if some is good, more must be better, many homeowners use pesticide or herbicide mixtures in concentrations higher than recommended, spray them more often than the manufacturers suggest, or spray them in areas not recommended by package directions. Add to this the fact that pesticides are often dangerous *even when used as recommended*, and you have the potential for serious health consequences.

A good example is the pesticide chlordane, used from 1948 to 1988 to kill termites in homes. Although chlordane was banned when doctors learned that it was a brain toxin, the chemical often persists for more than twenty years in treated homes. One 1995 study found that in homes treated years earlier with chlordane, air samples of the pesticide exceeded occupational standards. Moreover, the researchers found that the families exposed to chlordane in these homes "showed significant, and we suggest important, impairment of both neurophysiological and psychological functions including mood states."[7]

Even if your house has never been treated for termites, your children—especially the little ones—are likely to be getting a big dose of pesticides. Researchers report that indoor air contains concentrations of pesticides up to *ten times higher* than concentrations in outside air.[8] Furthermore, Wayne Ott and John Roberts say, "pesticides that break down within days outdoors may last for years in carpets, where they are protected from the degradation caused by sunlight and bacteria."

You'd think that schools would be more careful with pesticides than homeowners are, but that's not always the case. A review of research on schools' use of pesticides concluded, "Potentially dangerous pesticides are routinely applied in schools with little or no warning to parents or school staff." In some cases, so many children and teachers have become sick from improper spraying that entire schools have been shut down.[9]

Pesticides can cause behavior problems because many are, in effect, nerve gases. In fact, parathion and other organophosphate pesticides were first developed by German scientists during World War II as potential weapons. These pesticides interfere with nervous system functioning by preventing the breakdown of acetylcholine, a neurotransmitter, causing dangerous levels of this chemical to accumulate. The resulting brain and nervous system dysfunction leads to poor coordination, sensory and behavioral disturbances, and fuzzy thinking. In addition, pesticides can cause sore throats, breathing difficulties, swollen eyes, rashes, loss of appetite, and stomachaches.

The most dramatic case of pesticide toxicity I've seen in my own practice involved an adult, not a child. However, it's a graphic example of how dire the consequences of overspraying can be. Bob, my patient, was a longtime acquaintance, whom I'd known as a rosy, jolly, Santa Claus–like man. When he came to me, however, he was thin and looked weak and pale.

"I don't think you can do anything for me," Bob said gruffly, before I had a chance to ask any questions. "I've been to a doctor who tells me I have ALS. He says the only advice any doctor can give me is to get my affairs in order."

My heart sank when I heard Bob's words. ALS—amyotrophic lateral sclerosis, commonly known as Lou Gehrig's disease—generally kills its victims in two to four years. ALS is a terrible diagnosis for a neurologist to have to make, and it's even more terrible when the patient is a friend.

After briefly questioning Bob, however, I realized that I might not have to make that diagnosis at all. Bob didn't appear to have the classic signs and symptoms of ALS. In talking with Bob before I even started examining him, I got my first clue about his real problem.

Bob told me that his symptoms had started shortly after he started a new job at a pharmacy in a discount drug store. One of the first problems Bob noticed was an odd one: He was salivating excessively. He also developed a hyperactive bowel, necessitating a half dozen trips to the bathroom during work hours. He started feeling "spacey" and found himself making mistakes on prescriptions. And every few weeks, he'd experienced some flulike symptoms. "I don't think that has anything to do with my other symptoms," he said. "Everybody in the store complains about feeling sick or woozy or 'out of it' for a little while after the exterminators come."

"Exterminators?" I asked.

"We had a major problem with ants," Bob replied, "so the owner hired a company that sprays every two weeks."

That bit of information, combined with Bob's symptoms and the results of his lab tests, provided me with enough clues to make a tentative diagnosis of pesticide toxicity. Further investigation revealed that the exterminators spraying Bob's store were using unsafe concentrations of toxic insecticides. They were killing the ants—but they almost killed Bob as well. His coworkers were less affected, because they worked in other areas of the store that were less heavily sprayed.

Note that Bob's symptoms were primarily physical, *but his coworkers' symptoms frequently were primarily behavioral.* Some complained that they felt "out of it" or "drifty" after sprayings, and they had difficulty concentrating on their work. Generally, when people are poisoned by pesticides, they show *mental* symptoms before they show *physical* symptoms—and often hyperactivity and attention problems are the first symptoms that occur. That's why children suffering from chronic, low-grade pesticide poisoning are often labeled ADHD.

If your doctor finds evidence of *any* elevation of pesticides in your child's system—even if the levels are below those considered "toxic"—find out why. Check the labels of any pesticides you use regularly to see if you have been using them improperly. Call your pest-control company, if you use one, and ask what chemicals they use. If you don't use pesticides regularly, check with your child's principal and see if the school is sprayed. Also, if your child is older and has a job, find out if his or her workplace is treated with pesticides. Sometimes children in agricultural areas are exposed when farmers spray their fields or groves; your county's Agricultural Extension may be able to help you obtain details about agricultural spraying in your area. With the information you provide, your child's doctor should be able to help you identify and eliminate the source of your child's exposure.

Other Chemical Culprits

Pesticides are among the most toxic chemicals we use around our children, but there are plenty of other household products—including mothballs, disinfectants, furniture polishes, and air fresheners—that can affect an overexposed child's mental and physical health. These chemicals, although rarely a primary cause of hyperactivity, can exacerbate existing behavior problems. If you want to reduce your child's exposure to household chemicals, look for environmentally friendly products—and, more important, make sure you air out your home frequently.

Many parents smoke indoors, a habit that can cause or contribute to hyperactive behavior in their children. Cigarette smoke contains *four thousand chemicals*, many of which can affect brain function. Among them are carbon monoxide, which reduces the brain's supply of oxygen, and benzene, a highly dangerous chemical linked to cancer as well as brain dysfunction. If you smoke at home, do it outside, or at least in areas not frequented by your children. And make sure your house is well ventilated so smoke will dissipate. Better yet, quit.

Surprising Risks in Your Medicine Cabinet

Americans pop pills at the first sign of a sniffle, sore throat, or stomachache, and children are no exception. Unfortunately, those pills—both those prescribed by a doctor and the drugs you buy over the counter—can have drastic effects on children's behavior. But you usually won't find out about these effects unless you do some research on your own. Don't expect a doctor to warn you about all of the potential dangers of drugs, even when he or she prescribes them for your child.

Why? Because most doctors don't know as much about drugs as they think they do. Doctors spend only about three months studying pharmacology in medical school, and the small amount of information they pick up in school is out of date within a few years. Once in practice, physicians tend to rely heavily on blurbs from drug companies and on studies funded by those same drug companies—hardly impartial sources of information!

Furthermore, many drugs cause serious side effects only in a small minority of patients. As Joe and Teresa Graedon note in *The People's Pharmacy*, "Doctors rarely warn people about these kinds of complications because they are considered extremely rare and not worth worrying about." Unfortunately, as many hair-raising anecdotes in the Graedons' book show, even "rare" side effects are important to the few people who suffer from them.

The Graedons also note that physicians are all too human, and your doctor may shirk the responsibility of informing you about possible adverse drug effects, because "telling you about [side effects] will just tend to plant a seed of suggestion that could sprout into an annoying phone call in the middle of the night."[10]

Detoxing Your Child's Environment

Use cleaners sparingly. When possible, use biodegradable cleaners. Ventilate rooms thoroughly when using cleaning products. Open both doors and windows.

Be particularly careful with solvents, paints, aerosol sprays, air fresheners, mothballs, disinfectants, pesticides, auto care products, and gasoline.

Be extremely cautious with products listing the following ingredients: formaldehyde, toluene, methylene chloride, carbon tetrachloride, mineral spirits, petroleum distillates, and trichloroethane, hydrofluoric acid, and ammonium bifluoride. They are potent central nervous system toxins.

Read labels and follow directions carefully, especially if a product contains the words "caution," "warning," or "danger."

After you use potentially dangerous chemicals, wash your hands. If your clothing is contaminated, change it.

Many toxins are tracked in from outdoors. If your job brings you into contact with potential toxins such as pesticides or lead, consider leaving your shoes at the door when you get home.

Vacuum your carpet often and thoroughly, especially if you have infants or toddlers.

Do not allow young children to use bug sprays, solvents, or potentially toxic cleansers and disinfectants.

Keep children away from art and hobby supplies, except those specifically designed to be safe for children.

Contact your local Agricultural Extension to learn about nonpesticide means of killing or deterring home and garden pests.

To reduce the need for indoor pesticides, caulk all cracks around your home to keep bugs out.

Doctors and pharmacists also routinely fail to warn patients about the possibility of adverse effects when drugs are mixed with other drugs or foods. (Giving your child a glass of grapefruit juice along with some medications, for instance, can cause a dangerous overdose, because grapefruit juice reduces levels of an enzyme that breaks down many drugs.) Mixing three or four drugs is particularly risky, because generally these drugs have never been tested in combination.

In addiction, doctors often guess at the amount of medication to give children, because many drugs are formally tested only on adults. Furthermore, even the drugs that have been tested on children often are studied for only a few weeks or months, not long enough to discover what side effects might develop with chronic use.

It's impossible to list every drug that can cause hyperactive behavior or attention problems in children, because the list would be endless. I'm most concerned, however, about drugs that are used over long periods of time, long enough for a doctor to mistake their effects for ADHD. At the top of the list are asthma medications (see Chapter 5), steroids, and seizure drugs such as phenytoin. But watch out, also, for allergy, hay fever, or cold preparations containing pseudoephedrine. Most children can handle this chemical, but some develop behavioral symptoms, or even experience hallucinations. In *The British Medical Journal*, physician R. J. Sankey reported on three children who suffered hallucinations after taking small doses of Actifed, including a three-year-old girl who "presented screaming and unconsolable complaining of seeing crabs, snakes and spiders. She said that insects were biting her and that a crocodile was making a hole in her back."[11]

After publishing this report, Sankey and colleagues received information on at least 50 similar cases in which children taking drugs containing pseudoephedrine suffered visual hallucinations, behavioral disturbances, or both. Among the symptoms seen in children taking the drug were bad temper, irritability, impaired sleep, dizziness, and "general malaise."[12]

If your child routinely takes prescription or over-the-counter medications for asthma, hay fever, allergies, or any other condition, consider the possibility that the drugs are causing or contributing to behavior problems. Have a doctor do blood levels to check for overdoses of prescription drugs, and discontinue any OTC medications that aren't necessary. Also, if you can pinpoint a definite connection between a drug and a behavior problem, ask your doctor if another medication can be substituted.

One more word of advice: When you're trying to identify substances that might be causing your child problems, don't limit yourself to traditional drugs or to medications your child takes by mouth. Other common medicine cabinet items can also cause behavioral symptoms.

Insect repellants containing DEET, for instance, can be toxic to some children if used chronically and excessively. This chemical, which appears to be harmless for most children when used as directed, is linked to confusion, behavior changes, sleeplessness, and even seizures in some children.

After observing one child who suffered severe seizures following two applications of DEET, J. W. Lipscomb and colleagues suggested that "avoidance of high-concentration DEET formulations in pediatric patients should be considered."[13] According to physician Lorne Garrettson, DEET is a good example of a chemical that is used regularly on children but whose effects on children have gone virtually unstudied. "We . . . have some good basic data [about DEET's effects] on adults," Garrettson says, "but we do not have a good lead on why children seem more susceptible to the compound or what the metabolism or elimination characteristics for children might be."[14]

Until we have that data, use DEET with caution. If your child does need to use insect repellants on a regular basis, apply them sparingly rather than slathering them on—and look for repellants with lower DEET concentrations. Make sure a child who applies DEET washes his or her hands thoroughly before grabbing a burger or a soda. Also, consider switching your child to Avon's Skin-So-Soft lotion or bath oil; while these don't deter insects quite as well as DEET, they're reasonably effective substitutes.[15]

Another medicine cabinet hazard is lead, contained in several widely used traditional folk remedies. In 1992, the California Department of Health Services received forty reports of children suffering from lead poisoning caused by lead-based ethnic treatments.[16] The most common are greta and arzacon, used to treat constipation. (Indeed, lead does cure constipation, but at a high cost to mental health!) According to a report in *Science News*, as many as half of Mexican-American households in the Southwestern United States rely on folk remedies, many containing lead. Lead-based folk remedies used by other ethnic groups include paylooah (a Southeast Asian preparation) and surma (a preparation used by some immigrants from India). According to anthropologist Robert Trotter II, the lead toxicity and resulting brain dysfunction that these cures cause often go undiagnosed, because they are "hidden behind a cultural curtain."[17]

Be wary, also, of herbal teas. Most are harmless, but a few have ingredients that can cause physical or mental distress. A few years ago, for instance, seven people in New York City were poisoned by a South American herbal tea that turned out to contain belladonna; although none of the individuals died, a number developed agitation, hallucinations, and other symptoms of brain dysfunction.[18] Herbal teas aren't well regulated and sometimes contain ingredients that aren't listed on the labels, so exercise caution when giving these drinks to children on a regular basis. It's probably best to stick with brand-name herbal teas, so you know what you're buying.

Parent Problems

I'm not one of those doctors who blame hyperactivity on "toxic parents." The parents of hyperactive children I meet in my office are among the most intelligent, loving, and kind parents I've ever met. Furthermore, parent-blaming is an all too common cop-out for physicians too overworked or lazy to look for a real diagnosis. But it's true that occasionally, children's behavior problems stem from difficulties at home.

Sometimes children misbehave because they're frightened

about what's going on in their lives—or in their parents' lives. If you're experiencing marital difficulties, health problems, or financial troubles, try not to burden your child too much with these problems. Remember that children are just that—children, and not young adults—and they don't always have the maturity to deal with fighting parents, family members' illnesses, or money worries. Instead, they may express their frustrations and feelings of helplessness by misbehaving, both at home and at school.

If you're experiencing emotional or financial problems at home, be honest with your child about what's happening, but make an extra effort to reassure your child that things will work out. If you and your spouse aren't getting along, be mature enough to postpone your arguments until a time when your child isn't at home to hear you. And don't put your child in the middle of a divorce or a custody dispute.

Also, if you lead a busy lifestyle, and your child spends a great deal of time alone or with sitters, consider rearranging your life to spend more time with him or her. Some behavior problems are simply a child's way of saying, "Look at me!" These days, when both mothers and fathers usually work—and when many children are being raised by single parents—it's often hard for a child to get a parent's attention in positive ways. Be sure to set aside some family time each day, no matter how busy you are, and really focus on your child's interests, activities, successes, and concerns. You may find that your child's negative attention-getting behaviors dwindle as a result.

Hyper Couch Potatoes

This sounds odd, but it's true: Some hyper children aren't moving *enough!* It may seem as though hyperactive children are always in motion, but often that motion is in fits and spurts: leaping up from a chair, spinning around in the lunch line, bouncing in a chair while watching TV. Quite a few hyperactive children actually don't get enough sustained, strenuous exercise to stay healthy mentally and physically.

Obviously, exercise helps counter hyperactivity simply by wearing children out. But the benefits of exercise go far beyond simply burning off excess energy. Studies show that regular aerobic exercise can actually reduce moodiness and problem behavior in both nondisabled subjects and those labeled depressed, hyper, or even delinquent. For example:

- A Finnish study found that increased exercise, combined with relaxation training, significantly reduced the overactivity of foster care boys with elevated activity levels.[19]
- Researchers in Alabama found that teenage girls undergoing treatment for psychiatric problems showed "improvements in depression, anxiety, hostility, confused thinking, and fatigue" after a nine-week program of aerobics and running.[20]
- A study of runners and non-exercisers found that "runners had a significantly more positive mood profile" and concluded that "exercise, particularly aerobic exercise, helps the regular participant not only to cope with stress but also to have a generally more positive feeling of well-being."[21]
- In one study, thirty-two delinquents were asked to exercise vigorously and thirty-seven to do mild exercises, over a three-month period. Researchers reported that while the two groups were quite similar at the beginning of the program, the vigorous exercisers showed "improved self-concept [and] mood" in addition to better fitness.[22]
- Researchers studying the effects of large muscle exercise and relaxation exercises on hyperactive, impulsive males found that subjects who participated in the exercises performed better on a cognitive test than a control group who received no treatment. Their results, the researchers said, suggest that exercise can be an effective part of a treatment program for hyperactivity.[23]
- Studying forty-three depressed women participating in aerobic exercise, relaxation therapy (used as a placebo), or no-treatment groups, researchers reported that "subjects in the aerobic exercise condition evidenced reliably greater decreases in depression than did subjects in the placebo condition or subjects in the no-treatment condition."[24]

In short, exercise can make people happier, less anxious, less hyperactive, and less depressed. One reason is that exercise increases serotonin levels in the brain—exactly what Prozac, Elavil, and similar drugs do. However, exercise does it naturally, without dangerous side effects.

In addition, exercise causes the brain to pour out extra endorphins, "feel-good" chemicals that are similar to opium. These endorphins make children feel happier and also relieve the minor aches and pains of growing. And, of course, exercise makes all organs of the body work better. It increases blood flow to the brain, boosts oxygen levels, helps the digestive system function properly, and speeds the removal of toxins.

If your child doesn't participate in strenuous sports for at least half an hour four or five times a week, try to get him or her interested in swimming, jogging, tennis, cycling, or another form of aerobic exercise. Again, vigorous exercise seems to be far more useful in improving mood and behavior than mild exercise.

GRANTED, IT'S NOT POSSIBLE TO CONTROL EVERYTHING A child eats or drinks, or to eliminate every toxin that threatens a child's health. And it's not easy to tell a child—particularly a surly and uncooperative teen—to exercise every day, cut down on sodas, get plenty of sleep, turn off the TV at nine P.M., and avoid health hazards. But if you can alter even a few bad habits, you might be surprised at the behavioral changes you see.

In addition, lifestyle changes are usually cheap and often free—and, unlike Ritalin and other drugs, they're completely harmless. Furthermore, a healthful lifestyle will protect your child's mental and physical health long into the future. And isn't that better than jeopardizing your child's health with potent drugs that don't cure the problem?

PART 4

Getting *Real* Help for Your Child

CHAPTER 8

Is Your Child *Really* Hyperactive?

The more you study "hyperactivity" or "attention deficit disorder,"
the less certain you are as to what it is, or whether it is
a thousand different medical and non-medical
situations all called by the same name as if it were one thing.

A neurologist quoted by Richard Vatz and Lee Weinberg in USA Today

Some of you don't need to read this chapter.

You're the parents who know, without a doubt, that your child is indeed abnormally hyperactive. You know because your child is destroying your sanity (and your house), wreaking havoc at school, alienating friends and family, constantly committing dangerous or senseless acts, and making every day of your life a nightmare. Your child is sick, and you're worried. There's no question that something is seriously wrong.

If you fall into that category, I'll get back to you in the next chapter. This chapter is for the rest of you, those who aren't sure whether your child is a hyperactive hellion, or simply a normal, healthy kid. Luckily, you have an expert to help you make that decision. That expert is you.

Mom (or Dad) Knows Best

If you're reading this book, it's probably because someone—most likely a school nurse, teacher, or counselor—says that your child is hyperactive or attention disordered and needs help. You've most likely been told: "Your child is disrupting the entire class," "He can't sit still," or "Your child is smart, but she can't do the work."

This professional probably even presented you with a check-list, with the requisite number of hyperactivity symptoms checked off: *"squirms in seat," "often talks excessively," "has difficulty taking turns," "often interrupts others."* Maybe you were told that Ritalin is the best means of calming your child. Maybe school authorities warned that "something needs to be done," if your child is to stay in his or her current class—and that "something" is a label of ADHD and a pill. But if you're reading this chapter, you're still skeptical.

Good for you.

Often, parents are so intimidated by pressure from school officials that they buckle under and agree that their children need professional help, *even though the parents aren't sure their children really have a problem.* That's a shame, because nine times out of ten, when a parent disagrees with a professional as to whether a child is pathologically hyperactive, the parent is right.

That's right: You, not a doctor or teacher or counselor, are the best judge of whether your child has a real problem.

Why? Because a doctor, no matter how observant, gets only a snapshot of your child's behavior during the brief time you're in the office. You, on the other hand, have lived with the child for years. Furthermore, you know how your child acts at home, at school, and in other settings, while a doctor sees your child only in the artificial setting of a medical clinic.

Similarly, a teacher sees the child only in one setting, for nine months during a single year. You, on the other hand, know how your child behaved last year and the year before. You know if your child is having personal problems. You know if your child likes or hates that teacher. You know how your child feels about school in general. You know how your child acts at home, at other people's houses, at church, at soccer games, and at parties. You, not a professional, are the expert on your child's behavior, no matter how many degrees the professional has.

Bear in mind that hyperactivity isn't like a rash, or a broken bone, or a wart. There's no medical course in differentiating between hyperactive people and non-hyperactive people. You can't verify hyperactivity with a lab test or a brain scan. A label of hyperactivity is, to a large degree, simply an opinion. (Consider that American doctors label ten times more children hyperactive than European doctors do.[1] And doctors in Virginia prescribe nearly six times as much Ritalin as do doctors in Hawaii.[2] Are American kids really that different from European kids? And are kids in Virginia that much wilder than kids in Hawaii? Of course not. The difference lies in different doctors' *perception* of what's hyperactive and what's not.) A hyperactivity label is a judgment call, and in this case, *your judgment is more valid than anyone else's*, because of your extensive knowledge of your own child.

That doesn't mean that you shouldn't listen to your child's teachers, counselors, or doctors. Although they aren't as knowledgeable about your child's behavior as you are, they can sometimes identify a problem more objectively. (As a parent, I know it's not always easy to admit that a child has a serious problem.) If others perceive a significant problem, it's up to you to evaluate your child honestly and see if there's merit to what they're saying. That means asking yourself: Is my child simply guilty of normal childhood mischief and mayhem? Is her behavior most likely a passing phase, or perhaps a reaction to a divorce or other trauma? Is his school poorly equipped to deal with the energy and enthusiasm of a rambunctious boy? Or is my child truly troubled—and troubling others?

When you're evaluating your child's behavior, the following questions can help you determine whether a real problem exists. If possible, sit down with your spouse (or another relative familiar with your child) and get his or her input as well. Answer all of the questions as honestly as possible and then see if your answers support the concerns of your child's doctors or teachers.

Question: Is Your Child's Behavior *Really* Abnormal?

There's a big difference between a rowdy, active, curious kid and a restless, inattentive, irritable, troubled child. Unfortunately, it's a distinction that schools and doctors don't always make well, and hundreds of thousands of perfectly fine children—most of them boys—wind up with ADHD or ADD labels as a result.

As a parent, you are in the best position to make a distinction between normal and abnormal behavior. Ask yourself these questions:

- Is my child chronically hyper to the point of seriously disrupting my life?
- Is my child often irritable or hostile?
- Has my child gotten into trouble with the law?
- Does my child have difficulty handling schoolwork?
- Does my child suffer from extreme mood swings?
- Does my child suffer from obvious physical problems? (See the next question on p. 158.)

If you answer yes to any of these questions, it's time to get help. In particular, if your child's behavior scares you or endangers people, immediate medical evaluation is not optional but *necessary*. And if your child is constantly unhappy, defiant, or aggressive, it's important to find out why. Although defiance, aggression, unhappiness, and mood swings are all normal behaviors for children and teens, negative behaviors and emotions should be *occasional* and not chronic.

If your child doesn't exhibit any of these troublesome problems, you might be worrying over nothing. Is your child, in general, a happy and healthy kid? If your child is a girl, is she a tomboy who likes horseback riding, football, or other vigorous activities? If your child is a boy, is he a mischievous rascal who enjoys rough-and-tumble sports and lives life to the fullest? Then the problem probably lies not with your child but with society's perception of what normal childhood behavior is. And that's particularly true if you have a boy.

Let's face it: Boys are natural troublemakers. They're supposed to be. They're supposed to jump off fences, pull girls' pigtails, throw spitballs, make fun of their teachers, and occasionally hit each other. It's what boys do, and some do it better than others. But that doesn't mean they're sick. Unfortunately, some doctors and teachers don't know that.

A recent article in the *Wall Street Journal* shows how easy it is for a teacher to label a little rascal mentally disordered. The article focuses on Marty Wolt, who as a third grader was a classic Dennis the Menace. His crimes, the *Journal* notes, included "leading a class strike over a math assignment, persuading 25 other kids to repeatedly shout, 'no pay, no work!' " In addition, Marty eavesdropped on a teacher telling another staff member about her pregnancy and spread the news all over school. And he irritated other kids by following them around with a notepad, writing down everything they said.[3]

We've all known a Marty. Many of us have *been* Martys. Until recently, teachers made kids like Marty stay in during recess and write fifty times on the chalkboard, "I will behave in class." But this is a new age, and Marty's teacher instead reacted by calling in Marty's mother and telling her, according to the *Journal*, that Marty "probably had a mental disorder and should be medicated," or perhaps moved to a special education class.

Mrs. Wolt refused, instead enrolling Marty in advanced classes (he had an IQ of 132), implementing strict discipline, and working with teachers to channel Marty's energy and imagination into productive activities. Now, years later, Marty is in high school, taking college prep courses, writing screenplays in his spare time, and working part-time at Pizza Hut. "I turned out okay," he told the *Journal*.

What happened to Marty is happening all over the country. As therapist Michael Gurian comments in the *Journal* article, "the country is making the argument, without often realizing it, that boyhood is defective." The endless energy of boys, their silly pranks and impulsive acts, their desire to gain attention at any cost—all of these perfectly normal behaviors are being recast as illness. As a result, the parents of creative and mischievous kids like Marty are under tremendous pressure to medicate their children into a more "normal" state of docility.

This medicalization of normal boyish behavior stems, in part, from changes in schools' disciplinary procedures. In the old days, a boy who acted up often was spanked or caned by the principal. Then, when the boy got home, his mother or father often spanked him again. I'm not recommending this form of discipline, but the fact is, it discouraged a great deal of misbehavior. Nowadays, in contrast, corporal punishment is generally banned, but—more controversially—even verbal discipline is frowned upon if it lowers a child's "self-esteem." Some schools have actually been sued for attempting to discipline students who misbehave. The new philosophy, therefore, seems to be, "If you can't beat 'em, treat 'em." Teachers often see a disability label as the only effective means of getting help in dealing with students who are out of control but can't be disciplined in any effective manner.

Our redefinition of boyishness as deviancy also stems, in large part, from changes in our culture and our technology. Up until the early 1900s, boundless energy was a big plus because people's survival or at least their well-being often depended on hard physical work. Kids often got up before dawn to help with chores. They walked to school, often miles (yes, in the snow!), and then made the same trek back home. Lacking TV sets and Nintendos, they played and worked outdoors for hours. They chopped wood, picked apples, fished, ran races, skated, swam, and chased frogs. Even "perpetual motion machines" eventually wore out and fell asleep. In the late 1800s and early 1900s, parents rarely had to worry about overly active children; ironically, the drugs of choice back then included iron tonics and similar treatments for *under*active children.

For little boys and tomboys, today's world is a very different place. Mom drives them to school. Dad picks them up in the car. They spend their afternoons in front of the computer and their evenings in front of the TV. This leaves energetic children with lots of bottled-up energy and few positive outlets for it.

Furthermore, kids today are educated in large classes by teachers who expect them to sit quietly for fifty minutes at a time, to be polite, to take turns nicely, and to keep their mouths shut. For quiet, placid boys and girls, it's not a bad setting. For the Huck Finns and Dennis the Menaces, it's a complete bore. They react, quite naturally, by wiggling, giggling, and throwing things—behavior that often earns them a label of hyperactivity.

If your child is one of these kids, *don't let teachers or doctors convince you that he or she is ill.* The world is full of healthy, bouncy, active, curious children who have more energy than the adults taking care of them. These kids don't have a problem, and eventually they'll mature and calm down. In the meantime, they'll drive their teachers crazy and run their parents ragged. But wait and see: When they grow up, these kids are likely to be the company CEOs, the inventors, and the leaders. It's a cliché, of course, but many of history's brightest stars were absolute terrors in their early years. (For instance, Pope Paul VI's first-grade teacher claimed he was "a little pest," adding, "I never would have thought he would become Pope." When she met him at the Vatican after he was elected Pope, he said, "My dear teacher, do you remember when you used to pinch my ears because I was always distracted?") A naturally energetic and curious personality, tamed a bit by age and maturity, is a good kind of personality to have.

That doesn't mean you can ignore Dennis the Menace behavior if it's getting out of hand. Often, overly boisterous but otherwise normal kids need firmer discipline at home, or a different kind of classroom at school. You may need to look into private schools, which are often better equipped to handle kids stifled by regular academic programs. In addition, get your child involved in sports—the more strenuous, the better! Augment those activities with family activities such as cycling, swimming, or jogging. Your child will wear out faster, and you'll be in better shape to chase him or her around.

Question: Is Your Child Physically Healthy?

Is your child boisterous, well built, athletic—the kind of kid who loves to run and jump, and wins the hundred-yard dash every time? Or is your child chronically sickly, pale, prone to ear infections, stomachaches, or headaches?

Does your child have plenty of healthy energy for sports and activities, or does your child instead have nervous, jittery energy? Does he or she have trouble keeping up with the pack and often fall behind in races or tire easily at sports?

Is your child coordinated and graceful, or clumsy and prone to tripping and falling?

Does your child sleep well, or have marked sleep problems including insomnia, sleepwalking, nighttime tooth grinding, or bed-wetting? In the morning, is your child ready to face the day, or fatigued and cranky? Does your child still have trouble controlling urination and defecation long past the age when most children have their bowels and bladders under control?

Does your child have a hearty appetite, or does he or she pick at meals? Does your child eat nonfoods such as dirt or wood?

Does your child pick up every bug that's going around and stay sick longer than other kids? Or is he or she pretty good at fighting off colds, flu, and other common kid diseases?

Is your child generally good-natured and relatively happy, or does he or she lash out physically or verbally, break toys or household objects, or commit self-injurious acts?

Is your child's appearance normal, or does he or she have what doctors call minor physical anomalies—unusually placed ears, undescended testicles, unusual eye folds? Are your child's fingers and fingernails normal in appearance, or unusually shaped or colored?

Think about your child's health in general. If your child is a healthy, rosy-cheeked, sturdy, happy kid, his or her excess energy is quite likely a normal developmental phase. I almost never see a healthy kid whose hyperactivity is a real problem.

What's not normal, however, is chronic sick hyperactivity. A hyper child who's not sleeping, not eating well, not growing at the right rate, not keeping up with other kids mentally or physically, or not gaining weight (or gaining too much weight) isn't normal. Neither is a child who's chronically irritable, pale, sickly, unhappy, achy, or spacey, or a child with chronic allergies, headaches, or digestive upsets, or a child who soils himself or wets the bed long after most children are toilet trained. A child with minor physical anomalies may also be suffering from genetic disorders, toxic exposure, or other conditions that need attention. And a child who's violent, aggressive, distraught, hysterical, angry, or despondent much of the time also has a real problem. Such kids need medical attention, because their hyperactive behavior is just one of many symptoms crying out for a diagnosis.

Question: Has Your Child's Behavior Changed Markedly—and Is There a Logical Explanation?

Often, hyperactive behavior is a perfectly normal reaction to a major change in a child's life. Divorce, in particular, shakes up kids. Many act out because they're scared, angry, and want to get their parents' attention. Likewise, a death in the family, a move away from friends and family, or parental financial crises will affect how a child feels and behaves. Acting-out behavior can last for months or even years, but it doesn't mean that a child is sick and needs treatment. Rather, it means that the child needs support, attention, and possibly counseling.

If you can't point to a life change around the time your child's behavior problems started, talk with your child about whether he or she is happy. Ask about friends, school, and family issues. And really *listen*. Life can be hard for today's kids, and particularly for latchkey kids who often spend time alone. Children are faced with pressures we never experienced: Should they have sex at fourteen? Should they try coke at thirteen? Should they carry a gun? Often, a child's behavior problems stem from worry, fear, anger, and confusion—and from the lack of an adult to act as a guide through these emotional land mines.

Psychologist William VanOrnum tells the story of one girl labeled as having attention deficit disorder by doctors. VanOrnum asked the girl, "Hey, kid, how are you doing?" It turned out the girl's aunt and grandmother had died, and her father was suffering from Lyme disease. "She couldn't pay attention because of all this stuff," VanOrnum says, "not because she had ADD."[4]

Sometimes behavior changes stem from schedule upsets. One girl started causing trouble in school and getting poor grades shortly after her parents split up. They obtained joint custody, and the girl was shuttled between households every week. It was a great system for the parents, but the daughter was a stressed-out wreck. "My clothes are at Mom's house, my schoolbooks are at Dad's house, and my friends never know where I am," she said. She didn't sleep well—would you, if you changed bedrooms twice a week? She didn't eat well some days, because she was rushing from one household to the other. This girl didn't need Ritalin or even a medical workup; she needed parents more sensitive to her needs.

Not all rapid behavior changes, however, are attributable to life changes. Sudden behavior changes in the absence of emotional triggers need to be investigated, particularly if a child exhibits health problems. A child who's been an angel for years and suddenly turns spacey, weepy, or surly may just be going through puberty, but chronic or serious behavior changes can also signal anything from a brain tumor to drug abuse. If your child's behavior changes are alarming or inexplicable, he or she should be examined by a physician.

Question: Is Your Child Extremely Bright?

Ironically, thousands of children are put on Ritalin simply for being too smart. They're hyper not because their brains don't work right but because they spend most of the day waiting for slower students to catch up with them. These students are bored to tears, and people who are bored fidget, wiggle, scratch, stretch, and (especially if they're boys) start looking for ways to get into trouble. (In my experience, bright girls are more likely to daydream, doodle, and exhibit other behaviors that earn them a label of attention deficit disorder.)

It's no surprise that most geniuses were considered classroom troublemakers. Here's a sampling, compiled by Dr. Harold C. Lyon, Jr., an expert on giftedness: "Winston Churchill was last in his class at Harrow. Charles Darwin dropped out of medical school. Shelley was expelled from Oxford, James Whistler and Edgar Allan Poe from West Point. Gibbon considered his education a waste of time. Einstein found grammar school boring."[5] (Einstein, in fact, was considered a terrible student by many if not most of his teachers.) Thomas Alva Edison was castigated as inattentive and even addle-brained by teachers who couldn't stand him, and eventually he ran away from school. Poet Robert Frost was tossed out of school for "daydreaming." Famous women, too, tended to get into trouble. Florence Nightingale, who revolutionized the field of nursing, was considered highly neurotic as a child, largely because her staid and dull Victorian peers bored her literally to the point of illness. And author Virginia Woolf was the bane of her teachers' existence, because she wouldn't shut up and behave.

Lyon asks the question, "Why should children with unusual abilities experience trouble with ordinary school curricula?" and offers the obvious answer: "Precisely because the curricula are ordinary." He notes, "Education is a mass enterprise geared . . . to the abilities of the majority. Just as a child of less-than-average mental ability frequently has trouble keeping up with his classmates, so a child of above-average ability has trouble staying behind with them."

There are, according to Lyon, three paths open to gifted children stifled by boredom and endless waiting. Some children conceal their abilities, afraid of sticking out. Others—those we now frequently label ADD—"drift into a state of lethargy and complete apathy." And a third group—those we call hyperactive—turn their restlessness outward, becoming discipline problems. (Many of the students in this third group will grow up to be painters, writers, and musicians. According to researcher Bonnie Cramond, a 1986 study found that students who scored in the top third on a test of creativity were significantly more hyperactive than those scoring in the bottom third. The creative students talked faster, were more restless, preferred fast games, were more impulsive, exhibited more delinquent behavior, and had more nervous habits.[6])

The number of bright kids being labeled hyperactive or attention disordered is in the thousands or even tens of thousands—and it's growing, thanks to the cookbook lists doctors and educators use to identify hyperactivity. In a fascinating article in the *ERIC Digest*, James T. Webb and Diane Latimer recently compared the criteria for ADHD with the criteria for giftedness.[7]

Behavior Associated with ADHD (Barkley, 1990):

- poorly sustained attention in almost all situations
- diminished persistence on tasks not having immediate consequences
- impulsivity, poor delay of gratification
- impaired adherence to commands to regulate or inhibit behavior in social contexts
- more active, restless than normal children
- difficulty adhering to rules and regulations

Behaviors Associated with Giftedness (Webb, 1993):

- poor attention, boredom, daydreaming in specific situations
- low tolerance for persistence on tasks that seem irrelevant
- judgment lags behind development of intellect
- intensity may lead to power struggles with authorities
- high activity level; may need less sleep
- questions rules, customs, and traditions

Do you see a big difference between those lists? Neither do I. That's why a bright child with a teacher or counselor who's been trained to spot ADHD is likely to wind up not in an accelerated class but in a doctor's office. Stephanie Tolan, who researches the phenomenon of giftedness, says that "almost every parent I talk to has had to deal with, either as a casual observation/suggestion or as a very serious threat, 'your child can't come to school any more until you have him [or her] medicated.' " If you think this is happening to your bright child, look for educational solutions rather than medical ones.

If your child scores above average on IQ tests, aces exams, has no trouble with homework, has no apparent learning disabilities, and primarily exhibits behavior problems at school, consider the possibility that he or she needs a more challenging classroom. Ask your child if school is boring. Ask if he or she is among the first to finish tests and reading assignments and spends lots of time waiting for other students to catch up. If so, check into gifted classes or private schools. And if your child is gifted in music, art, acting, or other creative pursuits, look into special programs that nurture talent rather than stifle it.

Incidentally, parents of bright children can find some outstanding resources on the Internet. One that I highly recommend is the Web site of the National Foundation for Gifted and Creative Children. This site offers insight into the unique personalities of gifted children, and is rightfully skeptical about wholesale drugging of such children in the name of making them more normal.

Question: Is Your Child Struggling in School?

If your child is hyperactive *and* struggling academically, it's clearly necessary that you obtain a thorough medical examination. Hyperactive behavior in conjunction with learning problems can indicate any one of a wide variety of medical problems ranging from hearing and vision problems to toxic exposure to mixed dominance (a treatable condition in which neither side of the brain establishes clear dominance). And it's critical, for your entire family's sake, to determine whether a child's learning problems stem from a genetic condition (see Chapter 5).

Sudden declines in previously good academic performance, when these declines occur in children not reacting to a recent trauma such as a death or divorce in their family, also are a cause for real concern. Declines in *motor* skills such as handwriting, bike riding, or physical education skills are of equal concern, because they can signal the onset of diseases that affect the muscles and/or nervous system. If your child masters a skill, and then loses it, a doctor should certainly find out why.

Some children, however, struggle *emotionally*, not educationally. One category of children I'm always interested in is those who are victims of bullies. It's a situation that isn't as straightforward as you'd think, and it can offer clues to a doctor who really takes an interest in his or her patients. Children get bullied for different reasons, and these reasons can provide surprising diagnostic insights.

Many kids are bullied simply because they're the new kids on the block, or they're victims of racial prejudice, or they're poorer than their classmates. These are normal kids who act out because they're scared. They start sleeping badly, they feel sad, and they develop physical symptoms, especially if they think those symptoms will keep them home from school. Often, they can't concentrate in class, partly because they're worried and partly because they're suffering from sleep deprivation.

These children develop *real* physical problems. A 1996 study found that "there was an association between children reporting being bullied sometimes or more often and reporting not sleeping well, bed-wetting, feeling sad, and experiencing more than occasional headaches and stomachaches." Furthermore, the researchers said, as the bullying escalated, so did the physical symptoms.[8] And no wonder! If you were worried every day about being beaten up or verbally threatened on your way to or from work, wouldn't you feel miserable?

Obviously, for such children, the cure is not Ritalin (or imipramine for their bed-wetting) but an end to the bullying. Be sure to question your child carefully about his or her relationships with other children at school; and if you detect any evidence that your child is the victim of a bully, handle the situation. Sometimes a change of classrooms helps; other times, a teacher or principal may have to intervene.

There is, however, another type of bullied child. This is the chronic victim—the child who gets picked on no matter what setting he or she is in. Moving this child to a new class probably won't help. What will help is finding out why your child is the one who's always picked on.

It sounds like a heartless analogy, but these children are a little like the weaker members of a herd who are the first prey of any hunters. Generally, it's because they're physically more frail or slower, or because they have learning problems, or because they're socially inept. Several of my patients with cardiac problems were victims of bullies, because they were weak and tired and couldn't fight back.

If your child is a perpetual victim of bullying, he or she probably has physical problems that are causing fatigue, slowness, weakness, frailty, learning disabilities, or a general malaise that makes it difficult to keep up socially, academically, or physically. Arrange for a thorough physical checkup to determine the causes of these symptoms.

Question: Does Your Family Exhibit a Pattern of What Doctors Call Familial Hyperactivity? If So, Is It Healthy or Pathological Hyperactivity?

These days, doctors frequently label a child *and* the child's family members hyperactive. That's because these doctors believe that hyperactivity is a disease and that this disease runs in families.

In reality, hyperactivity does often have genetic roots, but not because it's a genetic disease in and of itself. Rather, hyperactivity can be a *symptom of any number of disorders* that run in families (see Chapter 5, on genetic diseases), or it can be a *normal personality variant* that's common in a family tree. If there's a pattern of hyperactive behavior in your family tree, it may be a good clue as to why your child is hyper.

Think about any adults in your family who have been labeled hyperactive or attention disordered. Include any who *haven't* been labeled but were hyper little hell-raisers as children. If attention disorders are your worry, make a list of relatives who tended to be absentminded or spacey children, or had problems in school. When possible, ask your relatives their recollections about what your cousins, aunt, uncles, or other adult relatives were like as children.

If you've turned up a number of relatives who would have qualified as children for a label of hyperactivity or ADD, ask yourself these questions:

- Are these adults functioning reasonably well?
- Is their behavior within societal norms?
- Are they happy, or at least not *unhappy*, most of the time?
- Is their physical health generally good? Is their intelligence normal or even above average?

If the answer to these questions is yes, then the high activity level that's common in your family members most likely is a normal personality trait. Like any trait, it has its advantages and disadvantages. Your relatives may be late for holiday dinners, forget to buy birthday presents, run you ragged when you go shopping with them, or lose the books you loan them, but they're probably also talented, quick-witted, bright, and funny. In fact, you may find that the relatives who were the most rowdy and least attentive as children are now the most interesting as adults. That's because, as I've noted, the characteristics labeled as ADHD or ADD are often linked to giftedness and creativity.

On the other hand, if many of your adult relatives have a history of physical illness, mental illness, serious behavior problems, long-term academic or career problems, or social problems, you may be looking not at a normal personality trait but at a genetically influenced disorder. In this situation, your child needs a complete evaluation to detect or rule out genetic disorders.

Question: Is Your Child Sick or Just Different?

Some children are just plain eccentric. That doesn't mean they have to be drugged into normality. In fact, it usually means they'll grow up to be interesting people. Think how dull the world would be if we had no one like Robin Williams, Liberace, David Bowie, or Elton John. Think how peculiar many Hollywood celebrities, famous inventors and scientists, successful musicians, and prominent writers are. Now think about the fact that these are the first people who would, if they were children today, be put on Ritalin, Prozac, or some other drug because they weren't normal.

If your child marches to a different drummer, think carefully about his or her behavior. Is it harmful or frightening, or is it just eccentric? If your child is a bit odd but does well in school *and* appears happy and healthy, you're probably raising a unique individual who'll grow up to do interesting things. Rather than worrying, foster your child's curiosity and creativity.

But, you may ask, how can you tell if your child's unusual personality is a sign of harmless eccentricity, or the first stages of some serious brain dysfunction? David Weeks, a researcher who's studied hundreds of eccentrics, says that an important difference is that while eccentrics are strange, they're happily and productively strange. The typical eccentric, he says, is nonconforming, creative, curious, idealistic, happily obsessed with one or more hobbies, intelligent, opinionated, outspoken, noncompetitive, "not in need of reassurance or reinforcement from society," and "possessed of a mischievous sense of humor." Above all, he says, eccentrics have an "indomitable spirit of hopefulness" and a tremendous enjoyment of life. People suffering from brain dysfunctions are miserable, Weeks says, while eccentrics "know they're different and glory in it."[9] If your child, like

Weeks's subjects, is enjoying life and comfortable in his or her uniqueness, leave well enough alone.

That said, I should exclude one group of unusual children from the "don't worry about it" category. If you have a child who sets fires, tortures animals, and/or seems completely, utterly amoral despite having a good upbringing, *worry about it*. These children are not eccentric, and they're not ADHD. They are, to put it bluntly, young psychopaths. These children rarely change, no matter how much love and attention they receive. (And contrary to popular belief, most of them come from good and loving families.) If you're afraid your child might fall into this category, I suggest reading the works of C. Robert Cloninger (who specializes in the biochemical roots of personality) and Robert Hare (a leading authority on dealing with psychopathic children and adults). Do be aware that psychotherapeutic approaches virtually never help such children. In rare cases, medical treatment can find underlying causes for psychopathic behavior, so an in-depth medical evaluation is warranted. But forget Ritalin—it's never cured a psychopath, and it never will.

Question: Is Your Child a Troubled Soul or Just a Brat?

Be honest. Are you the boss around your house, or does your son or daughter rule the roost? Did you establish firm rules and boundaries early on, or are you a permissive parent who lets your child get away with almost anything?

If your child is running the show at your house, your problem isn't that he or she is sick. It's that you're too lenient.

An ever-increasing number of children labeled hyperactive are merely underdisciplined children who need a firmer hand. I blame this rise in bratty kids not on their parents but on the psychological experts who have counseled these parents for several decades that children are fragile, easily traumatized little flowers who could be ruined for life by a cross look or a scolding. Psychologists, social workers, psychiatrists, and counselors reared on Freudian theory have warned us repeatedly that strict parents raise timid, repressed, permanently scarred children—and as a result, as Martin L. Gross notes in *The Psychological Society*, "the contemporary parent is constantly anxious about the child's precarious emotional state."[10]

Well, guess what? The Freudians were wrong. Children need firm discipline and strict rules, and often the worst-behaved kids respond to this approach with miraculous personality changes. I'm not talking about beating children or locking them in closets or otherwise abusing them. I'm talking about setting rules and standards, demanding that these standards be met, and exacting consequences—grounding, taking away allowances or driving privileges, etc.—when your rules are broken. In general, the higher your expectations are (within reason), the better your child's behavior and performance will be. In a recent Ann Landers column, a retired colonel passed on a humorous letter he'd received that illustrates my point perfectly:

> *Our son gave us nothing but trouble starting at age 13. Weird clothes, crazy hair, failing in school, scruffy-looking, smelly, ill-mannered. We didn't think he would graduate from high school. When he announced that he was enlisting in the Air Force, I said to myself, "If they take him, he'll be home within a month."*
>
> *[When he graduated from boot camp and returned home on leave] I was stunned when our handsome young airman got off the plane—neatly barbered, perfectly groomed, grinning from ear to ear. We still can't get used to all the "Yes, sirs" and "No, sirs" around the house. . . .*
>
> *His mother and I wanted to let you know that if this is our son, thank you not only for what you have done for him but also for what you have done to him. If there has been a mistake, and this is not really our son, can we keep him, anyway?*[*11]

Like this young man, many kids misbehave because they get away with it. These kids aren't hyperactive or conduct

* Permission granted by Ann Landers/Creators Syndicate.

disordered—they're spoiled. Put them in a situation where they can't get away with being brats, and their brain dysfunction miraculously vanishes. Psychologist John Rosemond discovered this with his own child, Eric, whom he says "would have rated a 9.5 on any scale of 10 measuring attention deficit." When Rosemond implemented some strict discipline, assigned household chores, and removed the TV set from his home, Eric turned into a straight-A student. Doctors who put children like Eric on Ritalin or label them ADHD, Rosemond says, are "making much ado about something that isn't very complicated."[12]

If you think your child falls into the spoiled but normal category, I recommend that you check out some library books on assertive parenting, try some tough love, and see if your child's problem behavior starts to clear up. What I most assuredly *don't* recommend, in such a case, is that you fall for a label of ADHD. The worst thing you can do for a child who's undisciplined is give him or her additional excuses for misbehavior.

One of the greatest sins of doctors who label normal children hyperactive is that they are telling children, in effect, "You're not responsible for your behavior." In addition, they are telling parents that simple discipline won't work, because their children have brain disorders that prevent them from behaving. Excusing out-of-control behaviors in a normal, healthy child simply causes more such behaviors—and the range of behaviors that are being attributed to hyperactivity and attention deficits, and which can thus be excused by children as out of their control, borders on the ludicrous. A popular book on ADD,[13] for instance, tells readers that behaviors attributable to ADD include:

- not being able to tell right from wrong
- being insensitive to other people's feelings
- being verbally assaultive
- being physically aggressive
- spending too much money on shopping
- lying

Now, if your child is undisciplined to begin with and is told that lying, insensitivity, yelling, overspending, hitting people, and not being able to tell right from wrong are symptoms of ADHD or ADD rather than controllable behaviors, do you think his or her behavior will get better or worse? You guessed it. So don't fall for the disability cop-out if you're raising a perfectly normal child who simply needs firm guidance. If you do, you'll be teaching your child that there's an excuse for being unpleasant, ill-mannered, irresponsible, or even violent. You'll also be setting the stage for your child to become a failure at school and work, and possibly even an out-of-control abusive spouse. You won't be doing your child, yourself, or your child's future spouse or children any favors.

Question: Is It Your Child Who's Hyperactive, or Is It Your Child's Lifestyle?

Judyth Reichenberg-Ullman and Robert Ullman noted recently, "We live in an extremely overstimulated society. Children spend hours playing Nintendo rather than romping through the woods or playing outside. Many are glued to the television set. Movies are speedier, scarier, and more violent than ever before. There is a growing atmosphere of hurriedness, intensity, and urgency. . . . We eat fast, play fast, and channel surf. . . . Our society places little value on tranquillity, quiet, solitude, and the simple joy of being in nature."[14]

This frantic pace takes its toll on children. As one nursery school teacher told Jane Healy, author of *Endangered Minds*, "These kids . . . come from houses where the TV is going all the time, ride in cars with the music blaring—it's no wonder some have blocked it out and others are bouncing off walls." It's not just the level of the noise but the type of noise that assaults children: movies full of gunshots and screamed obscenities, frightening news stories about rapes and robberies, and video games loaded with carnage. On top of that, many children (even very young ones, if they have teenage siblings) are exposed for hours a day to loud and often threatening rap and heavy metal rock lyrics. A heavy diet of this stuff isn't good for children's brains, especially if they're very young and easily overstimulated.

And that's not just an old fogy's opinion. In a 1998 study, R. McCraty and colleagues played New Age music, classical music, "elevator music," and "grunge rock" music to 144 subjects. After fifteen minutes of grunge rock listening, the researchers say, psychological profiles revealed "significant increases in hostility, sadness, tension, and fatigue, and significant reductions in caring, relaxation, mental clarity, and vigor." The other types of music, in contrast, produced either improved moods or no discernible pattern of mood change.[15]

(I'm reminded of a recent award-winning science project by a student who played either hard rock or classical music to laboratory mice for four weeks, and no music at all to a third group of mice. The student, David Merrell, found that non-music-exposed mice ran a maze in five minutes, while mice exposed to classical music completed the maze in only one and a half minutes. The hard rock mice, however, took thirty minutes to finish the same maze. The project had to be cut short, Merrell said, "because all the hard rock mice killed each other. None of the classical music mice did that." It's a funny story, but what's not so funny is scientific research indicating that, in addition to reducing mental clarity and increasing aggression, loud rock music can lower immune functioning, cause hearing damage, and even decrease visual acuity.[16])

Now a little rock music isn't going to make your child hyper. But if your child watches TV for three or four hours a day, spends another hour or two playing video games or computer games, and keeps a Walkman playing all evening, he or she may be getting more loud, fast-paced visual and aural stimulation than a young brain can handle. Healy says, "Increasing questions are being raised as to whether too much loud music might induce in a growing brain not real relaxation, but instead a habit of defensively 'tuning out' to active thought." Some researchers also wonder about the effects of the pulsating sound, rapid picture flashes, and frantic pace of children's TV programs, particularly in light of a recent incident in which hundreds of Japanese children became physically ill, with many having seizures, while viewing a cartoon show employing fast-paced visuals, colors, and music. (EEG testing, in fact, often uses flashing lights to stimulate seizures in susceptible children.)

You can't slow down society in general, but you can slow down your own household at least a little. Introduce some quiet into your child's life. Limit your child's TV viewing to an hour or so a day. Limit your *own* viewing and instead put on some classical music. (There's actually research showing that Mozart is good for kids' brains. No kidding. A 1995 study found that "listening to a Mozart piano sonata produced significant short-term enhancement of spatial-temporal reasoning in college students.") Try to interest your child at least occasionally in reading and other quiet activities. Plant a garden and have your child help with the digging, watering, and harvesting. Go for walks together. Introduce hobbies that take time and foster sustained attention skills, such as jigsaw puzzles.

At first, your child will probably rebel against these changes. A surprising number of overactive kids, however, become much less wired when their TV and video game time is cut down to reasonable levels. And an even more surprising number develop a taste for Mozart!

AS I SAID EARLIER, THE CONCLUSION AS TO WHETHER YOUR child has problem behavior is a judgment call. After reading the preceding questions, you should be equipped to make that judgment.

If you conclude after reading this chapter that you're dealing with a smart, creative, happy, healthy kid, put this book away in the bookcase and stop worrying. Make sure your son or daughter eats a good diet, gets plenty of exercise, receives lots of love and firm but fair discipline, and has plenty of creative outlets for any excess energy. If your child is very bright, consider a more challenging school program. And if your child is spoiled, lay down the law.

On the other hand, if the questions in this chapter left you feeling concerned, then it's time to look for good medical help for your child. And don't wait, because a troubled child won't get better and will probably get worse. How do you find such help? Read the next chapter for some solid advice.

CHAPTER 9

Before You See the Doctor: Some Detective Work on Your Part Can Help Your Child

The world is full of obvious things which nobody by any chance ever observes.

Sherlock Holmes

EVER WANTED TO PLAY SHERLOCK HOLMES? IF SO, THIS IS your moment. In this chapter, I tell you how doing some serious investigative work *before* you visit the doctor can help you catch the culprit that's making your child hyperactive or attention disordered.

Like Holmes, you're going to be looking for subtle and not-so-subtle clues about what's ailing your child—the kinds of clues that overworked and corner-cutting physicians often miss. Your investigative work will help you gain a clearer understanding of the symptoms you're seeing and will prepare you to be a valuable partner in your child's care. With luck, it will make your doctor evaluate your child more thoroughly and help you obtain referrals to the specialists your child may need to be seeing. And it may very well provide the information your child's doctor needs to make a diagnosis.

In an ideal world you wouldn't need this chapter, because your child's doctors would do this detective work themselves. In that ideal world, each physician would spend hours asking about your child's health and activities, taking complete medical histories of your child and your family, and examining your child from head to toe. But that world doesn't exist any-more, except on TV (and in the offices of a few old-fashioned physicians who have avoided the managed-care revolution).

In reality, your doctor probably has ten or fifteen minutes to take a history and do an exam—and that's not enough time for even Sherlock Holmes to make a diagnosis. Furthermore, as you're already aware, doctors who are willing to consider hyperactivity itself as a diagnosis may not be motivated to search deeper for real answers.

So, in effect, I'm asking you to do a little bit of the doctor's job yourself. The following questionnaires include a large number of questions about your child's physical and mental status, your family's medical history, and your child's lifestyle. The questionnaires are designed to turn up red flags—that is, unusual signs and symptoms pointing to possible diagnoses. Presented with these clues, a good doctor should feel com-pelled to investigate your concerns rather than dismiss them.

Here's an example. A doctor who hears that a child is rest-less may think hyperactivity. If the doctor hears that this same child is a poor sleeper, has stomach pains, and recently lived in South America, the doctor will be more likely to include parasites as one possible diagnosis. Hearing that the child's parents are restoring their old home, the doctor may think to check for lead poisoning as well. In short, the more clues you provide, the more likely you are to force your child's doctor to perform a thorough evaluation, explore a wide range of diagnostic possibilities, order appropriate tests and studies, and make appropriate referrals to specialists.

Let me stress, however, that *I'm not asking you to diagnose your child yourself.* Don't try to guess what's wrong with your son or daughter, based on the questions in this section. That is not the intent of these lists. Only a medical professional can assess the importance of the information you are collect-ing.

Furthermore, the answers to the questions in this chapter *are not sufficient to make any diagnosis.* The purpose here is simply to gather clues that may steer a doctor to any one of dozens of potential diagnoses. A physician will need to do a thorough evaluation, ask many, many more questions, and most likely order consultations, laboratory studies, EEGs, etc., before making any diagnoses.

Why did I choose these particular questions? Because they can be readily answered by parents, because harried managed-care physicians may fail to ask them, and because the answers may be extremely helpful in pointing physicians toward correct diagnoses. Your answers to these questions will give your child's doctor a good starting point, but they won't substitute in any way for a complete diagnostic workup.

You'll also notice that I don't explain *why* I ask each question. That's because, as I've said, any clue you uncover may point to a number of diagnoses. For instance, headaches could suggest allergies, brain cysts, certain toxins, medication reactions, or a dozen other disorders. So don't attempt to formulate diagnoses yourself—unless you happen to have a medical degree. I don't expect you to differentiate brain cysts from allergies. I do expect your doctor to follow through on the clues you provide.

Also don't worry when you answer yes to a question. Many of your answers will be of little or no significance, *unless* they point to a pattern.

The chapter contains several sections, and each is important. Make photocopies of these sections and take the copies to your child's doctor. *Don't* expect the doctor to read through these forms in their entirety, because he or she won't have time. Rather, *review your forms quickly with the doctor, pointing out red flags you've discovered.*

What's a red flag? It might be a behavioral symptom (for instance, frequent tantrums or anxiety attacks), or a physical sign or symptom (anything from skin rashes to oddly shaped toes). Or it may be a family pattern of illness or behavioral disorders that you detect. Here's a good rule of thumb: If a physical symptom, behavior, or family health pattern is noticeable enough to catch your attention, it's worth bringing to the doctor's attention. Let the doctor sort the wheat from the chaff; your job is to err on the side of presenting too much information, not too little.

Remember that specialists, like the proverbial blind men feeling an elephant, see only what they're trained to see. A cardiologist, for instance, is likely to be intrigued by ridged fingernails (a possible sign of cardiac insufficiency). A specialist in metabolic disorders, on the other hand, will be interested if you report that your child feels faint before lunch. A neurologist might overlook that clue and focus on sleepwalking or bed-wetting, both possible symptoms of petit mal seizures. The detail that one doctor dismisses as irrelevant may be the very detail that turns on the lightbulb over another doctor's head. Since you have no way of knowing what clues will be helpful to each specialist, your best bet is to review *all* of your concerns with each doctor.

Furthermore, don't limit yourself to telling a specialist about symptoms that seem related to his or her specialty. Remember that diseases can affect seemingly unrelated parts of the body. For instance, be sure to point out skin abnormalities to your child's neurologist, because the skin and the nervous system form from the same group of fetal cells, and many neurological disorders affect the skin as well. And thinning hair may interest an endocrinologist, because it can be a sign of thyroid disorder. Again, it's better to tell a specialist too much than too little.

Now, on to your detective work. Grab a pencil!

The sections included in this chapter are:

- **A '24-hour day' questionnaire**. This questionnaire asks important questions about your child's daily (and nightly) routine, including eating habits, sleeping patterns, hobbies, exercise, and mood changes.
- **Questions about your child's physical development.**
- **Questions about your child's cognitive and social development.**
- **A physical signs and symptoms list**. Often, seemingly minor and unrelated abnormalities are part of a diagnostic pattern. (Here's an example: loose joints, a long face, large testicles, and hyperactivity are all part of the constellation of symptoms associated with fragile X syndrome.) By listing the signs and

symptoms you've noticed, you may spot important clues a doctor could otherwise overlook.

- **Questions about your family history**. Ideally, your physician will query you closely about any mental or physical disorders in your family tree. If you make a list beforehand, however, you're more likely to give a complete answer, especially if you have an opportunity to check with relatives.

- **Questions about your child's lifestyle**. This section will help you identify any potential dangers presented by your family's careers, hobbies, or other aspects of your lifestyle.

I'm asking you to do a lot of work in this chapter, so set aside several hours at least. It's better to be too thorough than skimp on this section, because sometimes the tiniest clues can lead to a diagnosis. If an abnormality is obvious enough that you've noticed it, *then it's obvious enough to list*—no matter how minor it seems.

Once you've completed these questionnaires, I have just a few more "assignments" before you're done with your homework:

- Get a bright-colored pen or marker and highlight the red flags you think you've uncovered, so you can spot them easily during a doctor's appointment. If you have any doubts about whether an answer is important, go ahead and highlight it.

- Get reports from all physicians who have evaluated your child, including birth records and copies of any lab tests, MRIs, CT scans, PET scans, EEGs, or other medical workups. Most doctors will charge a small fee for sending you these reports, but it's well worth the cost. Give a set of these reports to each physician you see.

- If you have kept a thorough record of your child's development using a baby book, leaf through the book and note anything unusual that you may have forgotten. Consider taking the baby book to appointments with doctors, so you can provide accurate information about your child's early years.

- Before you visit a doctor, sit down with your child and ask, in a casual and sympathetic way, if there are any physical problems he or she is experiencing that you aren't aware of. Ask,

in particular, about headaches, stomachaches or other digestive problems, fatigue, or muscle or joint pains. A child may
reveal far more to a parent, in a casual conversation, than he
or she will volunteer in the more intimidating setting of a
doctor's office. If your child mentions a problem, put it on
your red flags list.

• If your child spends a significant amount of time with another
caretaker (a divorced spouse, grandparent, or baby-sitter), ask
for that person's input on this form. Also, see if your child's
teacher will help with the 24-Hour Day chart, and provide a
specific list of concerns about your child's academic, behavioral, and social status at school.

One more thing: Don't be limited by this list. If you have
concerns I haven't listed, write them down, too. As I've noted,
a physician knows a great deal about children's health in general,
but nobody knows your child like you do! And, again, don't
hesitate to list even seemingly minor anomalies. To quote Sherlock Holmes once more, "The little things are infinitely the
most important." Like Holmes, many a doctor has solved a difficult case thanks to a small and easily overlooked clue—and the
work you do in this chapter could very well provide such a clue.

The 24-Hour Day

A healthy child generally sleeps long and well, awakes refreshed, eats three good meals a day, and is reasonably happy, energetic, and productive at school and at home. By tracking your child's activities and behavior for a full day and night, you can often spot deviations from this healthy pattern. This 24-hour-day form will help you spot irregularities in your child's eating, sleeping, and daily activities that may point to physical disease or to lifestyle problems such as poor eating or sleeping habits. Flag any answers that concern you.

Bedtime

What time does your child go to bed?_____

Is your child ready to go to bed, or does he or she resist?_____
_____

Does your child have bedtime rituals (circling bed, lining up slippers, etc.)? How compulsive is he or she about these rituals?_____
_____

Does your child sleep alone or in the same room as siblings or parents?
_____

Is there a gas heater in your child's room? If so, is it an older heater? Is there any ventilation in the room?_____

Does your child sleepwalk?_____

Does your child grind his or her teeth during sleep?_____

Is your child a quiet or a restless sleeper?_____

Is your child a heavy sleeper, or easily awakened?_____

Does your child get up frequently during the night to go to the bathroom?_____

If your child is over age six, does he or she still wet the bed?_____
_____

If your child is over age two, does he or she ever have bowel movements while asleep?_____

Does your child frequently get up at night to drink water?_____
_____

Does your child get up at night to eat?_____

Does your child snore heavily?_____

Does your child have frequent nightmares or "night terrors"?_____
_____

Is your child's sleep pattern regular or irregular?_____

Is it difficult to get your child to sleep?_____

Is it difficult to awaken your child when he or she is sleeping?_____
_____

Morning

What time does your child awaken?_____

Does your child awaken refreshed or tired?_____

Does your child eat breakfast? If so, what does he or she eat?_____
_____

Does your child feel good after breakfast, or does he or she appear
    tired or sweaty, or regress behaviorally?_____

If your child is a toddler, does he or she nap during the morning? If so,
    for how long?_____

What is your child's behavior like in the morning?_____

What is your child's energy level like in the morning?_____

What is your child's mood like in the morning?_____

Does your child eat a morning snack? If so, what is it? Does it appear
    to affect your child's mood or energy level?_____

How does your child get to school (bus, car, bike, walking)?_____
_____

Does your child have tantrums in the morning? If so, at what time?_____
_____

If possible, ask your child's teachers to assess your child's morning
    behavior/mood/energy level, particularly as compared to that of other
    students._____

Afternoon

At what time does your child eat lunch? What does he or she eat?
    Does your child take a lunch, or eat a school lunch? Does your child
    trade lunches with other children?_____

Does your child feel weak or irritable before lunch?_____

Does your child feel good after lunch, or does he or she appear tired or sweaty?_____

If your child is a toddler, does he or she nap during the afternoon? If so, for how long?_____

What is your child's behavior like in the afternoon?_____

What is your child's energy level like in the afternoon?_____

What is your child's mood like in the afternoon?_____

Does your child eat an afternoon snack? If so, what is it? Does it appear to affect your child's mood or energy level?_____

Does your child have tantrums in the afternoon? If so, at what time?___
_____

If possible, ask your child's teachers to assess your child's afternoon behavior/mood/activity level, particularly in comparison to that of other students._____

Late Afternoon

How does your child get home from school (bus, car, bike, walking)?___
_____

What is your child's mood/energy level when he or she arrives at home?_____

Does your child snack upon getting home? If so, what does he or she eat?_____

How many hours does your child spend watching TV before dinner?___
_____

What other activities does your child participate in before dinner (sports, computer games or video games, hobbies, etc.)?_____
_____

How many caffeinated beverages (coffee, colas, tea, hot chocolate) does your child consume during the afternoon?_____

What is your child's behavior like immediately before dinner?_____
_____

Does your child have tantrums in the late afternoon? If so, at what time?_____

Evening

What does your child eat for dinner? How good is your child's appetite?___
_____

What is your child's behavior like immediately after dinner? Does your child feel good, or is your child fatigued or sweaty?_____

How often does your child go to the bathroom during the evening?_____
_____

How much water, soda, or juice does your child drink during the evening?_____
_____

How many caffeinated beverages (coffee, colas, tea, hot chocolate) does your child consume during the evening?_____

How much TV does your child watch during the evening?_____
_____

What other activities does your child participate in during the evening?
_____

What is your child's behavior like in the evening?_____

Does your child have tantrums in the evening? If so, at what time?_____
_____

What is your child's energy level like in the evening?_____

What is your child's mood like in the evening?_____

Does your child snack in the evening? If so, what does he or she eat, and how does he or she feel after eating?_____

Developmental History

Complications during pregnancy or delivery can sometimes cause or exacerbate children's hyperactive behavior or attention disorders. Infections, injuries, or other medical problems during infancy and childhood also can have a significant impact on a child's behavior and academic performance. By reviewing your child's prenatal and childhood development, you may identify birth complications, illnesses, injuries, or other medical conditions contributing to your child's current problems. Flag any answers that appear out of the ordinary.

Pregnancy

What was the length of your pregnancy?_____

Was your pregnancy supervised by a doctor?_____

How many pounds did you gain?_____

Did you use alcohol, drugs, or tobacco during the pregnancy?_____
_____

Did you use any prescription or over-the-counter drugs during pregnancy? Which?_____

Were there any complications during your pregnancy?_____

What types of drugs (if any) were used during labor?_____

Was labor induced or spontaneous? Did you require any anesthesia? If so, what type and for how long?_____

How long was the labor?_____

Were there any complications during labor or delivery?_____

Was it a breech or headfirst birth?_____

What was your baby's Apgar score (if known)?_____

What did your child look like following delivery?_____

Did your child cry spontaneously and move arms and legs immediately after birth?_____

Postnatal Development

Was your child breast- or bottle-fed? If breast-fed, for how long?_____
_____

Was your child good at sucking?_____

Did your child have colic?_____

At what age did your child sit?_____

At what age did your child stand?_____

At what age did your child walk?_____

At what age was your child toilet trained?_____

At what age did your child talk?_____

At what age could you tell whether your child was left-or right-handed?

_____

Which vaccinations has your child had? Were any vaccinations followed
  by high fevers, seizures, or other problems?_____

Has your child had measles, mumps, chicken pox, rheumatic fever, or
  other significant diseases?_____

Has he or she been hospitalized?_____

Has your child ever required surgery or emergency care?_____

_____

Has your child ever been under anesthesia? If so, for how long? Were
  there any adverse consequences?_____

Does your child have heart, liver, kidney, lung, or other disease?_____

Is your child allergic to anything?_____

Has your child ever experienced a concussion? Has he or she ever been
  involved in a significant accident, or suffered a head injury?_____

_____

Has a physician ever noted that your child exhibits any structural or
  biochemical abnormalities?_____

Has your doctor ordered any medical evaluations or tests? *If so, obtain
  reports of the physician's findings and bring them to your physician
  with this list.*

Cognitive/Social Development

Almost all children have a few cognitive or social problems—difficulty with math, for instance, or shyness. However, a child's cognitive and social problems sometimes form a pattern that can point an alert doctor toward a medical diagnosis. Conversely, some questions can help a physician rule out a problem. (For instance, language delays in a child learning a second language are generally less worrisome than the same problems in a child who only speaks one language.) The questions below may help your child's doctor identify potential problems. Flag any answers that concern you.

Do you have any concerns about your child's speech (too fast or too slow, difficult to understand, not appropriate for age level, stuttering, lisp, etc.)?_____

Does your child speak another language, and, if so, at what age did your child begin speaking English?_____

Is more than one language spoken at home?_____

Does your child have academic problems, or specific problems with reading, spelling, math, or handwriting?_____

Does he or she reverse letters such as *b* and *d*?_____

When reading aloud, does your child pronounce "saw" as "was," or "dog" as "God"?_____

Is your child's handwriting poor, or has it deteriorated recently?_____

Have other academic abilities or physical skills deteriorated from earlier levels?_____

Does your child have difficulty making or keeping friends? Why?_____

What activities does he or she participate in with friends?_____

Does your child have fantasies and daydreams—and, if so, does he or she understand the difference between fantasy and reality?_____

Does your child have obsessive or compulsive behaviors?_____

Is your child usually anxious, tired, sad, or angry?_____

Does your child hurt other children or animals regularly?_____

_____

Is your child physically aggressive to the point where he or she is a
danger to others?_____

Is your child verbally aggressive to a degree that causes problems at
school or at home?_____

Is your child emotionally mature or immature for his or her age?_____

_____

Does your child have trouble relating to other people? If so, why?_____

_____

Does your child exhibit play skills appropriate for his or her age (e.g.,
takes turns, understands and follows game rules)?_____

Is your child often the target of bullies? Or does your child often bully
other children?_____

Has your child's teacher mentioned any concerns about your child's
academic or social development?_____

Does your child show possible signs of illicit drug or alcohol use
("stoned" behavior, hangover-like appearance, etc.)?_____

_____

Do you think your child is sexually active?_____

Physical Signs and Symptoms

Flag any questions to which you answer yes.

Have you noticed that your child exhibits any abnormalities in any of these areas?

eyes (vision problems, squinting, or other abnormalities)_____

ears (hearing problems, pulling on ears, oddly shaped or placed earlobes, etc.)_____

nose (chronic discharge, stuffiness, etc.)_____

mouth (soreness, tooth grinding, etc.)_____

facial features_____

skin (dark or light patches, other unusual markings, difficulty tanning, etc.)_____

hair (unusually coarse or fine, hair whorl on same side as dominant hand or in the middle of head, or two hair whorls)_____

fingernails or toenails (brittle, ridged, discolored, or misshapen nails)

fingers or toes (webbing between toes, unusually long or short fingers or toes, etc.)_____

joints (double-jointed, pain in joints, etc.)_____

handedness (has no hand preference, has switched hand preferences, or does not use one hand at all)_____

genitalia (abnormally large or small, malformed, etc.)_____

Does your child have any of these problems?_____

difficulty gaining or losing weight_____

frequent headaches, stomachaches, or other pains_____

frequent diarrhea, constipation, nausea, gas, or vomiting_____

frequent vaginal yeast infections or urinary tract infections_____

chest pains_____

itching_____

heat intolerance_____

excessive thirst_____

excessive sweating_____

frequent episodes of dizziness_____

frequent episodes of breathlessness_____

frequent urination_____

fainting spells_____

chronic fatigue_____

frequent colds, ear infections, or bouts of the flu_____

tics such as grimacing or twitching_____

Does your child's gait (when walking, running, hopping, skipping, or climbing stairs) appear abnormal in any way?_____

Does your child's posture appear abnormal in any way?_____

Does your child tire more easily than other children?_____

Does your child sweat excessively following meals?_____

Does your child feel markedly better or worse following meals?_____

Is your child uncoordinated at sports?_____

Does your child have poor fine-motor control (has difficulty coloring, writing, or picking up small objects)?_____

List any significant sleeping problems noted on the 24-Hour-Day form you completed earlier (sleepwalking, tooth-grinding, snoring, frequent awakening to drink water or eat, or urination or defecation by older children during sleep)._____

Does your child eat nonfood items such as paste, laundry detergent, dirt, or crayons?_____

Does your child experience food cravings on a regular basis?_____

Has your child gotten any tattoos? Has your child had any body parts pierced? If so, who did the tattooing or piercing?_____

Does your child write right-handed and kick left-footed, or vice versa?
Is his or her dominant handedness different from that of the
parents? Did your child "declare" his or her handedness before one
year of age?_____

Family History/Activities

Your family history can provide a doctor with valuable information about diseases, even those not normally linked to hyperactivity, that may be influencing your child's behavior and health. In addition, information about your family members' hobbies, jobs, and other activities may provide clues about possible toxic exposure or other lifestyle risks. Flag any "yes" answers in the Family History section, and flag any answers in the Family Activities section that raise concerns.

History

Is there a family history of any of the following?

developmental disabilities or mental illness_____

learning disabilities_____

genetic diseases of *any* kind—even if they appear to be unrelated to your child's behavioral problems_____

diabetes or other metabolic disorders_____

abnormalities of the heart, lungs, other organs, or the skeletal, nervous, or circulatory system_____

consanguinity (marriages between close relatives)_____

Do any close relatives have any noticeable physical abnormalities? If so, does your child exhibit these abnormalities as well?_____

Did/do either of the child's biological parents abuse alcohol or drugs?

Activities

Do you or your spouse work in jobs that may bring you into contact with lead or other pollutants (car repair, battery repair, smelting, stained-glass work, home restorations, painting, pest control, farming, or industrial jobs involving lead or cadmium)?_____

Do you, your spouse, and/or your child do extensive gardening or yard work? If so, do you regularly use pesticides, herbicides, or fertilizers?_____

Is your house heated with gas? Have you had your furnaces checked recently? Do you ever smell gas in the house?_____

Do your family hobbies include shooting, model building, car
restoration, furniture refinishing, or any other activities involving
extensive use of solvents, glues, paints, or other chemicals?_____

Do you live in an older home? If so, have you done any large-scale
renovations, particularly sanding old paint off walls, or sanding
floors?_____

Does your home contain any lead-based paints?_____

Does your child frequently participate in any sports that have a high
risk of head injury (football, soccer, bike racing, skateboarding)?_____

Have you traveled to, or lived in, any foreign countries? If so, how
hygienic were your living conditions? Do you remember your child
being ill at any time during your stay in a foreign country?_____

Does your child routinely take any prescription or nonprescription
drugs? Does your child take any ethnic or herbal remedies or high
doses of any supplements?_____

Do your child's behavioral and/or physical symptoms:

occur in one setting but not in another (for instance, at school but
not at home)?_____

appear to be linked to any particular activity or time of day?_____

worsen outdoors or indoors?_____

appear to be either reduced or exacerbated by eating or drinking?___

occur more in one season than in others?_____

CHAPTER 10

In the Doctor's Office

You should never assume that all doctors are good. Of course, that
doesn't mean you can't find a good doctor. It just means you have
to consider every doctor carefully.

Marti Ann Schwartz, Listen to Me, Doctor

ARMED WITH THE INFORMATION IN THE LAST CHAPTER,
you're ready to start your search for a real diagnosis for your
child's behavior problems.

Now comes the hard part.

Obviously, I don't want to discourage you from searching
for good care and an accurate diagnosis. Far from it! But I
want to prepare you for the fact that the medical system isn't
set up to help you in this search. In fact, it often seems as
though the system is set up to *prevent* doctors from correctly
diagnosing hyperactive children.

But getting your child diagnosed and treated isn't impossible, as thousands of parents can attest. It's just a challenge,
and if you're determined, you can meet that challenge. To
help you, here's some advice on how to avoid "label-and-
drug" doctors and find a physician interested in giving your
child a real diagnosis.

First Things First: The HMO Issue

How much would you pay to protect your child's health? How
much would you pay to find out what's really causing your son's

or daughter's behavior problems and to learn how they can be treated without dangerous drugs?

Two thousand dollars?

Two hundred?

Maybe fifty?

You're probably thinking, "Whatever it takes." But the answer I usually get when I ask people this question is, "Nothing at all."

Of course, that's not how I'm phrasing the question. Here's what I'm asking: "When your HMO doesn't give you adequate medical care, do you go to a physician outside your plan?"

The answer I get, almost always, is, "Of course not. My insurance won't cover it."

This response never fails to amaze me. The average visit to a doctor's office, if you simply march in and lay down cash, costs between $50 and $150. Even a visit to a specialist generally won't cost more than a few hundred dollars. That's not a lot of money, when your child's health and future are at stake.

Yet many people who can afford good cars, good wine, good restaurants, and big-screen TVs tell me they "can't" get good care for their behavior-disordered children. Why? Because their managed care programs' physicians aren't up to the job, or because their HMOs refuse to fund referrals to specialists who could diagnose their children's baffling symptoms.

I'm not talking here about parents too poor to afford to pay for medical care, who are at the mercy—what mercy there is—of government health-care programs. I'm talking about reasonably well-off people who don't get their children diagnosed, because they've developed HMO mentality. That is, they believe that the only care available to them is the care their HMOs are willing to pay for. Many of these parents spend years fighting managed care bureaucrats, while their children grow worse instead of better.

It's not these parents' fault that they were forced into HMOs in the first place. For many Americans, that's the only type of coverage available. And it's not their fault that their HMOs sometimes provide medical care resembling that in third world countries. That's the fault of a managed care system that's pushed a profits-over-care philosophy beyond sane limits. But it *is* these parents' fault if they accept this level of care rather than biting the bullet and shelling out the cost of a new CD player or espresso maker in order to pay a non-HMO doctor who'll diagnose their children correctly.

Don't be brainwashed into thinking that you "can't" see a doctor outside your plan. Remember: Your child is not being forced at gunpoint to go to an HMO doctor. Use your HMO when it provides good care; when it doesn't, *leave and find better care*. If you're in the type of managed care program called an IPA (independent physician association or individual practice association) or PPO (preferred provider organization), your managed care program will even pay a portion of an outside physician's fee.

If your plan doesn't allow any flexibility in seeing outside doctors, talk to your company's human resources director and see if other types of plans are available. Before doing so, read up on the different types of plans, and the advantages and disadvantages of each. You'll find a number of good resources at your local library. One is *Managed Care Beware*, by Harvey M. Shapiro, M.D. Dr. Shapiro has a more optimistic view of managed care than I do, but he does an excellent job of telling consumers how to fight for good care from an HMO.

No matter what plan you have, don't let your efforts to help your child become stalled due to red tape and HMO cost cutting. At the very least, get an accurate diagnosis for your child from an outside doctor and then take that diagnosis back to your HMO and insist on treatment. If you do this, you'll have a hammer to hold over the managed care bureaucrats' heads: the threat of legal action if they refuse to provide adequate treatment for a diagnosed condition. Often, simply paying for one consultation with a specialist can give you the ammunition you need to get good care.

And if paying a few medical bills out of your own pocket lets your HMO off the hook for diagnostic services they should have provided in the first place—well, better to be cheated out of a few bucks than to have your child spend months or even years suffering from a diagnosable and treatable disease.

If you truly can't afford to go outside the system and your only choice is to go the managed care route, be assertive—and be prepared to challenge your doctors. I've already talked a bit in Chapter 2 about the hazards of managed care, but let me reiterate here: *Don't expect a managed care doctor to operate solely in your interest.* As Seth G. Spotnitz, president of Physicians Who Care, recently said, "Physicians in HMOs are ethically compromised. Patients have a right to know this. Their health and even their lives are at risk."[1]

The Starting Point

That said, let me add that there's no reason not to start your search by making an appointment with a family practitioner (also called a general practitioner) or pediatrician through your HMO or other managed care program. If you're lucky—*and* assertive— you should be able to persuade this physician to check your child for some of the most common causes of hyperactive behavior. This will save you money later, if and when you need to go outside the system.

Why start with a family practitioner? Because the first step in any diagnosis of behavior problems is a complete general checkup, and that's the forte of the generalist. These doctors are fully equipped to diagnose (or to rule out) several of the most routine disorders that cause behavior problems. A pediatrician or a family practitioner who conducts a competent physical evaluation is qualified to detect gross hearing and vision problems, lead toxicity, pinworms, and a number of other easy-to-diagnose problems. Also, this doctor should detect any obvious symptoms of cardiac abnormalities, genetic disease, or other problems requiring a referral to a specialist.

Furthermore, if you're lucky, the work you put into completing the 24-Hour-Day chart (see Chapter 9) and documenting your child's symptoms may pay off at this point. Insist, politely, that the doctor carefully review all of your red flags. Show him or her any oddities you've detected involving your child's sleeping, eating, or activity patterns. Insist, also, on giving the doctor a detailed account of your child's and your family's medical history, even if he or she doesn't ask.

During the doctor's examination of your child, don't be shy about pointing out any physical signs or symptoms that concern you—for instance, unusual fingernails, or areas of skin pigmentation or depigmentation. (Don't just assume that the doctor will notice these signs on his or her own. A doctor who conducts several dozen physical evaluations a day can sometimes wind up doing them on autopilot and missing a lot.) The more information you provide, the more likely it is that your doctor won't be able to brush your child off as merely hyperactive or ADD—and the more likely it is that you'll be referred to the proper specialists.

If you're lucky, this initial doctor will at least rule out a few diagnostic possibilities. But what if this first doctor is a firm believer in the hyperactivity/ADD myth? What if instead of listening to your concerns, he or she simply tells you that hyperactivity and ADD are diseases, that you're misguided in seeking any other diagnosis, and that you're harming your child by depriving him or her of Ritalin treatment?

Simple: Pick the next family practitioner or pediatrician on your managed care list. And if that doctor, and the next and the next, give you the same line, then go to Plan B: *Pay good cash to go to a doctor who's not on your plan.* Be sure to let this doctor know right off the bat that you're not one of his or her managed care patients, and that you're willing to pay privately for any consultations, evaluations, or laboratory tests that the doctor feels are appropriate. That way, you'll know the doctor has your child's interests, and not financial concerns, in mind.

Selecting the doctor you want won't be easy, of course. You can't just open up the Yellow Pages, shut your eyes, and point to a name; ninety out of one hundred doctors in the Yellow Pages are probably Ritalin fans. But the other ten doctors are out there somewhere, and there are several steps you can take to locate them.

First, try asking neighbors, friends, and coworkers for recommendations. Stress that you're looking for a physician who takes time with his or her patients, listens to their questions, and goes the extra mile when looking for a diagnosis. Also, if you know any physicians you admire, or have friends in the medical profession, ask them whom they recommend.

If you live near a teaching hospital, look for physicians affiliated with that hospital. Doctors at teaching hospitals, which are in the business of training new physicians to make difficult diagnoses, often are more attuned to diagnostic detective work than other doctors are. Conversely, be *extremely* wary of for-profit psychiatric hospitals. A number of these hospitals have actually been charged with fraud, for coercing patients into unnecessary treatments.

Physician referral services can help you in a very limited way, by providing information about whether a doctor is board certified, where the doctor went to school, and how long he or she has been in practice. Bear in mind, however, that doctors pay to be listed on the for-profit referral services. And hospital referral services will refer you only to doctors on their staffs.

If you're computer literate, searching the Internet for information about physicians can sometimes save you time, money, and frustration. If you're willing to wade through the Web sites of a trillion clinics promoting Ritalin for ADD or hyperactivity, you may find a few local doctors with Web sites critical of the ADHD and ADD labels. However, avoid any of these doctors who push a one-size-fits-all theory—that is, doctors who claim that *all* hyperactivity and attention problems are due to a single culprit such as food additives or immunizations. These doctors remind me of the old saying about a stopped clock being right twice a day. Like that clock, these doctors are right occasionally—but they're wrong *most* of the time, because hyperactivity has hundreds of causes. Any doctor pushing one cure-all for all hyperactive or attention-disordered children is wrong and should be avoided.

Here are some additional rules and recommendations that can help you avoid wasted time and effort in your search for a real diagnosis for your child.

See an M.D., Not a Psychologist

There are plenty of times when a psychologist can help your family, but this isn't one of them. Psychologists aren't doctors, and they receive no training whatsoever in diagnosing medical disorders. At most, a psychologist can conduct a few pen-and-paper tests (for instance, IQ tests), which may be helpful adjuncts to a physician's diagnosis but can't replace it.

After your child receives an accurate diagnosis and medical treatment, however, a psychologist can often be a valuable help in designing behavior modification programs to handle any residual behavior problems.

Traditional or "Holistic"?

Doctors who treat hyperactivity tend to come in two breeds these days. One is mainstream doctors. These doctors generally have a thorough classical training that enables them to diagnose a wide variety of ailments. Unfortunately, when it comes to hyperactivity, too many of these traditional doctors forget their diagnostic skills and reach for the Ritalin.

"Holistic" or "alternative medicine" doctors, on the other hand, generally reject stimulant treatment outright. That's a big plus. In addition, most alternative medicine doctors do a good job of evaluating a child for problems due to toxins, parasites, allergies, and nutritional deficiencies. Unfortunately, many don't go beyond that short list.

Both types of physicians often are limited by their biases: the traditional doctor by the concept that pills fix everything, and the holistic doctor by the idea that hyperactivity always stems from an unhealthful lifestyle. It doesn't: Children with the most healthful lifestyles can still have genetic diseases, cysts, metabolic disorders, infections, and other medical disorders.

My advice is to check out both traditional and holistic doctors, while being skeptical of both. If the traditional doctor offers your child a stimulant drug, turn it down. If the holistic doctor blames your child's problems on lifestyle, without conducting a thorough differential diagnosis and ruling out other causes, walk away. Whichever type of doctor you choose, don't fall for any simplistic treatment—diet, drug, whatever—that isn't based on a real diagnosis. How can you tell the difference between a pseudo-diagnosis and the real thing? The former takes only a few minutes, while the latter requires careful questioning, a thorough physical evaluation, and the consideration of many diagnostic possibilities.

Let the Doctor's Staff Know What You Expect Ahead of Time

Often, parents arrive at a doctor's office expecting a thorough evaluation while the doctor is expecting to do a ten-minute exam. It's a good idea, when you make an appointment, to tell the nurse or receptionist up front that you have *many* concerns about your child's health and that you need a long appointment. Otherwise, you're likely to be meeting with a doctor who's more worried about his or her crowded waiting room than about your child's problems.

Don't Be Too Polite

I'm not suggesting that you be rude to your child's doctor. In America, however, we tend to err in the opposite direction. Patients often worry that they're asking too many questions, taking up too much of the doctor's time, or being offensive by questioning a doctor's opinions. Phooey! If your questions haven't been answered, or you have reservations about a doctor's verdict, speak up. And if your child's doctor is spewing out incomprehensible medical terms, don't hesitate to request a translation into plain English.

Above all, stick to your guns and politely but firmly insist on a complete workup and a real diagnosis. You may anger a few doctors by doing this. Who cares? This isn't a popularity contest.

"Some people have told me that they can't imagine questioning a doctor," Marti Ann Schwartz says in *Listen to Me, Doctor*. "They don't want the doctor, or his staff, to see them as a difficult patient." But, Schwartz says, "I have never seen myself as a difficult patient. I am simply standing up for the care I need. . . . The questions I raise and the solutions I seek are for the express purpose of seeing that my family and I receive the quality health care we require."[2]

I know it's unpleasant to be considered uncooperative or even a crackpot by your child's doctor, but it's the price you may have to pay for persisting in your effort to get real help for your child. As physician Richard Podell notes, "To be able to operate effectively as a patient in the current health care environment, you must have the guts to stand up to your doctor and to ask him pointed questions. The alert—and safe—patient is the one who is able to be assertive, even aggressive, with her physician." So worry more about your child's health than about wounding your physician's ego or gaining a reputation as a problem parent.

Don't Be Afraid to Shop Around

You may have to see half a dozen doctors, or even more, before finding one who can help your child. Don't let anyone dissuade you from this search by deriding you for "doctor shopping." After all, you'd probably visit five or six car dealers before buying a car. And you'd most likely look at dozens of houses before buying one. Isn't your child's health as important as your car or your house?

There's no sin in visiting half a dozen, a dozen, or even a hundred doctors. When you find the right one, you'll be glad you kept trying. And it's far smarter to search for appropriate care than to accept a prescription for Ritalin from the very first doctor you see.

Keep Good Records

Save every piece of paper you get from a doctor. That includes all test results, in addition to records of office visits. Often, they'll save you time and money when you go to see the next physician. Furthermore, even normal test findings can serve as a baseline record if your child's condition changes later.

Also, consider taping your consultations with doctors. That way, if you have any questions about what was said, you'll have a complete record. Some doctors don't like having their conferences recorded, but good doctors won't object. (I tape conferences myself and give parents copies of the tapes.)

Be Assertive About
Getting Referrals to Specialists

If you do attempt to work within your managed care plan, re-member that even if you're referred to a specialist, your man-aged care company may do its best to keep you from seeing one. One trick they use is to allow only a certain number of specialists onto their approved provider lists. As one doctor explained re-cently, "The insurance companies see specialists as cost centers. They pick them by geographic zone, and make access to them difficult so patients will use them less."[3]

Furthermore, when you *do* see a specialist, your HMO may not agree to provide the treatment he or she recommends. For in-stance, many Arizona physicians contracting with Aetna US Healthcare are refusing to sign new contracts, because—accord-ing to the doctors—Aetna makes it too difficult for patients to ob-tain care recommended by specialists.[4] So be prepared for the possibility that you'll have to fight your managed care provider to get proper care for your child. Again, it's often easier to bite the bullet and pay for treatment yourself when you can afford it.

Why are specialists so important in your quest to obtain a real diagnosis for your child? Because we've learned more about medicine in the past twenty years than in the century before, and no one doctor can master all of modern medical knowledge. A cardiologist is far more qualified to detect a subtle defect of the heart wall than I am. Conversely, as a neurologist, I'm far more qualified to diagnose a brain cyst. Specialization works, because it allows doctors to develop true expertise rather than just superficial knowledge.

It may take one, two, three, or more specialists to pin down the source of a patient's problems. (I've diagnosed patients who've seen literally dozens of primary care doctors *and* spe-cialists who missed their diagnoses.) These specialists may not be cheap, but again, how much is your child's health worth?

Know What Those Specialists Do

Most likely, your child will be referred to a number of spe-cialists during the diagnostic process. You can prepare more efficiently for your visits to these doctors if you have a basic understanding of what each specialist does. Here's a quick look at each medical specialty's area of expertise—and some cautions about these specialties' limitations.

Family Practitioner or General Practitioner (GP). A generalist qualified to diagnose common problems including lead toxicity, pinworms, and hearing or vision problems. This physician also may detect signs and symptoms necessitating a referral to a specialist. **Caution:** Do not expect your family practitioner to be capable of diagnosing all causes of hyperactivity. Many of the subtle or rare disorders that can cause behavior problems are out of the GP's area of expertise.

Pediatrician. Also a generalist, a family practitioner who specializes in caring for children. Like a family practitioner, a pediatrician is qualified to diagnose common hyperactivity-causing problems and to detect symptoms necessitating referral to a specialist. **Caution:** Again, do not expect this generalist to be capable of diagnosing subtle or unusual causes of hyperactivity.

Pediatric Neurologist. A physician who specializes in diagnosing and treating disorders affecting a child's brain and/or nervous system. A neurologist can diagnose or rule out disorders that stem directly from brain dysfunction or brain injury, such as infectious diseases of the nervous system, genetic brain disorders, and developmental disorders. **Caution:** Most neurology training includes a rotation in psychiatry, where neurologists are exposed to the concept of psychiatric labeling as a substitute for diagnosis. Many neurologists do not like to treat behavioral problems and either label patients ADHD or hand off hyperactive patients to a psychiatrist. Furthermore, most neurologists do only very cursory evaluations, and many do little in the way of biochemical studies.

Another physician, the *Neurosurgeon,* is trained to perform surgery on the brain or nervous system. This specialist may be called in *after* a child is diagnosed with a surgically treatable lesion.

Pediatric Cardiologist. Focuses on cardiac problems, particularly developmental cardiac abnormalities and childhood cardiac problems stemming from infection or genetic defects.

Allergist. Focuses on allergies and related disorders altering the function of the immune system. **Caution:** Few children have hyperactivity caused solely by allergies. Be sure other cause of hyperactivity are identified, rather than relying solely on allergy treatments.

Pulmonary or Respiratory Medicine Specialist. Focuses on disorders that can impair the functioning of the lungs and respiratory system. Among conditions this specialist may diagnose in hyper children are sleep apneas, calcium/potassium/sodium imbalances, asthma, and metabolic disorders affecting the respiratory system.

Infectious Disease Specialist. Diagnoses and treats bacterial, viral, fungal, or parasitic infections. This specialist can often spot rare or exotic afflictions, such as schistosomiasis or rickettsial diseases, that generalists fail to identify.

Hematologist. Focuses on blood disorders. Generally works in the laboratory and does not see most patients directly. Can diagnose iron-deficiency anemia, sickle-cell anemia, other forms of anemia, blood cancers, and other blood disorders.

Endocrinologist. Focuses on diseases and disorders of the endocrine glands. Among the hyperactivity-causing conditions these physicians may identify are thyroid disorders and diabetes (which, in its earliest stages, is often missed by generalists).

Geneticist. A physician who can evaluate your child for genetic disease. Some geneticists see patients in person, while others work solely in the laboratory. Sometimes patients are referred to dysmorphologists, who specialize in evaluating children for physical anomalies. A patient with an identified genetic disorder may also be referred to a genetic counselor, who need not be a physician.

Psychiatrist. A physician who specializes in treating behavioral disorders, or in offering therapy for life issues. **Caution:** Because many psychiatrists have very limited hands-on medical training, consider them as a last resort. Most psychiatrists only offer ADHD or ADD labels and drug treatments. Furthermore, these physicians receive only limited training in the effects of the drugs they prescribe. Also, most psychiatrists do only cursory physical evaluations—in fact, many do *no* physical evaluations at all—and most psychiatrists do little or nothing in the way of biochemical studies.

Neuropsychiatrist. A physician with training in both neurology and psychiatry. These physicians, unlike basic psychiatrists, have extensive training in diagnosing and treating medical disorders of the brain and nervous system. **Caution:** See warnings under pediatric neurologist and psychiatrist.

Nonphysicians

Chiropractor. The chiropractor is not an M.D. He or she receives two or three years of training in spinal manipulation and generally uses X rays to identify spinal misalignment. **Caution:** The chiropractor is not trained in differential diagnosis and is not qualified to diagnose the causes of hyperactivity.

Psychologist. The psychologist also is not an M.D. He or she receives training in conducting pen-and-paper tests such as IQ tests and neuropsychological evaluations. Some psychologists are experts in behavior modification techniques. **Caution:** Psychological evaluations are of some limited usefulness but are not a substitute for medical evaluation and diagnosis. Psychologists are *not* physicians and are *not* trained to diagnose the causes of hyperactivity. However, they *are* qualified to assist in developing behavioral programs after your child is diagnosed.

Be Sure You've Found All the Culprits

Many hyperactive children are suffering from a *combination* of medical problems—for instance, elevated lead levels *and* caffeinism. If your child improves a little bit after one medical condition is identified but still has significant behavioral problems, keep searching for other culprits. A colleague of mine once said, "If your child has three nails in his shoe, and you remove one, he'll still have a sore foot." Don't quit looking until you find *all* of the causes of your child's aberrant behavior.

When Your Child *Does* Receive a Diagnosis, Make Sure the Doctor Follows Up

If a doctor diagnoses a condition that's causing or contributing to your child's hyperactivity, get that condition treated *and* be sure your doctor follows up to ensure that the problem really has been solved. If your child's behavior stemmed from exposure to toxins, for instance, make sure the doctor orders a follow-up toxin screen to make sure all sources of the toxin have been eliminated.

If Your Doctor Gives Your Child a Drug, Ask Why

I've already talked at length about the dangers of masking children's symptoms with Ritalin or other psychoactive drugs. Don't accept these drugs from a physician who's merely attempting to cover up your child's behavioral problems without diagnosing them. Likewise, if your child has seizures, make sure these seizures have been correctly diagnosed—and not just labeled epilepsy—before you accept a prescription for anticonvulsants.

But what if a doctor, after a careful evaluation, recommends a heart medication, an antiparasitic drug, or perhaps a drug to remove toxins from your child's system? When medications are appropriate—that is, when they actually treat the root causes of hyperactivity—they can be vital to your child's medical treatment. But it's still important to ask a number of questions about any prescription.

- Why is this drug being prescribed?
- What side effects, including rare side effects, does this drug have?
- How long will my child need to take this medication?

Also, when you get a prescription filled, ask your pharmacist about any possible interactions with other drugs or foods. Find out, too, whether or not the drug should be taken with meals. And read the package inserts. (Ask for them, if your pharmacist doesn't supply them.) A medication that's taken incorrectly can fail to cure your child's existing problem and can lead to new physical or behavioral problems, so don't take any chances.

Become an Informed Consumer

The more you know about your child's condition, the better an advocate you can be. Once your child receives a diagnosis, learn more about that diagnosis and about current treatments. PubMed (the National Library of Medicine's free Internet database at http://www.ncbi.nlm.nih.gov/PubMed) and your local medical school libraries can be of enormous help. Also, buy a paperback medical dictionary, so you can look up any terms you don't understand in your child's medical reports. And pick up a good, up-to-date book on prescription and nonprescription drugs, so you can learn more about the effects and side effects of any drugs your child's doctor prescribes.

I HOPE I HAVEN'T DISCOURAGED YOU WITH THIS LONG LIST of advice and cautions. It's true that finding good medical care for your hyperactive child will probably be difficult, but it won't be impossible. Thousands of parents have won the battle, and their children are happy and healthy as a result.

Your most important weapon, in entering this battle, is the attitude that your child's health is priceless. Don't let managed care bureaucrats or antagonistic doctors prevent you from seeking a diagnosis. The goal is to find out what's wrong with your child and fix it, *not* to save money for your HMO, or to save time for your doctor. So stick by your guns and resist the pressure to give in to the Ritalin establishment.

That establishment, by the way, includes members *outside* the medical profession as well. In the next chapter, I look at another powerful group—the education establishment—that all too often pushes parents into Ritalin treatment.

CHAPTER 11

The School Connection

Parents are very vulnerable when a teacher says, "Here's something
you can give your kid that will make him function better."
Howard S. Adelman

REBECCA KELLY DIDN'T THINK HER SON NEEDED RITALIN.
But the teacher, she told the *Houston Chronicle*, was "most
definite with me that Max needed to be on Ritalin to manage
his behavior. She made me feel terrible—she told me I'm
keeping him from doing his best work."

The teacher continued to press, even though Max's doctor
said the nine-year-old boy was fine. Finally, Kelly moved Max
to another school for a year. He's now a straight-A student.

Kelly isn't alone in feeling pressured. Denise, whose elementary school child was doing poorly, resisted when the
boy's teacher recommended Ritalin. Later, she found that he
had a correctable reading problem. "If I had medicated him,"
she told the *Detroit News*, "we never would have fixed the
problem."

These stories are being repeated all over the country. A
survey of parents of hyperactive children ten years ago found
that about half had been pressured by school officials to put
their children on Ritalin,[1] and the pressure has increased
substantially since then. I'd estimate that at least two-thirds
of the hyperactive kids I see are on Ritalin largely because
their teachers, school counselors, or school psychologists recommended the drug, and their doctors took the teachers'

advice—often without conducting more than a superficial evaluation.

Let me stress here that not *all* schools, *all* teachers, *all* counselors, or *all* school psychologists are pushing Ritalin. I'm impressed by the thousands of dedicated teachers who recognize the difference between hyperactivity and boisterousness and are creative enough to channel the energy of normal little boys and girls into productive outlets. I'm pleased that many schools recognize and cultivate their students' individual personalities. And I'm delighted to have met a number of teachers who realize that the relatively few truly hyperactive children they see in their classrooms need real medical help and not just a pill. Several of my patients wound up getting the treatment they needed thanks to such teachers.

Unfortunately, however, many schools are completely caught up in the hyperactivity craze, and too many doctors are using schools' recommendations as a reason to prescribe Ritalin.

Jane: A Case of Ritalin Cover-up

Jane was only seven when I first saw her, but she looked like the weight of the world was on her shoulders. She'd been put on Ritalin in kindergarten, when the teacher complained about Jane's wild behavior and poor attention span. "She said Jane had a brain disorder and the drug could make her more normal," Jane's mother told me. After a brusque physical and a ten-minute questioning, a doctor agreed, saying, "We don't want her to fail this early in life"—a comment that made Jane's mother feel guilty enough to accept the Ritalin prescription despite her reservations.

The Ritalin made Jane less crazy, but it also caused her to be sad, to the point that a label-happy doctor would have called her depressed (and most likely would have added Prozac to her daily diet of drugs). But Jane's parents were wary of more drugs, and rightfully so. Thinking that Jane might have some sort of treatable brain disorder, they brought her to me.

While examining Jane, I asked about her symptoms. These included attacks of severe abdominal pains and nausea. In addition, Jane was hypersensitive to noises, sometimes screaming in fear when she heard sirens or fire alarms. She had night terrors and sometimes walked in her sleep. She alternated between violent tantrums and phases of sad listlessness.

Obviously, Jane wasn't just hyperactive—she was sick. But what was making her sick? My evaluation and the laboratory workups, EEG, and glucose tolerance test I ordered pointed not to one culprit, but to two.

Jane, it turned out, had hyperthyroidism, a condition that can cause a racing mind, physical hyperactivity, tremors, sweating, and rapid heart rate. Hyperthyroidism alone could explain most of her symptoms, but it wasn't her only problem. Her sadness, it turned out, was a toxic reaction to the Ritalin that her kindergarten teacher had said would make her normal. It didn't; it merely threw her into a state of despondency bordering on psychosis.

THERE ARE THOUSANDS AND THOUSANDS OF CHILDREN LIKE Jane out there, and thousands of their parents are being told by school officials to find a doctor who will prescribe Ritalin. Often that advice is friendly, but all too often it's not. In fact, it can be downright intimidating.

School officials are fond of saying that they don't force parents to put their kids on Ritalin but merely recommend evaluations. However, that's not what many parents say. The pressure some schools put on errant parents who refuse to accept the Ritalin party line is fierce: Parents report being "ganged up on," sometimes by five or six school officials at once. Many of these professionals seem to be taking the advice of physicians Edward Hallowell and John Ratey, both firm believers in the "diagnosis" of ADD, who recommend to teachers: "What do you do as a teacher if a parent disregards your suggestions that a child needs an evaluation for ADD? [We] have three solutions to this

predicament: persist, persist, and persist. The first no is usually
the parents' own denial borne out of guilt. The second no is usually an 'ouch.' The third no usually means, 'I want to say yes if
only you can show me how.' So persist. Get support. Don't give
up. And give yourself and the parents time. It takes most people
a while to change their minds."[2]

What Hallowell and Ratey consider persistence sounds more
like browbeating to me. Phrased somewhat differently, their advice is: The teacher is always right, the parent who questions an
ADD or hyperactivity label is always wrong, and parents must
be harassed until they give in and find a doctor who will "diagnose" ADD or ADHD.

Many schools, unfortunately, take this advice. G. Pascal Zachary notes in the *Wall Street Journal* that "it is typical for
schools to use a tag-team approach: teachers, counselors, administrators, maybe even psychologists, all gathered around a
parent to press a disability designation." Often parents are called
to meeting after meeting after meeting, and at each meeting they
are outnumbered by "experts" pushing them to seek an ADHD
or ADD label and a prescription. In such cases, moreover, school
officials don't hesitate to play the guilt card; one parent in Montreal, for instance, reported that a school psychologist suggested
that if her son wasn't put on Ritalin, "he could end up dropping
out of school, becoming a delinquent and possibly committing
suicide."[3]

Parents who fight this pressure are sometimes ostracized, and,
even worse, so are their children. Richard Vatz and Lee Weinberg recently commented, "Schools insist that no pupil ever is
penalized for failure to follow up on school recommendations
for ADD diagnosis and therapy [but] anecdotal evidence indi-
cates otherwise." According to Vatz and Weinberg, children of
parents who refuse to buy into a school's ADD/hyperactivity
label "are punished informally by teachers who treat them with
irritation and/or contempt, and their mothers and fathers are
considered as irresponsibly uncooperative."[4]

Some parents have the guts to fight this kind of pressure, but
many—probably most—eventually give into it. Their children's
doctors give in, too, saying that if a child is causing school of-

ficials that much trouble, "Ritalin couldn't hurt." As a result, thousands of American children are taking a potent and potentially dangerous drug that's been prescribed *based almost entirely on a teacher's opinion*.

Skeptical? Consider this typical incident, reported in the *Houston Chronicle*:

> *A parent in Conroe Independent School District . . . said she had to contact her school board to get a teacher to stop insisting she medicate her child. At the teacher's insistence, she had her 9-year-old son evaluated by a psychiatrist, who said he lacked social skills but did not have ADD. Nevertheless, the psychiatrist said, if the school thought it was important, he would recommend Ritalin to calm the child down. After the parents refused, the teacher tried to have the boy removed from her class and demanded the results of his psychological tests. In frustration, the parents called a school board member, who told the teacher to back off. The following year, their son had a new teacher and was on the honor roll.[5]*

Here's another example, this time from Florida, described in a December 1977 story in *Good Housekeeping*:

> *[After several meetings], the school psychologist was brought in. "She said, 'Well, he doesn't meet all the criteria for ADD—attention deficit disorder,' Sue recalls, " 'but if he did, we could get him help with Ritalin.' Then they gave me a bunch of pamphlets—all pro-Ritalin.*
>
> *". . . They gave me their report to take to a pediatrician they suggested," Sue says. "We were with him ten to fifteen minutes. He didn't even look at the evaluation. He never talked to Chris. He just prescribed Ritalin and said, 'This is the best thing for him.' "*
>
> *. . . Sue and Tony took Chris off Ritalin when he was in the middle of second grade. "The school told us we were making a mistake," she remembers. Chris repeated second grade in mainstream classes. "And he was on the honor roll the whole year."[6]*

Think about these two families' stories. And think about the case of Jane, whose kindergarten teacher labeled her as hyperactive when she actually had hyperthyroidism.

Now ask yourself this: Would you let your child's teacher decide if your child needed heart medication or chemotherapy? Would you take a teacher's word if he or she recommended surgery for your child? If your child developed a shooting abdominal pain, would you expect a teacher to tell you whether it was appendicitis or a tumor? And, furthermore, if a teacher said your child had appendicitis, a tumor, leprosy, pneumonia, or heart disease, would you expect your doctor simply to take the teacher's word for it?

Of course not. Yet thousands of parents are being told by their children's teachers that these children have brain disorders and need to take psychoactive drugs. All too often, the parents are buying these "diagnoses" without question—and, more frighteningly, so are the children's doctors. It's a bizarre and incredibly dangerous situation.

It's Not the Teacher's Fault

I don't believe that *any* teacher recommends Ritalin for selfish reasons, or out of laziness. Like parents, teachers want the best for their students. They recommend Ritalin because they truly believe it's the right thing to do. In fact, it's often the most dedicated and concerned teachers who are the most fervent champions of the ADD and ADHD labels and Ritalin treatment.

The question is: *Why* do so many dedicated, committed, and caring teachers honestly believe that Ritalin is what's best for the children in their classes? In my opinion, teachers are as much victims of Ritalin hype as are hyperactive children and their parents. Here are some of the reasons teachers become convinced that up to 10 percent of their students are sick and need drugs.

Teachers Are Often Influenced by Information From Sources Who May Be Biased

If you doubt this, consider a 1994 educational video made with your tax dollars. This video was intended to be a tool to teach teachers and parents how to help children labeled as having hyperactivity and attention deficit disorder. The video featured members of CHADD, the leading group for children labeled hyperactive or attention disordered.

What the Department of Education didn't know, when it shelled out thousands of dollars to make this teaching tool for teachers and parents, is that a large part of CHADD's funding came directly from Ciba-Geigy, the manufacturer of Ritalin. By 1995, the drug manufacturer had donated more than $800,000 to the group, a fact CHADD kept fairly quiet until a PBS documentary[7] revealed the CHADD/Ciba-Geigy connection. "There's no mention of Ciba-Geigy in CHADD's introductory brochure, educators' manual, fact sheets, or annual reports," John Merrow, who produced the PBS show, reported. "These widely distributed materials describe CHADD as a grass-roots, parent-based organization."

The PBS exposé charged that since 1988, Ciba-Geigy (now Novartis) "has quietly propped up the national ADD 'support group' CHADD with more than $1 million in grants and valuable services." As a result, PBS concluded, "CHADD has been distributing misleading information to hundreds of thousands of parents and teachers that exaggerates the benefits of drug therapy, including Ritalin."

The educational video project came to a sudden halt when the Department of Education learned about CHADD's pharmaceutical company ties. The revelation led department officials to take a hard look at the video's contents—and when they did, some didn't like what they saw. As one official put it, "Some people watching the video could get the impression that medication alone was the best treatment, and we are saying there are many treatments for ADD."[8] (A writer for *The Education Reporter* put it more forcefully, after watching this video and another featuring CHADD members: "Parts of the videos sound like an infomercial for Ritalin."⁹)

Although the Education Department scrapped the video, CHADD's literature remains in wide use in schools. A look at this literature is enlightening. For instance, in "Treating a Child With Attention Deficit Disorder," CHADD mentions only one medical approach to treating ADD, which is—no surprise—stimulant drugs. In a section of this handout that discusses these drugs, only three of their mildest side effects (reduced appetite, weight loss, and sleep problems) are mentioned. There is not a word about Ritalin's potential addictiveness. And there's no mention of psychotic reactions, or Tourette's syndrome, or lowered seizure thresholds, or cardiac arrhythmia, blood pressure changes, angina, or abdominal pain. In fact, none of the most serious Ritalin side effects listed in the *Physician's Desk Reference* (which publishes information provided by Ritalin's own manufacturer) are mentioned. No wonder teachers reading this material get the impression that Ritalin treatment is harmless!

For its part, CHADD continues to assert that it is a grassroots organization and that it was never influenced by the hundreds of thousands of dollars it received from Ritalin's manufacturer. But as psychiatrist Peter Breggin told Merrow, "Money influences people. When people are being supported by some kind of institution, they tend to believe in it, they tend to be aligned with it, because if they don't they lose the support they need for their programs."

Incidentally, CHADD's other pet project is an effort to have Ritalin reclassified as a Schedule III drug, meaning that the manufacturer will be able to produce unlimited amounts of the drug. (Currently, because the drug is a Schedule II substance, the Drug Enforcement Administration sets limits on its production.) According to the Merrow Report, CHADD has hired a Washington, D.C., law firm to lobby the DEA to change Ritalin's classification.

CHADD, however, isn't the only group whose influence on the schools is questionable. Another financial conflict of interest results when schools contract with mental health centers staffed by psychiatrists who are big on Ritalin therapy.

Chappell Dew, a member of the Board of Education in a South Carolina county, told *Good Housekeeping*, "For the last three years, we contracted with a local mental health center to provide psychological services in the schools. The center's psychologists come into a school and conduct a forty-minute workshop . . . and all of a sudden the teachers are empowered to refer kids to doctors who prescribe Ritalin." Dew's conclusion: "I think it's just business. It's motivated by money."[10]

Pediatric neurologist Fred Baughman, Jr., agrees, saying, "Child psychiatry urges its members to establish service contracts with schools. For-profit psychiatric hospitals place personnel in schools, targeting children by providing free assessments—a sham and prelude to drugging. . . . Not only do they invent diseases, they invent entire epidemics."[11]

Teachers Are Influenced by the Media

Like the rest of us, teachers get much of their medical information from TV and magazines—and in recent years the media have treated hyperactivity as a legitimate epidemic and Ritalin as its only cure. As reporter John Lang commented recently, hyperactivity "is like halitosis in the 1960s, impotence in the '70s, and herpes in the '80s. Everybody seems to have it or to be afraid they do."[12] Teachers, like the rest of us, have been deluged with hundreds of popular magazine articles and TV shows promoting hyperactivity and ADD as the explanations for virtually every childhood or adult behavior problem.

Only recently have major magazines begun reporting that the epidemic we're experiencing is not of hyperactivity but of unnecessary labeling and drugging. I'm glad to see that the pendulum is finally swinging, but it will take years to undo the media hyperactivity hype of the past decade—and for teachers, the time lag may be longer. That's because in education, media fads quickly translate into seminars, conferences, and workshops. Virtually every teacher in America has, by now, attended a conference on how to identify ADHD and ADD, and how to encourage parents to consider Ritalin treatment.

Teachers Often Fall for the
Self-Fulfilling Prophecy

If you've taken a psychology class, you know how self-fulfilling prophecies work. Tell a teacher that Janie is brilliant and that Suzie is slow, and the teacher will treat the two children differently even if they're really equally smart. In the long run, Janie usually *will* outperform Suzie—not because the children are different, but because the teacher expects them to be. Thus, the teacher's prediction comes true, even though that prediction was based on false information.

A similar phenomenon often occurs with Ritalin. Gail Furman likes to demonstrate this by telling a teacher that a child has started taking Ritalin, when in fact the child isn't taking the drug. "And, lo and behold," she says, "the child remarkably [gets] better. I've done it several times, and it's never failed. Which is really a sad commentary."[13]

What does this mean? It means that teachers *think* kids do better on Ritalin even when they don't. And, in many cases, it means that the teacher could have caused the same behavioral improvement simply by treating the hyperactive child differently. But the teacher, not realizing this, believes that Ritalin made the difference, and thus is likely to keep recommending Ritalin.

Incidentally, teachers aren't the only ones who fall for a placebo effect when it comes to Ritalin. Carol Whalen and colleagues told fifteen boys that they were taking either stimulants or a placebo and then asked them to evaluate their performance. The researchers found that "the boys predicted better performance when told they were on medication versus placebo," and that "boys actually taking placebo [rated] themselves more positively when told they had taken medication versus placebo."[14] In a related study, Esther Sleator identified children who responded positively to Ritalin and later gave these children pills that, unbeknownst to the subjects, contained no active ingredients. Of the twenty-eight children taking placebos instead of Ritalin, eleven continued to behave just as well as they had on the drug.[15] (Perhaps doctors thinking about prescribing Ritalin should prescribe placebos instead, without telling either the children *or* their teachers!)

Simplistic Checklists Give Teachers, School Psychologists, and School Nurses the False Sense That They Can Diagnose Hyperactivity

As I've explained, hyperactivity and attention deficit disorder are identified by physicians using checklists from the *Diagnostic and Statistical Manual of Mental Disorders*, published by the American Psychiatric Association. Check off a sufficient number of symptoms—fidgets, talks too much, answers questions out of turn—and, presto, you have a diagnosis.

It's not surprising that laypeople assume that this job can be done by *anyone*. After all, a teacher is as good at diagnosing fidgeting as a doctor. A school nurse can diagnose running about excessively as easily as someone with years of medical school training. And a school psychologist is as qualified as a doctor to diagnose a child as too talkative. So teachers and psychologists and school nurses, who wouldn't dream of trying to diagnose heart conditions or thyroid disorders, are now attempting to diagnose brain disorders using handy checklists.

Teachers who find themselves doing this should ask themselves: "Am I qualified to diagnose brain dysfunction? Can I tell the difference between hyperactivity caused by a brain cyst and hyperactivity caused by pesticide toxicity? Can I differentiate between attention deficits caused by anemia and attention deficits stemming from seizures? Do I have the medical training necessary to tell the difference between conduct problems stemming from fetal alcohol syndrome and misbehavior caused by a reaction to asthma medications?" The answer, obviously, is no.

Actually, one study shows that teachers who label children hyperactive can miss even the most simple reasons for misbehavior. Nancy J. Cohen and Klaus Minde asked kindergarten teachers in one community to list the names of students the teachers believed suffered from hyperactivity. The teachers identified sixty-three children as hyperactive, but the researchers discovered that two-thirds of these children suffered from easily identified problems ranging from poor nutrition to lack of sleep.[16]

Young Teachers See Hyperactivity and ADD Everywhere

The teachers most likely to be labeling many of their students ADD or ADHD are young teachers who are new to the class-room. One reason, I suspect, is that these teachers are fresh from college psychology courses where hyperactivity is hyped as a medical epidemic, and budding teachers are told to be on the lookout for it. However, there's another good reason why young teachers see hyperactivity everywhere—even where it doesn't exist.

Older, seasoned teachers have met all types of children: shy wallflowers, class clowns, counterculture types, cheerleaders, sports nuts, geeks, lazy kids, energetic kids, talkers, silent types, cheerful kids, whiners, and all the rest. What do they learn from this? They learn that it takes all kinds. In other words, they know that there's plenty of range in normal childhood behavior, and that virtually all of these children, even the ones who are bouncing off the walls in second grade, will probably grow up to be well-adjusted adults. In addition, older teachers usually have raised a few of their own children, and they know that youngsters—and especially little boys—are naturally a little nuts.

Younger teachers, on the other hand, frequently haven't met that many real, live children. Instead, they've read about the symptoms of hyperactivity—symptoms that are actually common, normal behaviors in many children, particularly in the early grades. A second-grade teacher who's unfamiliar with little boys, and who's been told by the psychiatrists who wrote DSM that fidgeting, talking out of turn, running, climbing, and blurting out answers may be pathological signs of illness, is likely to think *every* little boy is sick. I'll bet that if someone did a study comparing twenty-three-year-old teachers and forty-three-year-old teachers, they'd find that the former label ten times as many kids hyperactive as do the older, more experienced teachers.

Sometimes Children Are Scapegoats for Problems with the System

Another reason that teachers think so many of today's students are hyperactive has nothing to do with the students themselves. With classrooms averaging thirty or more students, and the teacher-to-student ratio growing worse, even a few rowdy or troublesome students can bring the educational process to a standstill. Generally, a child labeled hyperactive is moved to a special education class, or provided with a special aide or extra services, or tamed by a daily dose of Ritalin. Thus, the problem is solved—not because the child has really changed, but rather because an overstressed teacher in an overcrowded classroom has gotten a little relief. In short, teachers often mistake the failures of the system for failures of the children trapped in it.

This can be particularly true in the case of younger children, who are accustomed to one-on-one care and often react badly to crowded classrooms run by stressed teachers. Such children may react to a less than optimal setting with behavior that appears hyper and crazy. The solution, of course, is to change the classroom rather than drugging the child. Cornell professor Lorraine Maxwell notes, for instance, that preschool children placed in smaller groups "exhibited higher cooperation and compliance, more reflection and innovation, more verbal initiative, less aimless wandering, less hostility, and fewer squabbles than the children in the larger groups."[17]

Children Mature at Different Ages

Some children may simply be too young for school. Not every child magically becomes school-ready at five or preschool-ready at three or four. In the past, schools often recommended to parents, "Keep him home till next year, and he'll be ready."

Nowadays, of course, families with one parent or with two working parents don't have that option, and a large percentage of American children enter preschool at four or even three years of age. Frankly, that's just too early for some perfectly normal toddlers, particularly some boys (who tend to develop at a slower rate than girls). These children don't have brain disorders. These children don't need to be drugged. They just need to grow up a little.

Unfortunately, far too many of these children are labeled hyperactive or attention disordered, because their behavior fits DSM criteria. This is ludicrous, because DSM criteria for hyperactivity or attention disorders are so close to the expected normal behavior of toddler-age boys as to be almost indistinguishable. Toddlers, for instance, are supposed to fidget, climb, run, be easily distracted, lose things, blurt out things, have trouble taking turns, interrupt other people, and butt into games. Yet all of these, according to the DSM, may be signs of illness.

It's true that the DSM specifies that for ADHD or ADD these behaviors should be inconsistent with developmental level, but too few teachers—and too few doctors, for that matter—realize just how wide the range of normality is at that age. A teacher with twenty preschoolers may believe that the most hyper two or three children are abnormal, *simply because they're so much more active than the best-behaved children*. In fact, however, the hyper four-year-olds are as likely to be perfectly normal as the least active students.

When teachers recommend these highly active children for evaluation, many of them wind up on Ritalin—*even though Ritalin is not approved for use in children under the age of six*. Thousands of prescriptions for Ritalin and other stimulants are being written for children five years of age or younger. That's extremely troubling when you consider that the brains of very young children are still plastic and developing, and that drugs often alter brain structure and functions in ways that aren't detectable for years or even decades.

Sometimes Parents Are to Blame

I've been very critical in this chapter of school officials who are overzealous about pushing hyperactivity and ADD labels and Ritalin, even when parents resist. But it's only fair to point out that sometimes the positions are reversed. There are, indeed, times when schools find themselves fighting parents determined to have their children classified as handicapped by hyperactivity or attention deficit disorder.

Why? Because a hyperactivity label can open the door to a plethora of special services. For poor families, the label can mean money: low-income parents can qualify for Supplemental Social Security Income benefits—up to $484 monthly—if their children are labeled as having hyperactivity or attention deficit disorder.[18] And for wealthy students competing to get into prestigious colleges, a hyperactivity label can provide an added edge. That's because, under the Americans with Disabilities Act, students labeled as having ADHD or ADD can take untimed SAT tests, and, if they go to law school, untimed bar exams. The label works for aspiring doctors, too: They can get extra time to take medical school exams. (Of course, this won't translate into real life: When a patient is dying in the emergency room, a doctor isn't going to get an extra two hours to save the patient's life.)

"I can't tell you how many letters I've received from parents asking that their children be classified with a learning disability," one high school guidance counselor told *Forbes* reporter Dyan Machan. Machan notes, "One wealthy New York City mother boasts that her son's ADD diagnosis added 100 points to his combined verbal and mathematical SAT score."[19]

The news that an ADD or ADHD label can boost SAT scores is getting around. In the 1991–92 testing year, 18,000 students labeled as learning disabled received "special administration" SATs. By the 1996–97 testing year, 40,000 students requested this special treatment. The labeling of many normal children as handicapped, in order to give them an advantage over other students, sometimes reaches the point of the ridiculous. In *The New Republic*, Ruth Shalit cites the case of Michael F., a student making A's in honors classes and testing in the ninety-ninth percentile academically. Despite Michael F.'s outstanding performance—"he had also written a book," Shalit notes, "[and] played in the school band"—his family was dissatisfied with his special accommodations. Labeled as ADD, learning disabled, and having neuro-motor dysfunction and tactile sensitivity,

Michael F. had already received more than three hours a week of special tutoring, extra time to complete homework and tests, stretch breaks in class, permission to chew gum to aid his concentration, seat assignments close to his teachers, and access to tapes and transcripts of lectures. When Michael F. did poorly on one honors midterm geometry test, however, his parents wanted him labeled with a new math disability that would allow him to obtain summer math tutoring. The case, Shalit says, is an example of parents seeking disability labels because they "are unwilling to believe their progeny is less than perfect."[20]

Fortunately, parents who attempt to have their children labeled as ADHD or ADD in order to gain money or an academic advantage are in the minority. Far more troubling is the number of college students looking for a hyperactivity label and a prescription for Ritalin. Their numbers are increasing, because Ritalin can give any student—hyperactive or not—an artificial boost, like caffeine or the uppers an earlier generation of college kids took to get through finals. And more than a few athletes are using Ritalin as a legal way to boost their performance on the field or in the gym. (Amazingly, in a country where racehorse doping is a big scandal, the use of Ritalin to give *human* athletes an edge is little discussed—although the Olympic Committee is aware of the issue and does not allow its athletes to use the drug during competition.)

What Should Teachers Be Doing?

So far I've focused on what teachers, counselors, and school psychologists *shouldn't* be doing. In my opinion, that includes browbeating parents into agreeing that their children are hyperactive or ADD, or telling parents that stimulants are the key to school success. And it certainly includes taking an adversarial position against parents brave enough to buck the Ritalin-promoting establishment.

But, as I said at the beginning of this chapter, thousands of teachers are providing *real* help to children with behavior problems and their families. Here's what they're doing:

- Identifying bright children and providing extra classroom stimulation for them, rather than expecting these children simply to sit still and be quiet no matter how bored they are.
- Having gifted children tested and put in programs that can nurture their talents rather than squelch them.
- Attending workshops and training programs on behavior modification. Many quite simple behavior modification techniques can make a huge difference in the behavior of *both* normal and overactive children (see Chapter 3). In fact, behavior modification is the most powerful nonmedical treatment for hyperactivity and other childhood behavior problems.
- Incorporating movement or even exercise into classroom routines, to help active children let off steam.
- Contacting parents when behavior problems occur, to identify any personal problems—divorce, a new baby in the family, a family member's illness—that might be affecting a student's emotions and behavior.

All of these techniques will help teachers deal with normal or mildly hyper students. Some of them—behavior modification, for instance—will often cure behavior problems caused primarily by a lack of discipline or motivation.

Even more remarkable things can happen when entire schools, and not just individual teachers, begin focusing on alternatives to simply labeling disruptive children hyperactive or conduct disordered. A good example is North Lincoln Elementary School in Alliance, Ohio, which has drastically reduced both behavior-disordered and normal students' behavior problems, *and* improved their academic performance, using a few simple behavior modification techniques.

Sheila Billheimer, principal of North Lincoln, implemented a schoolwide behavior modification program after the 1993–94 school year, when she handled 1,081 office referrals for major behavior problems, suspended 73 students, and had to contend with 6 assaults involving students. "My teachers were fed up," Billheimer told *Morning Journal* reporter John Campanelli. "We knew we had to do something."

Billheimer called on William Pelham, an expert on behavior modification techniques for both hyperactive and nondisabled children. Pelham set up six simple rules for students to follow: be respectful, stay in your assigned seat, raise your hand to speak, work quietly, use materials correctly, and obey adults. Then, to get the students' attention, he implemented a system of rewards and consequences. Children begin each day with 200 points (or, for younger students, 10 chips). If they break a rule, they lose 20 points. If they do their homework consistently, they get 50 bonus points. Students who end the day with 260 or more points get special privileges, including the right to chew gum and to sit with friends in class. Additionally, students with enough points at the end of each week are invited to a special Friday activity. Those who break too many rules, on the other hand, wind up in the "task room," which Billheimer says is "worse than regular school work."

Parents also have to perform. They must review daily homework assignment sheets, or their children lose points. And children with behavior problems, including hyperactive behavior, get daily report cards.

The results of the program, Billheimer told the *Morning Journal*, are nothing short of astonishing. The year the program was implemented, only 11 students were suspended, and only 120 students were sent to the principal's office. There were no assaults, and 85 percent of homework got done (up from less than 50 percent before the program started).

"It's great," one teacher said. "There's been a big change, especially in problem children who need structure." Amy Palmer, a psychology student who helps monitor the program, says that it "seems to really be helping marginal kids—kids that may have fallen apart as the year progressed." Undoubtedly it's cutting down on drug prescriptions, too.

How Teachers Can Help the Real Victims of Hyperactivity

The North Lincoln Elementary School program is working miracles with normal children and with borderline children at high risk of being labeled hyperactive and being drugged. But what about children who truly are troubled? Every teacher encounters a few children who are wild enough to endanger themselves or others, or who are failing classes and falling farther and farther behind due to attention problems. A behavior modification program may help these children a great deal, but it won't address their underlying problems.

Here again, however, a teacher can be of great help to both parents and physicians. How? By being a good observer and documenting not just behavioral problems but also any physical symptoms that troubled children exhibit.

Here's a good example. One special education teacher, noting that a little girl in her class was behaving more erratically than usual, kept a close eye on her. That afternoon, she sent a note home to the girl's mother, saying, "I think Laura might need to see her doctor. After lunch, I noticed that she was staring into space, and her hand was twitching a little. I could be wrong, but she might be having petit mal seizures." Indeed, Laura *was* having seizures. The seizures were so subtle that her parents hadn't noticed them—and they could have been overlooked for months or even years, if the alert teacher hadn't reported her concerns.

It's not often that a teacher spots a symptom that dramatic. But often, teachers—because they see children in a different setting and doing different activities—notice physical or behavioral problems that parents might miss. Among the trouble signs that teachers are likely to spot:

- Does a child have more difficulty with class work, or exhibit more behavior problems, either shortly before or after meals?
- Does a child have trouble keeping up physically with other

children on the playground? Is he or she easily tired or winded?

- Does a child have periods where he or she spaces out? If so, is the child oblivious to others at these times? Does he or she look blue or gray, twitch, or exhibit any peculiar mannerisms during these periods?
- Does the child appear to have any hearing or vision problems?
- Does he or she appear to have an unusual number of headaches or stomachaches at school?
- Does the child become irritable and cranky after going several hours without eating?
- Is he or she a frequent victim of bullies, because of frailty or slowness?
- Does the child have *specific* problems with schoolwork—difficulty with penmanship, math, spelling, etc.?
- Does the child tend to fall asleep in class?
- Does the child take far more bathroom breaks than is normal?
- Is he or she thirsty more often than other students?
- Is the child a nail-biter? Does the child ever eat paste, crayons, or other nonfood items in class?
- Does the child have more episodes of wetting or soiling than is appropriate for his or her age?
- Does the child seem to be ill, sniffly, or under the weather more than other children his or her age?

Children who truly are pathologically hyperactive are sick, and observant teachers often spot subtle symptoms of illness. The clues teachers can provide, particularly when combined with the clues that parents spot, can be powerful diagnostic leads.

In short, teachers can make a huge difference in the lives of hyperactive students—for better or for worse. They can change these children's lives by pressuring their parents into putting them on potentially dangerous drugs that don't solve their real problems. Or they can change their lives for the better, by helping the truly sick children get proper medical care—and protecting the rest from unnecessary labels and drugs.

Afterword:
The Expanding Epidemic of Hyperactivity and ADD—and How You Can Fight It

Things usually get worse before they get better.
Old folk adage

I HOPE THIS BOOK HAS GIVEN YOU THE TOOLS AND THE courage you need to take on the medical and educational establishments and obtain a real diagnosis for your child. If you persevere, you'll succeed in the end—but you're probably in for a struggle. You'll need to be strong, and you'll need to be assertive. In fact, you'll probably even need to be "difficult." At the moment, America's doctors and many of its school administrators are firmly in the grip of hyperactivity hysteria, and talking sense into them isn't easy.

I want you to be realistic about this *before* you begin your search for a real diagnosis for your child. That way you can prepare yourself. And you'll need to be prepared, because when you question teachers and doctors, you're likely to be labeled as a bad parent, or at best as foolish or misguided. Most likely, you're going to encounter as much opposition as help from the medical and educational establishments. And that situation, unfortunately, isn't likely to change any time soon.

In fact, if I weren't an optimist, I'd be discouraged about

the odds of *ever* talking sense into the professionals who have bought into the ADHD/ADD myth. At the moment, there's no end in sight to America's hyperactivity epidemic and our love affair with Ritalin. Indeed, things are getting worse instead of better.

Why? Because right now we're actually *expanding* our use of the hyperactivity and ADD labels. Doctors, it seems, weren't content to give millions of America's young children these labels and drug them with Ritalin. Now they're doing it to adults as well.

If you're reading this book, it's because you're worried about your *child* being labeled as hyperactive or ADD and put on Ritalin. But as a parent of a behavior-disordered child, you also need to worry about the new phenomenon of adult ADD—because you're a target.

The Newest Fad: Adult ADD

Twenty years ago, everyone had hypoglycemia. Ten years ago, everyone had depression. Now adult ADD, the fad disease of the '90s, is sweeping America. Every month, doctors are labeling thousands of adults "ADD disabled" and putting them on Ritalin, Prozac, or similar drugs. While parents of children labeled hyperactive or ADD are particularly vulnerable (as I'll explain in a bit), any adult is at risk of receiving this dangerous pseudodiagnosis.

Like their younger counterparts, a number of the adults labeled as having ADD truly are ill. They're suffering from diseases and disorders that cause anxiety, memory problems, fatigue, restlessness, insomnia, mental fogginess, and other symptoms. They're going to their physicians seeking medical help for these disorders—but, like hyperactive children, the only help they're getting is a label and a drug to cover up their symptoms. These cases are particularly disturbing because adults' mental symptoms are far more likely than children' symptoms to have *serious* causes such as cancer or dementias, so getting a label instead of a diagnosis can be even more dangerous in adulthood than in childhood. Doctors who hand out hyperactivity and ADD labels to adults are, in many cases, endangering these patients' lives.

Here's a case in point. Several years ago, I saw a woman who was, according to current criteria, suffering from a bad case of ADD. She was rude and sometimes vicious to her husband. She neglected the housework. She couldn't keep a job. She drank too much. She had insomnia and suffered from anxiety attacks. All of these symptoms, according to various self-help books, can be symptoms of adult ADD. But they weren't; they were symptoms of a parathyroid tumor, which left untreated eventually would have caused outright psychosis and serious physical illness.

Patients like this woman have real diseases and need real diagnoses and treatments. By feeding them drugs and giving them faddish labels instead of diagnosing them, physicians are condemning these patients to a continuing struggle with disorders ranging from thyroid problems and menopausal hormone imbalances to genetic diseases and toxin-induced brain dysfunction.

It's important for you to know this, because if you have any attentional problems or other behavioral symptoms, a DSM-oriented doctor may tell you that both you and your child have ADD and recommend Ritalin for both of you. In fact, I've heard of whole families being put on Ritalin, because physicians are convinced these days that attention deficit disorder and hyperactivity run in families. This is, indeed, the new slogan of the hyperactivity establishment: "Hyperactivity and ADD are genetic disorders."

As mentioned earlier, this is a serious semantic and logical error. If both you and your child have problems with hyperactivity or attention deficits, these problems indeed may be genetically influenced—*because hundreds of different genetic diseases can cause these symptoms*. Or you may not have a genetic problem at all. It's possible that both of you are suffering from transmissible diseases such as parasitic infections. Or you may both be suffering from a common toxic exposure. (I've treated several families in which not only the children but also the parents had toxic levels of lead.) It's possible that you're both living in a house that's leaking carbon monoxide, or a home that was treated years ago with the termite-killing chemical chlordane, a chemical that lingers for years and causes attention deficits. The list of disorders that may be affecting both you and your child is a long one, and Ritalin won't cure *anything* on that list.

It's also possible (in fact, it's quite likely) that you're suffering from symptoms brought on by the stress of dealing with a behavior-disordered child. Living in a perpetual crisis situation can wreak havoc on your emotional and physical health, leading to sleeplessness, anxiety, tension, and poor concentration at work. If your symptoms stem from stress and exhaustion, the only solution is to find a real diagnosis and real treatment for your child—not to drug both of you.

Conversely, you may be one of the millions of adults who have no symptoms at all and who are being labeled as having ADD merely because doctors, like patients, fall for fads. And right now, ADD is just about the biggest fad in behavioral medicine.

One of the best ways to tell a fad disease from a real disease is by its symptoms, and the list of woes blamed on adult ADD is revealing. If you think the list of symptoms attributed to child-hood hyperactivity and ADD is vague, broad, and unscientific, take a look at this collection of symptoms of adult ADD, culled from several best-selling books.

- "I haven't lived up to my potential."
- "I get bored on the job."
- "I act immaturely."
- "Sometimes I'm insensitive to my wife."
- "I'm hotheaded."
- "I'm promiscuous."
- "I have a tendency to say embarrassing things."
- "I'm not good at small talk."
- "I have trouble balancing my checkbook."
- "I only seem to fall in love with married men."
- "I'm irresponsible."
- "I'm disorganized."
- "I don't get my work done on time."
- "I have low self-esteem."

- "I pick fights with my husband."
- "I 'act out' sexually."
- "I have trouble making commitments."
- "I'm addicted to shopping."
- "I can't make decisions."
- "I'm a slob."
- "I'm rude."
- "I'm overwhelmed by my responsibilities."
- "I'm absent-minded."
- "I'm shy."
- "I make impulsive purchases I later regret."
- "I can't find things in my purse."
- "I spend much of my time looking for things I've lost."
- "I tend to make too many commitments."

These are not symptoms of a disease. Some, such as shyness, absent-mindedness, and slobbiness, are simply personality traits. (And do we really want to get into the dangerous business of medicating away normal traits?) Others are almost universal complaints—for instance, feeling bored at work or having trouble balancing a checkbook. Some of these alleged symptoms, such as adultery, are shameful behaviors that we shouldn't excuse as evidence of illness. And many other problems on this list— for instance, taking on too many commitments and feeling overwhelmed by responsibilities—are in fact symptoms of modern life, rather than symptoms of disease. Millions of adults are being labeled as ADD when they're actually suffering from problems stemming from the pressures of overwork, children's and spouse's demands, and a stressful lifestyle.

Not surprisingly, many of the people in this last group are women—and if you're the mother of a demanding, overactive child, you're probably one of them. As a test, I asked a female associate of mine to read a new book on female ADD and to tell me how many of her friends met the criteria described in the book. Her reply: "All of them—and I do, too." Most of her friends, especially those with jobs and children, feel overwhelmed trying to juggle work and family. Many find it impossible to finish everything they're supposed to accomplish. Many of them have trouble coping with difficult children. Most find it necessary to make long lists and still forget to pick up bread at the store or make cupcakes for the PTA. Many live in messy houses scattered with unread newspapers, half-read books, and unanswered letters. All of these, according to the books, are symptoms of adult ADD.

But is this really adult ADD? No. It's not a disorder at all. It's merely a symptom of real life. Women (or men) trying to work full-time, raise children, and run a household all at the same time are usually overworked. They cut down on sleep, eat meals on the run, and are always doing three things at once. Thus, they're often tired and spacey, they frequently take on more jobs than they can handle, and they have no time for housework. This isn't a medical problem; it's a lifestyle problem.

IN SHORT, THE PROBLEMS THAT DOCTORS LABEL ADULT ADD can be more correctly divided into several groups: medical disorders, lifestyle problems, or (in the case of promiscuity or overspending) plain bad behavior. None of these is a good reason for prescribing Ritalin or Prozac. Clearly, the adult ADD fad is as big a fraud as the childhood hyperactivity fad.

Of course, that won't stop doctors from labeling and drugging millions of adults, any more than it has stopped them from labeling and drugging two million children. It seems, sometimes, as though many doctors won't be satisfied until *everyone* is taking Ritalin or other psychiatric drugs. Medical journals, in fact, seem to be taking the tack that both childhood hyperactivity and adult ADD are *underdiagnosed*, and are telling doctors not to be hesitant in identifying and medicating these conditions.

I'm worried about the new fad of adult ADD, which is why I've discussed it at length. As the parent of a hyperactive or attention-disordered child, you need to know about this dangerous fad so you don't fall for it. But I'm far more worried about the epidemic of drugging and labeling children. That's because adults have the power and authority to take their medical care into their own hands—and if they say yes to a label of adult ADD and a prescription for Ritalin, it's as much their fault as their doctors'. Children, on the other hand, can't stand up for themselves. Unlike an adult, a child is virtually helpless when doctors, teachers, and parents gang up and say, "You need to take this drug."

Moreover, I worry more about children because they're likely to be put on Ritalin not just for a few years but for a lifetime. As I pointed out earlier, we don't know what the long-term effects of this drug will be—because *no one has ever thoroughly studied them.* There's evidence, as I discussed in Chapter 6, that Ritalin constricts blood vessels in the brain, just as amphetamines do. In the case of amphetamines, this constriction can eventually lead to cortical atrophy ("amphetamine brain") and to early dementia. Will Ritalin have a similar effect on some children? Will it lead, years down the line, to presenile dementia in forty-year-olds or fifty-year-olds? Is the brain underdevelopment being seen in MRI scans of Ritalin-treated hyperactive children a symptom of disease, or the result of drugging with Ritalin? I don't know. Neither do researchers—although they're promising answers "in a few years." What I *do* know is that giving this amphetamine-like drug to small children, and continuing to administer it for decades—when we have no clue about what it may be doing to their brains—is taking a terrible risk.

There's still another reason why I worry more about children being labeled and drugged than about adults in the same situation. Adult ADD is a fad that's likely to blow over, just like dozens of other medical crazes. In the past few years alone, we've seen adults' problems blamed on repressed memories, multiple personalities, subclinical depression, and codependency. These fads are passing, and so will adult ADD. But the treatment of *children* with Ritalin, which has become a burgeoning business that benefits drug companies, cost-cutting doctors, and overcrowded schools, is likely to be around for a long time. None of these groups has any interest in stopping this ever-expanding pseudo-epidemic, and several—drug companies and managed-care programs in particular—have a significant financial interest in promoting it.

However, as I said at the beginning of this chapter, I'm an optimist. I don't think the next generation of children will be subjected to wholesale drugging with Ritalin, Prozac, or other powerful medications. I don't think two million of them will be labeled hyperactive when many are actually ill and the rest are perfectly normal. I think the hyperactivity epidemic will eventually be stopped, and I know who will stop it. You will.

Patient Power

Ritalin-oriented doctors are a powerful group, and they have the full weight of the medical establishment behind them. School administrators are powerful, too, and they know how to intimidate parents. But parents, too, are powerful. Parents are the ones who actually fill the prescriptions for Ritalin. Parents are the ones who patronize Ritalin-prescribing doctors. And parents are the ones who can refuse the prescriptions, find better doctors, and complain—loudly and assertively—when physicians or schools attempt to pressure them into accepting labels and drugs. And more and more parents are doing just that.

Every week, I hear from parents who have rejected Ritalin and are searching for the true causes of their children's hyperactivity. The numbers of these parents are growing slowly but surely. They're beginning to communicate with each other through newsgroups on the Internet. They're writing books and articles critical of the pressures being put on parents to drug their children. They're taking on schools and sometimes entire school districts. And, as often as not, they're succeeding in their battles.

I think that in time, these parents (and the ones who will join them) will topple the label-and-drug industry and win better medical care not just for their own children but for *all* children. I think they'll force doctors to abandon silly labels and potentially dangerous drugs and really diagnose and treat sick children. It will be a formidable task, but not an impossible one. I know, because I was around in the 1950s and 1960s, when a similar battle was joined—and the parents won that one, hands down.

Back then, the psychoanalysts held America in the grip of similarly misguided and destructive ideas. Then, as now, millions of children and adults with different diseases were labeled mentally ill and subjected to useless or even harmful treatment. Today, it's Ritalin and other drugs, but back then, it was years and years of psychotherapy aimed at rooting out the early childhood traumas that allegedly caused every childhood behavior problem from bed-wetting to schizophrenia.

For decades, the psychoanalysts were the only recognized authorities on treating children's mental disorders. The only treatment they offered was psychoanalysis, and patients who balked were denigrated (or sometimes forced into treatment against their will). It's hard to imagine, at this time, just how extraordinarily powerful these white-coated Freudians and post-Freudians were. They ran the mental hospitals, advised the schools, and dictated how learning-disabled students, neurotic children, and psychotic children were to be treated. And the fact that their treatments almost never cured anyone didn't make a dent in their arrogance.

So what happened? Put simply, a consumer revolution. Tired of spending years in expensive therapies, trying to uncover parenting flaws that had supposedly made their children troubled or even psychotic, thousands of parents eventually said, "Enough!" These parents refused to settle for the status quo of useless psychoanalysis. Instead, they quit taking their children to analysts, organized into support groups—the forerunners of today's medical consumer groups—and demanded better care for their children and better research into the causes of their disorders. And they got both. Within a decade or so, research was focusing on the *biological* causes of children's mental disorders, and the psychoanalysts' reign—the "Fraudian" era, as author Arthur C. Clarke calls it—was over (except in Hollywood). The revolution that toppled these demigods was led not by the medical community—which, for the most part, wholeheartedly supported the psychoanalysts—but by consumers who recognized that the accepted treatments of the time were hurting, rather than helping, their children.

It's time for a similar consumer revolution, aimed this time at stopping the hyperactivity epidemic. Now, as then, it won't be easy. But it *can* be done. And the more parents who join that revolution, the faster it will be won. (This time around, there are even a few doctors and other professionals fighting on your side. Groups such as the People's Medical Society are on the forefront of the war against the managed care mentality that I believe is largely responsible for the replacement of diagnoses with labels and drugs.)

If you choose to join this battle, keep reminding yourself that you're not "difficult"—you're *right*. You're right to reject Ritalin, a powerful and potentially addictive drug that masks symptoms without treating disease—and whose long-term effects on the brain are completely unknown. And you're right to reject drugs like Cylert, which can cause fatal liver disease, and Norpramin, which can cause sudden death.

Above all, you're right to reject pat labels and seek the real causes of your child's behavior problems, and real solutions for these problems. If your child has a true medical disorder, you're right to find out what it is and get it treated. And if you're raising a perfectly fine, happy, boisterous, active little boy or girl, you're right to resist drugging your child simply to make life easier for school officials.

You won't win many friends in the medical profession or the educational establishment if you join this battle against the misdiagnosis and nondiagnosis of hyperactive children. You will, however, make life better for your own son or daughter. Furthermore, if enough people join you, you'll make life better for millions of other children. And that goal—not drug company profits, the convenience of educators, or managed care cost-cutting—is what's *really* important.

Notes

Chapter 1: Symptoms in Search of a Diagnosis

1. Dr. Valentine is quoted in John Lang, "Hyperactivity Is the New World Disorder," *Naples Daily News*, 1997.

2. Salvatore Mannuzza et al., "Adult Outcome of Hyperactive Boys," *Archives of General Psychiatry* 50, no. 7 (July 1993): 565–576.

3. Eric Taylor et al., "Hyperactivity and Conduct Problems as Risk Factors for Adolescent Development," *Journal of the American Academy of Child and Adolescent Psychiatry* 35, no. 9 (September 1996): 1213–1226.

4. H. R. Huessy et al., "8–10 Year Follow-up of 84 Children Treated for Behavioral Disorder in Rural Vermont," *Acta Paedopsychiatrica* 40, no. 6 (1974): 230–235.

5. "Learning Disabilities: A Report to the U.S. Congress." Report of the Interagency Committee on Learning Disabilities, 1987.

6. Michael Rutter, ed., *Developmental Neuropsychiatry* (New York: Guilford Press, 1983).

7. James Gray, "They Really Should Call It Managed Doctors," *Medical Economics* 68, no. 8 (22 April 1991): 64–70.

8. Thomas J. Garvey, "Physicians Must Create Their Own HMOs," *Managed Care Magazine* (September 1996).

9. Harvey M. Shapiro, *Managed Care Beware* (West Hollywood, Calif.: Dove Books, 1997).

10. Cited in Thomas Armstrong, *The Myth of the A.D.D. Child* (New York: Plume, 1997).

11. Cited in Alfie Kohn, "Suffer the Restless Children," *Atlantic Monthly* (November 1989): 91–100.

12. Interview with Douglas Eby, posted on the Internet.

13. Figure cited by Richard Vatz in "Attention Deficit Delirium," *Wall Street Journal*, 27 July 1994.

14. H. A. Nasrallah et al., "Cortical Atrophy in Young Adults with a History of Hyperactivity in Childhood," *Psychiatry Research* 17, no. 3 (March 1986): 241–246.

15. Warren A. Weinberg et al., "Attention Deficit Hyperactivity Disorder: A Disease or a Symptom Complex?," *Journal of Pediatrics* 130 (1997): 665–669.

16. Quoted in Lang, "Hyperactivity Is the New World Disorder."

Chapter 2: Ritalin and Other Pharmaceutical Cover-Ups

1. Vernon H. Mark and Frank R. Ervin, *Violence and the Brain* (New York: Harper, 1970).

2. Marja Mikkelsson et al., "Psychiatric Symptoms in Preadolescents with Musculoskeletal Pain and Fibromyalgia," *Pediatrics* 100, no. 2 (August 1997): 220–227.

3. "Ritalin: The Smart Pill?," CNN, 1997.

4. Patricia Chisholm, "The ADD Dilemma: Is Ritalin the Best Way to Treat Attention Deficit Disorder?," *Maclean's*, March 11, 1996, 42–44.

5. S. L. Jaffe, "Intranasal Abuse of Prescribed Methylphenidate by an Alcohol and Drug Abusing Adolescent with ADHD," *Journal of the American Academy of Child and Adolescent Psychiatry* 30, no. 5 (September 1991): 773–775.

6. William J. Bailey, "FactLine on Nonmedical Use of Ritalin (Methylphenidate)," IPRC *FactLine* no.9 (http://www.drugs.indiana.edu/pubs/factline/ritalin.html.) (November 1995).

7. John Lang, "Ritalin Nation: Little Boys on Drugs," *Naples Daily News*, 1997.

8. Report of the International Narcotics Control Board, United Nations Publication no. E.96.XI.1, 1995.

9. Joyce Price, "DEA Restless about Ritalin," *Insight on the News* 12, no. 25 (1 July 1996): 39.

10. Comments made by Gene R. Haislip, deputy assistant administrator, Office of Diversion Control, Drug Enforcement Administration, at the Conference on Stimulant Use in the Treatment of ADHD, San Antonio, December 10–12, 1996.

11. Lang, "Ritalin Nation."

12. Research by Schenk and Lambert cited by Alison Motluk in "Calm Before the Storm," *The New Scientist*, 18 April 1998.

13. Cited in Armstrong, *Myth of the A.D.D. Child*.

14. Esther K. Sleator et al., "How Do Hyperactive Children Feel about Taking Stimulants and Will They Tell the Doctor?," *Behavioral Pediatrics* 21, no. 8 (August 1982): 474–479.

15. "A Tale of Two Stimulants," *Harvard Mental Health Letter* 12, no. 8 (February 1996): 6.

16. Cited in Lang, "Ritalin Nation."

17. "Attention Deficit Disorder: A Dubious Diagnosis?," *The Merrow Report*, PBS, 1995.

18. Theodore J. La Vaque, "Kids, Drugs, and ADD," Dr. La Vaque's Web Page (August 1997).

19. Susan Gaines, "Attention Disorders: Whose Deficit?," *Minnesota Parent*, October 15, 1997.

20. Dennis Cantwell, "Attention Deficit Disorder: A Review of the Past 10 Years," *Journal of the American Academy of Child and Adolescent Psychiatry* 35, no. 8 (August 1996): 978–987.

21. P. H. Lipkin, I. J. Goldstein, and A. R. Adesman, "Tics and Dyskinesias Associated with Stimulant Treatment in Attention-Deficit Hyperactivity Disorder," *Archives of Pediatric and Adolescent Medicine* 148, no. 8 (August 1994): 859–861.

22. *Physician's Desk Reference*, Montvale, N.J.: Medical Economics Company, Inc., 1998.

23. D. G. Ririe et al., "Unexpected Interaction of Methylphenidate (Ritalin) with Anaesthetic Agents," *Pediatric Anaesthesia* 7, no. 1 (1997): 69–72.

24. "Methylphenidate Studies Give 'Weak Signal' of Carcinogenic Potential," *American Journal of Health-System Pharmacy* 53, no. 6 (15 March 1996): 610.

25. T. A. Henderson and V. W. Fischer, "Effects of Methylphenidate (Ritalin) on Mammalian Myocardial Ultrastructure," *American Journal of Cardiovascular Pathology* 5, no. 1 (1995): 68–78.

26. C. K. Varley and J. McClellan, "Case Study: Two Additional Sudden Deaths with Tricyclic Antidepressants," *Journal of the American Academy of Child and Adolescent Psychiatry* 36, no. 2 (March 1997): 390–394.

27. M. Berkovitch et al., "Pemoline-Associated Fulminant Liver Failure: Testing the Evidence for Causation," *Clinical and Pharmacological Therapy* 57, no. 6 (June 1995): 696–698.

28. *FDA Medical Bulletin* 27, no. 1 (March 1997).

29. Michael J. Maloney and Jeffrey S. Schwam, "Clonidine and Sudden Death," *Pediatrics* 96, no. 6 (December 1995): 1176–1177.

30. Y. Epstein et al., "Heat Intolerance Induced by Antidepressants," *Annals of the New York Academy of Science* 813 (15 March 1997): 553–558.

31. R. J. Leo, "Movement Disorders Associated with the Serotonin Selective Reuptake Inhibitors," *Journal of Clinical Psychiatry* 57, no. 10 (October 1996): 449–454.

32. S. L. Dubovsky and M. Thomas, "Tardive Dyskinesia Associated with Fluoxetine," *Psychiatric Services* 47, no. 9 (September 1996): 991–993.

33. Michael Lemonick, "The Mood Molecule," *Time*, 29 September 1997.

34. Figure cited by Jennifer Hewett in "Prozac for Kids," *Sydney Morning Herald*, 23 August 1997.

35. Harold Koplewicz, *It's Nobody's Fault: New Hope and Help for Difficult Children and Their Parents* (New York: Times Books, 1996).

36. "Critics Say Ritalin Has Become Panacea for Children's Scholastic, Behavioral Problems," *Houston Chronicle*, 23 May 1996.

37. Mike Hurewitz, "Ritalin Finds New Niche on Campus," *Albany Times Union*, March 15, 1998.

38. Kessler quoted by Jeanie Russell in "The Pill That Teachers Push," *Good Housekeeping* (December 1997).

39. Lawrence Diller, "The Run on Ritalin: Attention Deficit Disorder and Treatment in the 1990s," *The Hastings Center Report* 26, no. 2 (March–April 1996): 12–18.

Chapter 3: Nondrug Therapies: What They Can and Can't Do

1. Katherine S. Rowe and Kenneth J. Rowe, "Synthetic Food Coloring and Behavior: A Dose Response Effect in a Double-Blind, Placebo-Controlled, Repeated–Measures Study," *Journal of Pediatrics* 125, no. 5 (November 1994): 691–698.

2. Bonnie J. Kaplan et al., "Dietary Replacement in Preschool-Aged Hyperactive Boys," *Pediatrics* 83, no. 1 (1989): 7–17.

3. Y. Rong et al., "Pycnogenol Protects Vascular Endothelial Cells from T-butyl Hydroperoxide Induced Oxidant Injury," *Biotechnology Therapeutics* 5, no. 3–4 (1994): 117–126.

4. J. E. Cheshier et al., "Immunomodulation by Pycnogenol in Retrovirus-Infected or Ethanol-Fed Mice," *Life Sciences* 58, no. 5 (1996).

5. Claudia Wallis, "Life in Overdrive," *Time*, 18 July 1994.

6. Alison Gendar, "Biofeedback: Alternative to Drugs for Attention Deficit?," *Westchester Today*, 9 December 1997.

7. Thomas R. Rossiter and Theodore J. La Vaque, "A Comparison of EEG Biofeedback and Psychostimulants in Treating Attention Deficit Hyperactivity Disorders," *Journal of Neurotherapy* (summer 1995): 48–59.

Chapter 4: The Invaders: Pests and Poisons

1. Ann Louise Gittleman, *Guess What Came to Dinner* (Garden City Park, N.Y.: Avery Publishing, 1993).

2. Sarah R. Cheyette and Jeffrey L. Cummings, "Encephalitis Lethargica: Lessons for Contemporary Neuropsychiatry," *Journal of Neuropsychiatry and Clinical Neurosciences* 7, no. 2 (1995): 125–134.

3. D. G. Thomas, "Outcome of Paediatric Bacterial Meningitis, 1979–1989," *Med. J. Aust.* 157, no. 8 (19 October 1992): 519–520.

4. Susan Swedo et al., "Pediatric Autoimmune Neuropsychiatric Disorders Associated with Streptococcal Infections: Clinical Description of the First 50 Cases," *American Journal of Psychiatry* 155, no. 2 (February 1998): 264–271.

5. M. Uhari et al., "Xylitol Chewing Gum in Prevention of Acute Otitis Media: Double Blind Randomised Trial," *British Medical Journal* 313, no. 7066 (9 November 1996): 1180–1184.

6. Wayne R. Ott and John W. Roberts, "Everyday Exposure to Toxic Pollutants," *Scientific American* 278, no. 2 (February 1998): 86–91.

7. The Ethyl Corporation's position on MMT is published on the Ethyl Corporation Web site. Information on manganese risks is cited by Gina Solomon in "MMT—Manganese in Gasoline: Potential Public Health Effects," position paper of the Greater Bos-

ton Physicians for Social Responsibility, 12 August 1998; by the Sierra Club in "Sierra Club of Canada Denounces Chrétien Government Decision to Life Ban on MMT," 12 August 1998; and by A. Iregren in "Using Psychological Tests for the Early Detection of Neurotoxic Effects of Low Level Manganese Exposure," *Neurotoxicology*, vol. 15, no. 3 (1994): 671–677.

8. Cited in Steven Waldman, "Lead and Your Kids," *Newsweek*, 15 July 1991.

9. Figure cited in "Carbon Monoxide Awareness Week," *Kidsource Online*, Internet, 9 December 1997.

10. R. O. Pihl and M. Parkes, "Hair Element Content in Learning Disabled Children," *Science* 198 (1977): 204–206.

11. All studies cited in Sharon Doyle Driedger, "The Furor over Fillings: The Battle Lines Are Drawn over Mercury," *Maclean's*, 18 March 1996, 60–61.

12. Cited ibid.

Chapter 5: The Body Against Itself: Genetic, Metabolic, and Endocrine Diseases That Can Make Children Hyper

1. Mary Ann Block, *No More Ritalin* (New York: Kensington Books, 1996).

2. R. E. Weiss, M. A. Stein, and S. Refetoff, "Behavioral Effects of Liothyronine (L-T3) in Children with Attention Deficit Hyperactivity Disorder in the Presence and Absence of Resistance to Thyroid Hormone," *Thyroid* 7, no. 3 (June 1997): 389–393.

3. Andrea Eberle, "Hyperactivity and Graves' Disease," *Journal of the American Academy of Child and Adolescent Psychiatry* 34, no. 8 (August 1997): 973–974.

4. Karen Bellenir, ed., *Genetic Disorders Sourcebook*, vol. 13 (Detroit: Omnigraphics, 1996).

5. H. Winter Griffith, *Complete Guide to Prescription and Non-Prescription Drugs* (Los Angeles: The Body Press, 1990).

6. T. L. Lowe et al., "Stimulant Medications Precipitate Tourette's Syndrome," *Journal of the American Medical Association* 247, no. 12 (26 March 1982): 1729–1731.

Chapter 6: The Injured Brain: Structural Defects That Can Cause Hyperactive Behavior

1. H. H. Khahil et al., "Cerebral Atrophy: A Schistosomiasis Manifestation?," *American Journal of Tropical Medicine Hygiene* 35, no. 3 (May 1986): 531–35.

2. H. A. Nasrallah et al., "Cortical Atrophy."

3. G. J. Wang et al., "Methylphenidate Decreases Regional Cerebral Blood Flow in Normal Human Subjects," *Life Sciences* 54, no. 9 (1994): PL143–146.

4. P. A. Filipek et al., "Volumetric MRI Analysis Comparing Subjects Having Attention-Deficit Hyperactivity Disorder with Normal Controls," *Neurology* 48, no. 3 (March 1997): 589–601; F. X. Castellanos et al., "Quantitative Brain Magnetic Resonance Imaging in Attention-Deficit Hyperactivity Disorder," *Archives of General Psychiatry* 53, no. 7 (July 1996): 607–616.

5. J. G. Millichap, "Temporal Lobe Arachnoid Cyst-Attention Deficit Disorder Syndrome: Role of the Electroencephalogram in Diagnosis," *Neurology* 48, no. 5 (May 1997): 1435–1439.

6. Mark Linzer et al., "Cardiovascular Causes of Loss of Consciousness in Patients with Presumed Epilepsy: A Cause of the Increased Sudden Death Rate in People with Epilepsy?," *American Journal of Medicine* 96, no. 2 (February 1994): 146–154.

7. *Alcohol Alert.* National Institute on Alcohol Abuse and Alcoholism no. 13, PH 297, July 1991.

8. Ann P. Streissguth et al., "Fetal Alcohol Syndrome in Adolescents and Adults," *Journal of the American Medical Association* 265, no. 15 (17 April 1991): 1961–1967.

9. Ann P. Streissguth, Helen M. Barr, and Paul D. Sampson, "Moderate Prenatal Alcohol Exposure: Effects on Child IQ and Learning Problems at Age 7½ Years," *Alcoholism: Clinical and Experimental Research* 14, no. 5 (September–October 1990): 662–669.

10. Salvatore Mangione and Linda Nieman, "Cardiac Auscultatory Skills of Internal Medicine and Family Practice Trainees: A Comparison of Diagnostic Proficiency," *Journal of the American Medical Association* 278 (3 September 1997): 717–722.

11. Stephen Garber, Marianne Daniels Garber, and Robyn Freedman Spizman, *Beyond Ritalin* (New York: Villard, 1996).

Chapter 7: Self-Inflicted Wounds: Causes of "Lifestyle Hyperactivity"

1. "Debate about Diagnosis, Treatment Rages," *Decatur Herald & Review*, 27 September 1997.

2. Ann B. Bruner et al., "Randomized Study of Cognitive Effects of Iron Supplementation in Non-Anaemic Iron-Deficient Adolescent Girls," *The Lancet* 347, no. 9033 (12 October 1996): 992–996.

3. Jun-Bi Tu et al., "Iron Deficiency in Two Adolescents with Conduct, Dysthymic and Movement Disorders," *Canadian Journal of Psychiatry* 39 (August 1994): 371–375.

4. L. M. Richter, C. Rose, and R. D. Griesel, "Cognitive and Behavioural Effects of a School Breakfast," *South African Medical Journal* 87, sup. 1 (January 1997): 93–100.

5. D. Lonsdale and R. J. Shamberger, "Red Cell Transketolase as an Indicator of Nutritional Deficiency," *American Journal of Clinical Nutrition* 3, no. 2 (February 1980): 205–211.

6. Long-term effects identified by N. Solowij, "Do Cognitive Impairments Recover Following Cessation of Cannabis Use?," *Life Sciences* 56, no. 23–24 (1995): 2119–2126. Short-term effects identified by H. G. Pope Jr., A. J. Gruber, and D. Yurgelun-Todd, "The Residual Neuropsychological Effects of Cannabis: The Current Status of Research," *Drug and Alcohol Dependency* 38, no. 1 (1995): 25–34.

7. K. Kilburn and J. Thornton, "Protracted Neurotoxicity from Chlordane Sprayed to Kill Termites," *Environmental Health Perspectives* 103, no. 7–8 (July–August 1995): 690–694.

8. Wayne R. Ott and John W. Roberts, "Everyday Exposure to Toxic Pollutants," *Scientific American* 278, no. 2 (February 1998): 86–91.

9. "Our Children at Risk," National Resources Defense Council, 1997.

10. Joe Graedon and Teresa Graedon, *The People's Pharmacy* (New York: St. Martin's Press, 1996).

11. R. J. Sankey, A. J. Nunn, and J. A. Sills, "Visual Hallucinations in Children Receiving Decongestants," *British Medical Journal* 288, no. 6427 (5 May 1984): 1369.

12. J. A. Sills, A. J. Nunn, and R. J. Sankey, "Visual Hallucinations in Children Receiving Decongestants," *British Medical Journal* 288, no. 6434 (23 June 1984): 1912–1913.

13. J. W. Lipscomb, J. E. Kramer, and J. B. Leikin, "Seizure Following Brief Exposure to the Insect Repellent N,N-diethyl-m-toluamide," *Annals of Emergency Medicine* 21, no. 3 (March 1992): 315–317.

14. Lorne Garrettson, "Commentary—DEET: Caution for Children Still Needed," *Clinical Toxicology* 35, no. 5 (1997): 443–445.

15. G. J. Magnon, L. L. Robert, D. L. Kline, and L. W. Roberts, "Repellency of Two Deet Formulations and Avon Skin-So-Soft Against Biting Midges (Diptera: Ceratopogonidae) in Honduras," *Journal of the American Mosquito Control Association* 7, no. 1 (March 1991): 80–82.

16. J. Flattery et al., "Lead Poisoning Associated with Use of Traditional Ethnic Remedies—California, 1991–1992," *Morbidity and Mortality Weekly Report* 42, no. 27 (16 July 1993): 521–524.

17. "A Cure That's Worse Than the Ailment," *Science News* 135, no. 4 (28 January 1989): 60.

18. C. K. Hsu et al., "Anticholinergic Poisoning Associated with Herbal Tea," *Archives of Internal Medicine* 155, no. 20 (13 November 1995): 2245–2248.

19. E. Rauhala et al., "Relaxation Training Combined with Increased Physical Activity Lowers the Psychophysiological Activation in Community-Home Boys," *International Journal of Psychophysiology* 10, no. 1 (November 1990): 63–68.

20. S. W. Brown et al., "Aerobic Exercise in the Psychological Treatment of Adolescents," *Perceptual and Motor Skills* 74, no. 2 (April 1992): 555–560.

21. J. B. Dyer III and J. G. Crouch, "Effects of Running and Other Activities on Moods," *Perceptual and Motor Skills* 67, no. 1 (August 1988): 43–50.

22. J. R. MacMahon and R. T. Gross, "Physical and Psychological Effects of Aerobic Exercise in Delinquent Adolescent Males," *American Journal Dis. Child.* 142, no. 12 (December 1988) 1361–1366.

23. S. A. Klein and J. L. Deffenbacher, "Relaxation and Exercise for Hyperactive Impulsive Children," *Perceptual and Motor Skills* 43, no. 3 (December 1977): 1159–1162.

24. I. L. McCann and D. S. Holmes, "Influence of Aerobic Exercise on Depression," *J. Pers. Soc. Psychol.* 46, no. 5 (May 1984): 1142–47.

Chapter 8: Is Your Child *Really* Hyperactive?

1. Dyan Machan, "An Agreeable Affliction," *Forbes*, 12 August 1996, 148–50.

2. DEA statistics, 1995, cited in John Lang, "Ritalin Use Appears Determined by Doctors, Not Need," *Naples Daily News*, 1997.

3. G. Pascal Zachary, "Boys Used to Be Boys, But Do Some Now See Boyhood as a Malady?," *Wall Street Journal*, 2 May 1997, A1.

4. "Debate About Diagnosis Rages."

5. Harold C. Lyons, former director of education for the gifted and talented, U.S. Office of Education, January 1974. Cited on Web page of the National Foundation for Gifted and Creative Children.

6. Bonnie Cramond, "The Coincidence of Attention Deficit Hyperactivity Disorder and Creativity," published by the National Research Center for the Gifted and Talented, 1995.

7. James T. Webb and Diane Latimer, "ADHD and Children Who Are Gifted," *ERIC Digest* 522 (1993, ED358673).

8. K. Williams et al., "Association of Common Health Symptoms with Bullying in Primary School Children," *British Medical Journal* 313, no. 7048 (6 July 1996): 17–19.

9. David Weeks and Jamie James, *Eccentrics: A Study of Sanity and Strangeness* (New York: Villard, 1995).

10. Martin Gross, *The Psychological Society* (New York: Random House, 1978).

11. Ann Landers, October 8, 1997.

12. Cited by Randi Henderson, "Relying on Ritalin," *Common Boundary* (May–June 1995).

13. Edward Hallowell and John J. Ratey, *Answers to Distraction* (New York: Pantheon, 1994).

14. Judyth Reichenberg-Ullman and Robert Ullman, *Ritalin-Free Kids* (Rocklin, Calif.: Prima Publishing, 1996).

15. R. McCraty et al., "The Effects of Different Types of Music on Mood, Tension, and Mental Clarity," *Alternative Therapies in Health and Medicine* 4, no. 1 (January 1998): 75–84.

16. Information on immune function is from D. O. McCarthy et al., "The Effects of Noise Stress on Leukocyte Function in Rats,"

Research in Nursing and Health 15, no. 2 (April 1992): 131–137. Information on hearing loss is from B. A. Bohne et al., "Irreversible Inner Ear Damage from Rock Music," *Transactions of the American Academy of Ophthalmology and Otolaryngology* 82, no. 1 (January 1976): ORL50–ORL59. Adverse effects of loud music on visual acuity are noted in T. J. Ayres and P. Hughes, "Visual Acuity with Noise and Music at 107dbA," *Journal of Auditory Research* 26, no. 1 (January 1986): 65–74.

Chapter 10: In the Doctor's Office

1. "HMO Survey Exposes Patient Concerns About Managed Care," Physicians Who Care Web site, 1996.

2. Marti Ann Schwartz, *Listen to Me, Doctor* (Aspen, Co.: MacMurray & Beck, 1995).

3. John MacDonald, "This Is Sick," *Arizona Republic*, 10 December 1997.

4. Max Jarman, "Aetna Gives Doctors a Bitter Pill," *Arizona Republic*, 5 February 1998, D1.

Chapter 11: The School Connection

1. William E. Schmidt, "Sales of Drugs Are Soaring."

2. Hallowell and Ratey, *Answers to Distraction*.

3. "Drugging Kids Draws Fire at School Board as Parents Complain Staff Pushed Use of Ritalin," *Montreal Gazette*, 26 October 1995.

4. Richard Vatz and Lee Weinberg, "Overreacting to Attention Deficit Disorder," *USA Today Magazine*, (January 1995): 84–85.

5. "Critics Say Ritalin Has Become Panacea."

6. Jeanie Russell, "The Pill That Teachers Push," *Good Housekeeping* (December 1997).

7. John Merrow, "Attention Deficit Disorder: A Dubious Diagnosis?" broadcast by the Public Broadcasting System, 1995.

8. Jessica Portner, "Worried About Message, E.D. Halts Video Distribution," *Education Week on the Web*, 8 November 1995.

9. "Reading, Writing, 'Rithmetic, and Ritalin," *The Education Reporter* (July 1996).

10. Russell, "The Pill That Teachers Push."

11. Fred Baughman Jr., "The Future of Mental Health: Radical Changes Ahead," *USA Today Magazine*, 1 March 1997.

12. Lang, "Hyperactivity Is the New World Disorder."

13. Russell, "The Pill That Teachers Push."

14. C. K. Whalen et al., "Messages of Medication: Effects of Actual Versus Informed Medication Status on Hyperactive Boys' Expectancies and Self-Evaluations," *Journal of Consulting and Clinical Psychology* 59, no. 4 (August 1991): 602–606.

15. Cited in Kohn, "Suffer the Restless Children."

16. Ibid.

17. Cited by Jeanne Mackin, "Crowded Kids Lag in Social and Scholastic Skills," publication of the Cornell Cooperative Extension (http://www.cornell.edu/News/extension_news).

18. John Lang and Jim O'Connell, "Ritalin Means Big Money for Schools, Parents, Drug Maker," *Naples Daily News*, 1997.

19. Machan, "An Agreeable Affliction."

20. Ruth Shalit, "Defining Disability Down," *The New Republic*, 25 August 1997.

Index